INCOME INEQUALITY AROUND THE WORLD

RESEARCH IN LABOR ECONOMICS

Series Editor: Solomon W. Polachek

IZA Co-Editor: Konstantinos Tatsiramos

Recent Volumes:

RESEARCH IN LABOR ECONOMICS   VOLUME 44

INCOME INEQUALITY AROUND THE WORLD

EDITED BY

LORENZO CAPPELLARI
Università Cattolica Milano and IZA

SOLOMON W. POLACHEK
State University of New York at Binghamton and IZA

KONSTANTINOS TATSIRAMOS
University of Nottingham and IZA

IZA

Emerald

United Kingdom – North America – Japan
India – Malaysia – China

Emerald Group Publishing Limited
Howard House, Wagon Lane, Bingley BD16 1WA, UK

First edition 2016

British Library Cataloguing in Publication Data
A catalogue record for this book is available from the British Library

ISBN: 978-1-78560-944-2
ISSN: 0147-9121 (Series)

ISOQAR certified
Management System,
awarded to Emerald
for adherence to
Environmental
standard
ISO 14001:2004.

Certificate Number 1985
ISO 14001

INVESTOR IN PEOPLE

CONTENTS

EDITORIAL ADVISORY BOARD

PREFACE

At least since the 1950s, rising income differences *between* rich and poor nations began to wane as poorer nations started to catch up to richer ones, but inequality *within* many countries rose. Not only have the rich been getting richer since the 1980s, but this trend of rising inequality holds true for most countries with the exception of a number of countries in Latin America (the world's most unequal continent). In short, the ultra-wealthy gained much prominence in both developed and developing countries. Typically, a population's poorest half controls less than 10% of a nation's wealth, and this gap is now getting bigger. According to Pew and other global attitudinal surveys, growing inequality within countries is becoming one of the biggest concerns facing the world economy. Whether this inequality is good or bad is open to debate. On the one hand, inequality stimulates risk taking and hence innovation and growth; on the other hand, inequality promotes jealousy, political protest, and even revolution. Thus enumerating and understanding inequality is important. Whereas Volume 43 dealt primarily with inequality in the United States, this volume concentrates on other countries. It leads with an overview paper presenting cross-country and time comparisons of inequality measures gleamed from five sources of data. In some countries, primarily Mexico and South America, inequality is decreasing, while in others, primarily Europe and China, inequality is increasing. Of the remaining papers, three concentrate on changes in the distribution over time, one examines inequality at a point in time relative to other countries, one looks at the effect of public policy on wage distribution, and finally one employs longitudinal data to get at earnings mobility of a given population.

To date, practitioners typically use five sets of data to analyze income distribution: the World Income Inequality Database (WIID), Standardized World Income Inequality Database (SWIID), the Luxembourg Income Study (LIS) Key Figures on Inequality, World Development Indicators (WDI) of the World Bank, and finally the Estimated Household Income Inequality (EHII) data set developed by the University of Texas Inequality Project. The latter EHII is a panel currently containing estimated Gini coefficients for 167 countries from 1963 to 2008. Each data set has positive and negative attributes. To get consistency, each data set is based on harmonizing information across countries. Clearly this process entails controversial judgement calls, many of which can be questioned. Thus it makes sense to compare each set of data. In the first paper, James K. Galbraith, Jaehee Choi, Béatrice Halbach, Aleksandra Malinowska, and Wenjie Zhang present Gini coefficients by country and year based on the EHII. They compare these income inequality measures with three of the other data collections. They generally find the EHII to be highly consistent with LIS, OECD, and EU-SILC, notwithstanding the difference in concepts measured, or differences in tax systems and welfare states. However, they argue EHII's coverage and historical depth are far greater.

Looking at an overview of all countries simultaneously might miss the specific nuances differentiating one country's trends from another. The remaining papers address this concern by examining aspects of income inequality in specific countries separately. First, take the case of Brazil. From 1995 to 2012, the wage distribution became less dispersed, but why? Otavio Bartalotti, Nora Lustig and Yang Wang utilize various decomposition techniques to show that the narrowing of the wage distribution coincided with the expansion of education. Rising education pulled up those that previously would be at the bottom, but at the same time educational premiums fell as more got educated. The latter, which the authors call a change in the wage structure, decreased prospects on the top, thus narrowing the overall distribution.

Peru also experienced a narrowing of its earnings distribution. From 2004 to 2013, poverty declined from 54% to 24% and the size of its middle class doubled to 39%. In the next paper, Adrian Robles and Marcos Robles decompose the changes in inequality and changes in welfare indicators based on counterfactual simulations. They find government transfers had only a very small effect, followed by demographic changes in the size of the working age population and changes in hours. However, as in the case of Brazil, the biggest impact was with education. Rising education levels increased earnings, but the rate of return declined given the greater proportion of the population getting more school. This decline in the rate of return lowered relative earnings on the top, thus narrowing the distribution.

Unlike Brazil and Peru, inequality in Spain increased in recent years (2008–2012) and is high relative to other European countries. In the next paper, Carlos Gradín uses the EU-SILC data to see why Spain's relative inequality rose. By comparing Spain to Germany, France, Italy, Sweden, and the United Kingdom, he is able to isolate household and economy-wide characteristics associated with inequality. First, he finds both Spain's higher unemployment rates, especially among the youth, and Spain's higher incidence of self-employment caused by the recession, to be important. Second, he finds factors prevalent before the recession, particularly lower educational attainment, high immigration, and weak redistributive tax and family allowances, were also related to increased inequality. On the other hand, he finds structural factors such as relatively few high-skilled jobs, relatively few finance sector jobs, relatively generous transfer payments such as pensions, and transfer payments from extended family members, reduced inequality.

Explicit public policies can also affect a country's earnings distribution. The next paper by Carl Lin and Myeong-Su Yun examines how raising the minimum wage affects income distribution in China. China is a country now experiencing extremely rapid growth, but also dramatic increases in income inequality. The deterioration of what was a realtively equal distribution led the Chinese government to consider and adopt policies aimed at increasing equality. The minimum wage is one such initiative. Beginning in January 2004, new minimum wage regulations required local governments to introduce a minimum wage increase at least once every two years. The legislation also increased coverage. Between 2004 and 2009, the average nominal minimum wage increased by 80%, but provinces, municipalities, and autonomous regions were able to legislate their own minimum wage, so there was lots of variation, enabling the authors to identify its effects. Using OLS and IV panel regressions with aggregated city level data, Lin and Yun examine the effect of minimum wage changes on the earnings gaps at the bottom and upper end of the earnings distribution. Their analysis shows that minimum wage increases significantly reduced earnings gaps, particularly at the bottom end of the distribution.

One can analyze upward mobility of a given set of individuals when using longitudinal instead of cross-sectional data. In the final paper, Rafael Novella, Laura Ripani, Agustina Suaya, Luis Tejerina, and Claudia Vazquez do that for Chile and Nicaragua, two countries that are similar in their levels of inequality, but different with regard to their opportunities to achieve success at work. To do so, their paper estimates autoregressive models using transitional matrices where the ranking of each individual depends on a set of past rankings conditional on personal characteristics. The authors find earnings mobility is lower in Nicaragua than in Chile after controlling for age, education, and work hours, but that previous rankings remain important in explaining an individual's current position in the income distribution. However, in Chile, previous rankings are not significant in explaining one's position in the distribution. Thus, a country's basic underlying institutional governance structure can be important.

As with past volumes, we aim to focus on important issues and to maintain the highest levels of scholarship. We encourage readers who have prepared manuscripts that meet these stringent standards to submit them to *Research in Labor Economics* (RLE) via the IZA website (http://rle.iza.org) for possible inclusion in future volumes.

Lorenzo Cappellari
Solomon W. Polachek
Konstantinos Tatsiramos
Editors

A COMPARISON OF MAJOR WORLD INEQUALITY DATA SETS: LIS, OECD, EU-SILC, WDI, AND EHII

James K. Galbraith[a], Jaehee Choi[b], Béatrice Halbach[b], Aleksandra Malinowska[b] and Wenjie Zhang[c]

[a]*LBJ School of Public Affairs, University of Texas at Austin*
[b]*The University of Texas at Austin*
[c]*Luxembourg Income Studies*

ABSTRACT

We present a comparison of coverage and values for five inequality data sets that have worldwide or major international coverage and independent measurements that are intended to present consistent coefficients that can be compared directly across countries and time. The comparison data sets are those published by the Luxembourg Income Studies (LIS), the OECD, the European Union's Statistics on Incomes and Living Conditions (EU-SILC), and the World Bank's World Development Indicators (WDI). The baseline comparison is with our own Estimated Household Income Inequality (EHII) data set of the University of Texas Inequality Project. The comparison shows the historical depth and range of EHII and its broad compatibility with LIS, OECD, and EU-SILC, as well as problems with using the WDI for any cross-country

Income Inequality Around the World
Research in Labor Economics, Volume 44, 1−48
ISSN: 0147-9121/doi:10.1108/S0147-912120160000044008

comparative purpose. The comparison excludes the large World Incomes Inequality Database (WIID) of UNU-WIDER and the Standardized World Income Inequality Database (SWIID) of Frederick Solt; the former is a bibliographic collection and the latter is based on imputations drawn, in part, from EHII and the other sources used here.

Keywords: Inequality; inequality databases; Gini coefficient

JEL Classification: D63

THE STATE OF WORLD INEQUALITY DATA

Since the landmark publication by the World Bank in 1996 of the Klaus Deininger − Lyn Squire (DS) data set of worldwide inequality measures, comparative, time-series and panel studies of economic inequality have become a significant field of economic research. But the ambitions of researchers have often run ahead of the quality, consistency, and coverage of the data, so that many empirical questions remain open to dispute.

As discussed in the works of Atkinson and Brandolini (2001, 2009), secondary data sets on cross-country income distribution have long been plagued by problems of data quality and consistency. Within countries, official statistical agencies may switch between different data sources − such as from household surveys to income tax records − in different time periods, leading to data breaks or implausible jumps or drops in coefficients. Statistical agencies may also change methodology over time, altering weights, equivalence scales, reference periods and units, population coverage, and definitions of income or expenditure. When inequality measures are analyzed at the individual-country level, such inconsistencies are simple enough to account for, especially if they are well documented. However, data inconsistencies can become extremely problematic when assembled in large cross-country data sets, especially if such data is used mechanically and without reference to their original source (Atkinson & Brandolini, 2001, 2009). This situation has spurred new efforts to develop better and more consistent comparative measures of economic inequalities.

The data sets now available are of five broad types. There are, first, large bibliographic data sets, of which the preeminent example is the World Income Inequality Database (WIID) of the World Institute for Development Economics Research (WIDER) of the United Nations University (UNU) at Helsinki. WIID is the successor to DS, and is a diverse collection of reported coefficients, chronicling the struggle to measure inequality around the world over the past six decades, with careful documentation as to the concepts and sources of information. But the WIID is not, itself, a data set of comparative measures. It is rather a source, from which such measures may be extracted according to the preferences and criteria of the researcher.

The opposite approach consists of synthetic measures, represented at large scale by the Standardized World Income Inequality Database (SWIID) prepared by Frederick Solt at the University of Iowa. SWIID contains 4,625 Gini coefficients each for market and disposable income, covering the world almost comprehensively. But the numbers in the SWIID, while consistent, are not actually measures. They are in many cases imputations, based on relationships across time or between countries, so as to fill in gaps in the statistical record. The imputations are in turn based partly on other data sources, including those examined here.

Original, consistent measures are to be found in two significant data sets: the Luxembourg Income Studies (LIS) Key Figures on inequality, and the Statistics on Income and Living Conditions (EU-SILC) data set of the European Union. LIS is based on an intricate process of international harmonization of existing data sets; EU-SILC was based on the European Community Household Panel (ECHP) survey from 1994 to 2001, and since 2003/2004 is derived from individual-country household surveys harmonized to common guidelines, procedures, concepts, and classifications aimed at maximizing comparability. Both are limited in coverage, in the case of LIS because of the demanding preparation required and because the underlying sources are of higher quality in richer countries. In the case of EU-SILC the surveys are restricted to member states of the European Union.

A fourth type of data set consists of measures supplied to international agencies, mainly (if not exclusively) by the statistical services of their member states. The World Development Indicators (WDI) of the World Bank have achieved wide use as a standard source of worldwide Gini coefficients, in part because of the authority of the Bank and the easy access afforded in the WDI to inequality measures alongside other indicators of economic and social performance. Meanwhile the Organization for Economic Co-operation and Development (OECD) has presented a table of inequality measures, concentrated on the OECD countries, which has also achieved wide recognition for similar reasons.

The final approach to be mentioned here is that of the University of Texas Inequality Project, which in 2005 introduced the Estimated Household Income Inequality (EHII) data set (Galbraith & Kum, 2005). EHII is a panel of estimated Gini coefficients, based on a table of measures and a simple model. The table of measures is called UTIP-UNIDO,

consisting of the between-groups components of Theil's T statistics calculated across industrial categories from the Industrial Statistics of the
United Nations Industrial Development Organization. UTIP-UNIDO was
introduced in 1999 (Galbraith, Lu, & Darity, 1999), and was updated most
recently by Amin Shams as reported in Galbraith, Shams, Halbach,
Malinowska, and Zhang (2014), with 4,054 country-year observations over
167 countries, dating from 1963 through 2008.

The between-groups component is (of course) the *only* component of the
overall Theil's T statistic that can be computed from grouped administrative
data such as industrial or geographic categories. In the UNIDO case one has
some 29 industrial categories and no further detail is available. However
Conceicao, Galbraith, and Bradford (2001) demonstrate that the between-
groups component of inequality across industrial or geographic classifications, even at such a coarse level of disaggregation, is an excellent instrument
for the evolution of inequalities at progressively finer levels, of which the ulti-
mate but unobservable level would be separate individuals. The common
sense of this is that much difference and especially most changes occur across
broad categories such as between industries, countries, or major regions, and
not within particular small locales, narrowly defined sectors, or establish-
ments, where relative stability and institutional rules tend to govern.

The calculations behind EHII are based on a regression (presented in
Appendix C) that shows the very close relationship between inequalities of
industrial pay and household income inequalities, both through time and
across countries. This relationship was originally measured by matching
overlapping country-year observations in UTIP-UNIDO and in the original
DS data set, with controls to specify whether the original DS measure represented inequality of household or persons, of income or expenditure, and
whether it is gross or net of tax, and to capture the degree of industrializa-
tion, measured very simply as the share of manufacturing employment in
total population. Once these are taken into account, the coefficients relating
industrial pay to income inequality are very precise and very stable and it is
possible to use them to produce a large table of estimated Gini coefficients
on a consistent gross household income inequality basis, with 3,872 observations covering 149 countries from 1963 to 2008 in the most recent version.[1]

The literature broadly distinguishes household income inequalities of
three types: market income, gross income, and net or disposable income. Of

---

[1]For present purposes, we dropped the estimate for Macau, reducing the country count to 148
and the observation count to 3,842.

these, "market income" is a relatively new concept; it is based on a distinction between private and welfare-state-based income sources such as state pensions, and tends to show very high inequalities in advanced countries, for two reasons: the concentration of capital incomes and the fact that advanced welfare states permit the existence of many households, notably those headed by retirees, with zero market income. High inequality of market income is therefore not a good indicator of a highly-unequal society. Net or disposable income is most appropriate for judging the distribution of economic welfare across households; however to estimate net income inequality with our technique, which admits only a single adjustment coefficient for all countries, would tend to blur the clear distinction between nations that do and do not have effective redistributive tax systems. EHII therefore focuses on the third concept, gross income, which is income after transfers but before tax; for the purposes of comparison this provides the best measure of pre-tax inequality across countries and through time.

The proliferation of inequality measures since DS also posed a technical question: would it be necessary to re-estimate the relationship between industrial pay inequality and household income inequality with a larger set of overlapping measures, drawn from one of the newer data sets such as the WIID? We considered this question and decided against it, because the EHII estimates as originally calculated can be shown to match quite closely with survey-based measures of gross household income inequality for most countries, where the latter are available. While the 430 original DS observations used to recalibrate the model may be "old" in the sense of having been in the record for a long time, there is no reason to think these measures unrepresentative and 430 is surely a statistically valid sample. In short, there would be little gain to justify the time and expense of matching still more observations across data sets, and developing the broader set of controls that would be required, because of the larger number of distinct income/expenditure categories now in use.

Why does the EHII data set succeed in matching and extending survey-based measures of inequality?[2] The reason is that in almost all countries

---

[2]The specific tracking of *gross household income* inequality stems from construction of the EHII model, which adjusts for six categories of measures in the original DS high-quality data set: gross versus net; household versus personal; and income versus expenditure. In the EHII model gross, household and income-based measures are given a zero dummy value, which tends to center the resulting estimate effectively on survey-based based measures of gross household income inequality. See Table C1 in the appendix for the coefficient estimates.

inequalities of industrial pay form an especially active element of economic activity and therefore of levels and changes in inequality. Industrial workers span the spectrum from low-paid textiles to the well-paid precincts of automotive, aerospace and petroleum engineering, and the existence of these latter sectors tends to prefigure the existence of still higher-paid households in the financial sectors. The existence and fluctuations of inequality across industrial pay thus tend to mirror those of the full household income distribution, even though large elements of the latter are not observed directly in industrial data. Peasant farmers and low-end service workers may be far more numerous, but they contribute less to inequality; workers in these sectors are almost never rich. It is true that EHII does not capture very well the capital market rents that are important especially in certain US household incomes, and it also tends to undershoot measured inequality in certain large developing countries, notably Brazil, Mexico and South Africa.[3] But for a very large selection of countries and a long period of time, the simple EHII model does an effective and inexpensive job of estimating gross household income inequality. Galbraith et al. (2014) provides evidence.

Fig. 1 presents year-by-year kernel density estimates of EHII inequality observations for four major regions: Europe and Eurasia, the Americas, Asia and Oceania, and the Middle East and Africa. For the European/ Eurasian the shift to the right in the early 1990s is largely due to the inclusion of the transition economies, which experienced especially large increases in inequalities during this time. In Asia and Oceania, the pattern is marked by an apparent reduction in the number of low-inequality countries over time, and in the Americas, by significant increases in inequalities, mainly in Central and South America, although coverage varies from year to year.

Solt (2016, p. 11) states: "For the UTIP data, comparability is compromised by differences across countries in the share of all employment that is

---

[3]For the South African case, we note that household income surveys tend to report up to a third of households as having no economic income at all, which fact will necessarily distort the Lorenz curve and inflate the Gini coefficient. It suggests that the definition of "income" or perhaps of "household" used in the surveys may not be standard, or else that South African respondents are unusually reticent to report income to survey takers. In the case of Brazil, a very large country with a massive regional divide, it is plausible that inequality measures for the South and for the Northeast, taken separately, would each be lower than the national measures; whereas industrial pay inequality measures would tend to be overwhelmingly based on the situation in the industrial South of the country.

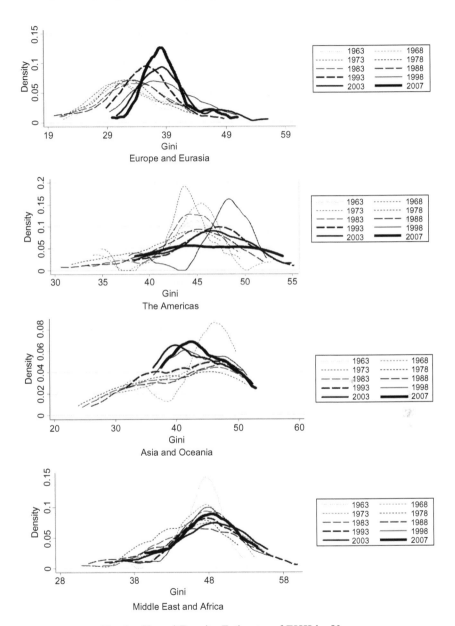

Fig. 1.   Kernel Density Estimates of EHII by Year.

in agriculture or services rather than in industry [...]." This is not correct: the EHII model controls explicitly for the share of employment in manufacturing. Solt is correct that EHII cannot capture the share of income originating in capital markets; however as a practical matter this appears to distort EHII's estimate only in the case of the United States, and to a minor degree that of the United Kingdom. In no other country do we find significant gaps between EHII's gross income inequality estimates and those of (sporadically available) surveys that can be traced plausibly to capital market income. Solt's remaining comment, which is with respect to within-group inequalities, has been addressed above.

Although EHII is not a direct measure of income inequality, unlike the SWIID every observation reported is based on a direct measurement for that country in that year; there are no imputations across years or countries. The advantage of the EHII approach is thus dense coverage without loss of degrees of freedom for statistical purposes. In Galbraith et al. (2014) we show that for at least 40 countries, the EHII measures are mostly plausible as estimates, since they track the movement of other measures well and tend to lie quite close to the (relatively few) direct measures of gross income inequality that exist. However, there are so many different measures of each type of inequality in most countries, with such differences of concept and coverage, that systematic evaluation of data quality against the whole literature is impractical. Comparison to the full literature remains a matter of eyeballs on the page.

The question we take up here is: how does EHII compare to other data sets that each purport – or have been widely taken – to present tables of comparable inequality measures? These are the OECD, the WDI, the EU-SILC, and the LIS.[4] The WIID has 6,950 Gini observations for 172 countries from 1,867 to 2013. We exclude it however on the grounds that summary measures of its diverse contents are not very meaningful; any conceptually consistent subset of measures would necessarily be considerably smaller. The SWIID offers a complete table of 4,627 Gini estimates each for market and net income inequality for 174 countries from 1960 to 2013. However, we exclude it because it is based on multiple imputations across years and countries and is derived, in part, from EHII and the other data sets, so that a close relationship is not

---

[4]The LIS, OECD, EU-SILC, and WDI data sets may be found at http://www.lisdatacenter.org; http://www.oecd.org; http://ee.europa.eu/eurostat/web/main/home and http://data.world-bank.org/data-catalog/world-development-indicators. EHII and UTIP-UNIDO may be found at http://utip.gov.utexas.edu

surprising. The exclusions are not meant to imply criticism. The WIID is invaluable as a resource, and the SWIID does appear to be largely consistent with EHII (see Galbraith et al., 2014), allowing for the fact that SWIID estimates market and net income inequality, but not gross income inequality. The World Top Incomes Data set covers 30 countries from 1870 to 2014, but provides mainly income shares and is therefore not strictly comparable to the other data sets (Alvaredo, Atkinson, Piketty, Saez, & Zucman).

PREVIOUS ASSESSMENTS OF CROSS-COUNTRY INEQUALITY DATABASES

There has been a recent surge in research assessing and comparing cross-country data sets on inequality, many of which have been recently published in the *Journal of Economic Inequality*'s special issue on Cross-National Inequality Databases. In one way or another, each of these authors highlights a trade-off between data quality and breadth of coverage across countries and over time. Our hope is that the EHII is a step toward making this trade-off less inevitable, by providing a panel that is both broad in coverage and of generally acceptable quality.

Jenkins (2015) presents assessments of the SWIID and WIID. With respect to the WIID, Jenkins argues that many of the issues raised by Atkinson and Brandolini in their 2001 and 2009 papers regarding DS are still relevant to the WIID. He highlights the need for researchers to be highly sensitive to the inherent limitations of such data. Regarding the SWIID, he emphasizes that the same limitations apply, since it is partially derived from WIID. Jenkins also highlighted problems with the validity of the SWIID estimates for several countries (Finland, United Kingdom, United States), which he attributed to the quality of the underlying data (particularly in the WIID), as well as to the imputation procedure used to derive the estimates. Jenkins notes that the SWIID estimates are also problematic for developing countries, including China and Kenya, due to the impact of high imputation variability in these countries on the precision of the estimates.

Gasparini and Tornarolli (2015) reviewed the OECD Income Distribution Database, with some comparisons to LIS, EU-SILC, and the Chartbook of Economic Inequality by Atkinson and Morelli (AM). They found the main advantage of the OECD database to be the relatively high comparability of measures across countries, given that statistics are based on a common welfare concept and collected with a standardized methodology from similar sources across countries. The main weakness seems to be gaps in coverage across time and place. For instance, although data are available from 1983 to 2013, the authors show that close monitoring of inequality patterns in most countries is only possible from the mid-1990s. The OECD data is less amenable to historical reviews of changes in inequality that are possible with LIS, but provides greater breadth than the EU-SILC. The AM data are longer and more complete in time than OECD, but with smaller country coverage.

Ravaillon (2015) addresses the strengths and limitations of LIS. He finds the main value-added of the database to be its very high level of standardization of data across countries compared to other similar efforts, although this comes at the cost of limited country coverage. In particular, Ravaillon notes that LIS has not greatly expanded coverage to middle-income and developing countries despite the increased availability of survey data in the developing world. Ravaillon also notes that the lag between the availability of surveys in countries and the time that LIS makes these measures available (due to the time required by its harmonization process) may pose a disincentive to users, since the more recent raw data are available elsewhere. Ravaillon also criticizes some aspects of the methodology LIS uses to construct its Key Figures on inequality and poverty. With respect to the key figures on inequality, he disagrees with the decisions to conduct top- and bottom-coding, not to impute missing values, to exclude consumption-based measures, to use exclusively the square-root equivalence scale, and with some price-adjustment practices. Finally, Ravaillon addresses deeper problems of underlying survey-based data that are common to all data-bases that use them, including the effect of non-response bias on the Gini coefficient, among others.

Smeeding and Latner (2015) reviewed PovcalNet, WDI, and "All the Ginis." These three data sets are largely overlapping. PovcalNet, for example, is an online tool used to analyze the more comprehensive WDI data. All the Ginis (ATG) is a compilation of high-quality Gini coefficients from eight different sources, which are used to create one standardized Gini variable for each observation. In contrast to the other data sets mentioned above (EU-SILC, OECD, LIS, SWIID, WIID), these three are focused on measuring inequality and poverty in middle- and low-income countries. Smeeding and Latner point out that rich countries tend to measure economic resources in terms of income, while consumption expenditure is far more common in developing countries. Consumption-based measures generally report lower levels of inequality than income-based measures. They also note that WDI and PovcalNet lack clear and easily accessible documentation on the sources of data and the method of calculation for the estimates, making it difficult for researchers to define accurately the concepts on which the estimates are based. This problem is compounded by the fact that users cannot directly access the micro-data on which the harmonized WDI (and thus, PovcalNet) is based. In comparison, the ATG is more transparent and provides more complete source and methodological documentation, although it does not give definitions in most cases of consumption/expenditure or income.

Several additional recent papers assessing cross-country data sets include Brandolini (2014) on the World Top Incomes Database (WTID) and Bourguignon (2015) on CEPALSTAT and SEDLAC, the main income inequality databases covering Latin American countries. Since we focus on EU-SILC, LIS, OECD, and WDI here, we direct readers directly to the papers above for assessments of WTID, CEPALSTAT, and SEDLAC.

CRITERIA OF COMPARISON

There are two criteria that can be deployed to compare data sets of this type. The first is *coverage*. Given the scope of the data set, in terms of countries and years, how many actual observations are to be found and therefore how dense and complete are the measures? This is a relatively straightforward thing to measure, but there are subtleties, including the question of balance across countries and time. Other things equal, a data set that spans a matrix of countries and years in a fairly even way is preferable to one that has an over-representation of observations in some countries and a dearth in others.

The second major criterion is *accuracy*. Here there is a problem: there is no objective standard of accuracy in this field. As a matter of principle, we cannot simply compare two Gini coefficients for the same country-year observation and declare one to be more accurate than another. We can of course rely on the properties of the data set and our confidence in the underlying techniques, or in the authority of the publisher, but these are often subjective and risky judgments. What we can observe is the *consistency* of measures *across* data sets.[5] Where two data sets compiled

---

[5]Our use of the word "consistency" differs from that of Atkinson and Brandolini (2009) who use it to refer to abrupt changes in Gini coefficients. We are referring here to divergences in matched observations from data set to another.

by different techniques and from different sources broadly arrive at similar measures, our confidence in the joint accuracy of the two data sets will
rise. Where overlapping measures diverge, we should be inclined to
caution.

Coverage

Table 1 presents coverage ratios for the data sets under study. For each
data set, we give the following information: total number of countries in
the data set; range of years covered; total number of country-year observations. Then we provide the following pairwise comparisons to EHII: total
number of EHII observations in the same range of years for the countries
covered; total number of EHII observations for the countries covered, over
the full range of years in the EHII data.

EHII has a strong coverage advantage in both the span of countries and
depth of time. Only LIS has comparable historical reach, with some observations as far back as 1967, but with a sixth of the observations over a
quarter of the countries. Only the WDI has a comparable breadth of countries,[6] but the WDI starts 15 years later and has barely a third of EHII's
observations even within the years that it covers. The remaining two data
sets are (by design) much smaller in time and country coverage, as well as
in number of observations.

A significant advantage of the four comparison data sets is the presence
of observations for the most recent five-year interval, 2009–2013. This
stems from the ability of these data sets to include new surveys as they are
published, and of course to draw them from the same sources. It also
reflects the increasing availability of surveys in recent years, as more
resources have been devoted to measuring household income inequalities.
A pending update to EHII will narrow this gap, to 2010 or 2011, depending
on the source data.

In all cases, the EHII all-years coverage, going back to 1963, for the
countries covered by the other data sources exceeds their own coverage of
those same countries by large factors. In all cases except the EU-SILC, the
EHII coverage is much greater even for the period after the other data set

---

[6]However they are not the same countries; the WDI includes 28 countries not covered by
EHII, most of them small island states, while omitting an almost-equal number of countries
that EHII covers.

Table 1. Comparison of Coverage across Data Sources.

Data Set	Total Observations	Countries Covered	Years Covered	Observations through 2008, Countries Covered by Both EHII and the Comparison Set	EHII Observations Matched by Countries and Years covered in Both Data Sets	EHII Observations Matched by Countries Covered in Both Data Sets, 1963–2008
LIS	261	45	1967–2013	206	1,319	1,415
WDI	1,110	149	1978–2013	846	2,676	3,793
OECD	382	34	1983–2012	286	711	1,266
EU-SILC	443	33	1995–2013	288	371	1,118
EHII	3,872	148	1963–2008	n.a.	n.a.	n.a.

begins. The EU-SILC exception arises because EU-SILC begins only in 1995 and extends to 2013, whereas the EHII data set reaches only to 2008; thus a large fraction of EU-SILC's observations lie outside of EHII's current range. In the other cases, EHII coverage for the same countries and years is on the order of two to six times as dense.

The most challenging comparison is with the World Development Indicators inequality measures published by the World Bank. It is not entirely clear what purpose these indicators are intended to serve, since they include a hotchpotch of income and expenditure, and gross and net inequality coefficients. Nevertheless, they are widely cited for comparative purposes, and often taken as authoritative; indeed on its website the Bank claims that they represent "the most current and accurate global development data available."

Unlike LIS, the OECD or EU-SILC, the WDI inequality measures have global reach, covering 149 countries with 1,110 total observations over the years 1978−2013, including 107 observations for 28 countries not covered in EHII (many small island states, Laos, Vietnam, Palestine, DR Congo, Belarus, Turkmenistan, Tajikistan, Uzbekistan, and Montenegro), and 178 observations for the years 2009−2013. However, also unlike the three other data sets, the WDI does not offer any consistency in the conceptual basis of its coverage: it includes both expenditure and income-inequality measures, and among the income-inequality measures the difference between net and gross is not clearly specified. Therefore it seems to us that an adjustment of the kind made for the other three data sets is not appropriate in this case.

There are 1,003 WDI observations for the 147 countries also covered by EHII, not necessarily exactly overlapping in years covered, and 932 observations in the same countries over the span of 1978−2008. EHII has 2,676 observations for this period, including observations in 26 countries that have no observations reported in the WDI: Afghanistan, the Bahamas, Barbados, Cuba, Cyprus, Eritrea, the GDR, Hong Kong, Korea, Kuwait, Libya, Luxembourg, Malta, Myanmar, New Zealand, Oman, Portugal, Puerto Rico, Qatar, Singapore, Somalia, Taiwan, Tonga, UAE, Yugoslavia, and Zimbabwe. WDI thus overlaps EHII in 121 countries.

To make a comparison, we broke the WDI and EHII down into four large regions: the Americas, Eurasia, Asia, and the Middle East and Africa. This permits us to compare coverage and values in manageable portions. Table 2 summarizes the coverage for each region.

Table 2. EHII and WDI Coverage by Regions, for Countries in EHII.

Regions	WDI Observations 1978–2013	WDI Observations 1978–2008	EHII Observations 1978–2008	EHII Observations 1963–2008	Number of Countries (EHII)	Number of Countries (WDI)	Mean Difference EHII − WDI
Americas	349	293	518	750	29	25	−6.04
Eurasia	382	323	919	1,245	44	39	4.75
Asia and Oceania	107	92	496	692	24	16	5.29
Africa and Middle East	165	138	743	1,155	50	41	3.98
Total	1,003	932	2,676	3,842	147	121[a]	1.23

[a]WDI has in addition 28 countries with 107 total observations that are not covered in EHII; They are excluded above.

Conceptual Consistency

Comparing inequality measures, even with matched country-year observations, has a major pitfall. Different data sets may measure different inequality concepts. The prevailing data sets from certain sources (the LIS, EU-SILC, and OECD data sets are examples) have concentrated on providing measures of net or disposable household income inequality. This measure will differ from gross household income by the extent to which direct taxes have progressive effect. And that will vary substantially from one country to the next, depending on political history, economic system, and level of development.

In advanced countries gross income inequality is substantially higher than disposable-income inequality, but by how much? Wang and Caminada (2011) give estimates of fiscal redistribution based on LIS data, but we find that they do not effectively bridge the gap between EHII and disposable-income inequality estimates in the three data sets.

To free an analysis-of-differences from bias due to the difference in concepts, we simply add the mean difference between the EHII estimate of gross income inequality to all values in the disposable-income-based data sets; this value is about 6.7 Gini points for LIS, 6.9 Gini points for the OECD, and about 7.5 Gini points for the EU-SILC. This is obviously an artificial procedure; it does not prove that gross income inequality exceeds net income inequality by these amounts in any particular case. Still, the striking consistency across data sets of these mean differences in these mostly wealthy countries with similar welfare states – despite differences in the specific country-year observations that are matched with EHII – is a reassuring sign. And in general the country-year specific differences between EHII's observations and those in the comparator data sets are also reassuringly small.[7]

Atkinson and Brandolini (2001, 2009) recommend against using a global additive or multiplicative adjustment to deal with differences between gross and net income, since the redistributive impact of taxation may vary over time. However, our choice of an additive adjustment in this case is justified

---

[7]The tables that make these comparisons clear cannot be rendered for publication in print but may be consulted online at http://utip.gov.utexas.edu; working paper #69. There are clearly in these data sets some countries – for instance Turkey and the Baltics – where fiscal redistribution is minor and the mean adjustment is too high, but making a better one would require having reliable calibration specific to the country, for which there is no reliable source.

in that when we plot the changes over time in EHII together with the changes in series drawn from LIS, EU-SILC, or OECD data for individual countries, the trends follow each other remarkably well. As noted previously, Galbraith et al. (2014) provide country-by-country comparisons of the EHII data set with a wide range of measures and estimates drawn from other work, along with documentation of all the measures and estimates. These comparisons show that EHII is a generally reliable reflection of trends, and a reasonable, though not perfect, estimator of the levels of inequality found in surveys.

PAIRWISE COMPARISONS

EHII-LIS

It is important to note that the Luxembourg Income Study is primarily a database service for researchers in comparative micro-economics. It is not specifically oriented to the production of inequality statistics, and it would not be fair to judge the LIS by inequality statistics alone. However LIS does produce a table of summary Gini coefficients, carefully adjusted to consistency on various concepts, and these have achieved wide acceptance and use.

The most obvious point of comparison is the far greater coverage of EHII. However, it is also clear that the two data sets are highly compatible; they share rankings and also trends to a high degree. Only China appears far out of place in the cross-country rankings, but this could be because China is ranked on its average EHII value, including low values from earlier years, whereas there is only one LIS value for China, from among the (more recent) peak years in Chinese inequality.

For the United States, after adjusting for the mean difference in overlapping observations, LIS shows higher *relative* values than EHII — a point of difference likely due to the fact that incomes based on capital values are very important in US data, and are not picked up in EHII. Since EHII is estimated from pay statistics rather than tax records or income surveys, this suggests that EHII is not based on a model appropriate to capture non-earnings sources of income. However, this appears to be a problem very specific to the United States. Apart from the United Kingdom in the OECD comparison below, the same cause does not appear to produce

observed discrepancies for other countries. Galbraith et al. (2014) explore
this issue in depth.

The LIS Gini is lower for Greece than EHII's − an unexplained
divergence − and there is an anomalous one-year discrepancy for France.
LIS has one value for Japan that is considerably lower than the EHII estimate, even after adjusting for the mean degree of fiscal redistribution.
Otherwise the two data sets broadly coincide. A notable instance of agreement is the high (singleton) LIS value for India − far out of step with the
consumption-based WDI Gini coefficients for that country, but very close
to the EHII estimates.

EHII-OECD

Comparing EHII and the OECD data sets, again the major difference is in
coverage, which is dense in EHII going back to 1963, but very spotty in the
OECD's own collection before 2004.

Again we adjust for the conceptual difference by shifting the OECD
measures by the mean difference for overlapping values, in this case 6.9
Gini points.

Once this adjustment is made, the two data sets are largely consistent.
As does LIS, the OECD shows higher values for the United States than
EHII, and also for the United Kingdom, which is the other major economy
with large amounts of well-recorded capital-asset-based incomes. Korea is
one country for which the OECD reports a lower average inequality ranking than EHII, however OECD data for Korea are all very recent, and the
ranking of that country in the EHII data set is influenced by high values
earlier in its history. Recently Korean scholars have noted the problems of
under-coverage of top income earners in Household Income and
Expenditure Survey, collected by Korea's Statistical Office and the survey
tends to underestimate inequality in market and disposable income (Kim &
Kim, 2013). The OECD Database publishes Gini coefficients based on this
Survey, which may explain the lower average in the OECD measures.

EHII-EU-SILC

The EU-SILC is a data set of disposable-income inequalities, and therefore
the raw Gini values are comprehensively lower than those in EHII or any
other data focused on gross household income. Our comparison is

therefore again with the EU-SILC values after adjusting for the mean difference between the two data sets; in this case the adjustment is 7.5 Gini points.[8]

The advantage of EU-SILC, as noted previously, is excellent coverage over the most recent years. The disadvantage is lack of historical depth and of course the narrow focus on the EU and its near neighbors alone. Discrepancies against EHII within this range of countries appear to be subtle; both data sets show Scandinavia and Eastern Europe to be on the low side, and Southern Europe and especially Turkey to be high.

EHII-WDI

A glance at Table 2 shows the dominance of EHII over the WDI in coverage of every region. However a striking aspect of the comparison is the areas of disagreement over inequality values.

The WDI uses a variety of concepts, including both consumption and income measures of inequality, without attempting to standardize them. Differences in consumption and income measures of inequality can be very large. Still, outside the OECD most estimates of fiscal redistribution (gross to net) are very small, and the mean difference between the WDI as a whole and EHII for some 846 matched observations is only about 1.7 Gini points. Mean differences between the WDI and EHII for the various regions are larger, however, and are reported in Table 2.

For the Americas, the two data sets are in broad agreement, with just a few anomalous values for the WDI in Jamaica and Peru. Both show only a handful of countries in the moderate-to-low-inequality range typical of the advanced world; in EHII these are Cuba, Canada, and the United States, with Uruguay, Costa Rica, and Nicaragua during the revolutionary period coming in just above. Uniquely, average values for the Americas in WDI are higher than they are in EHII; otherwise EHII measures tend to exceed those in WDI, especially in Asia where WDI incorporates numerous consumption-inequality measures.

---

[8]We thank a referee for pointing out that (except for the United Kingdom and Ireland) the EU-SILC data are based on surveys of income for the year prior to that reported. We have not adjusted the comparison for this as the effect for present purposes is likely to be very small.

For Eurasia, the main area of disagreement is over the inequality values in the countries of the former USSR. In EHII, outside the Baltics these are all relatively close to each other, and with inequality measures above those for Western Europe, as indicated by their grouping together by rank on the matrix. For the WDI, they are highly diverse, with the Ukraine, Moldova, and Kazakhstan showing as much more egalitarian than Russia, almost from the start of the separate existence of those countries. In our view, countries with closely related economic structures and histories – such as those of the former USSR – likely shared common inequality characteristics at the outset and even now, although they may diverge as time passes.

For Asia, the most important disagreements are over India and Indonesia, as well as Bangladesh, Nepal, Pakistan, and Sri Lanka, which are ranked by the WDI as low-inequality countries – with inequality values below those of Australia, in some cases. This is evidently because of the use of consumption-inequality measures for those countries, which tend to run some 20 Gini points below the corresponding income measures. All six countries are ranked as high-inequality by EHII, and (as noted above) the EHII measures for India come very close to the singleton income-inequality measure for that country recently published by LIS. It seems obvious that even if the expenditure-inequality measures are to be taken at face value, they are not comparable with income-inequality measures and it is essentially meaningless to include them in the same table.

For Africa and the Middle East the two sets of measures are discordant. Notably, the EHII value for South Africa is lower than that reported by WDI and also by almost all studies in the survey literature. We are inclined to distrust our estimate, although the large number of respondents in South African surveys reporting zero household income may be distorting the Lorenz curve and Gini coefficient in ways not found in most other countries. On the other hand, the cluster of oil producers in the high-inequality range for Africa and the Middle East, from Qatar and Kuwait to Angola, makes sense to us, as do the (relatively) egalitarian measures for Malta, the Seychelles, Algeria, Mauritius, The Gambia, pre-occupation Iraq and post-revolutionary Iran. In contrast, the WDI measures for Sub-Saharan Africa do not appear to follow any particular logic of regional or economic structure.

Still, whichever source one chooses, for much of Africa there is very little to go on. On one side, surveys are rare and there is no reason for confidence that they were taken in a consistent manner at different times, let alone across different countries; in fact given the mixture of consumption and income inequality measures in this table it is clear they were not. On the other side, the industrial sectors of most African countries are small, and so the foundation of the EHII estimate for this region is comparatively weak. We like our model and the fact that it gives results for many countries that track survey measures very well. For Sub-Saharan Africa, however, it may be best to conclude that while inequality is certainly high, and broadly similar to that found elsewhere in developing countries, all precise measures for the region are open to doubt.

The WDI measures, in addition to being sparse, are sometimes volatile within countries over short periods of time. Notable instances of large jumps in Gini scores in adjacent observations over short intervals — usually less than five years — occur for Angola (59 → 43), Bolivia (42 → 54), Central African Republic (44 → 56), Kenya (57 → 42), Kyrgyzstan (26 → 53), Paraguay (41 → 58), Peru (35 → 56 over one year!), Senegal (54 → 41), the Seychelles (43 → 66!), and Venezuela (53 → 44). Apart from the collapse of communism in the early 1990s, there is little known basis in the political history of these countries — or almost any country — for such shifts.

For these reasons, in our view the WDI measures of inequality are haphazard. They do not meet the standards set by any of the other comparison data sets, for coverage or comparability.

Summary of Comparisons

Table 3 presents summary information on the divergences between matched values of EHII and the other data sets. The mean divergences are as reported previously, while the standard deviations of divergences from EHII give an impression of the general correspondence of values in the pairwise comparisons. The "volatility" reported in the final two columns provides a summary measure of the stability of inequality coefficients measured through time, in the penultimate column for the various comparator data sets, and in the final column for the EHII values for the same countries and years covered. A higher volatility results from larger reported changes within particular countries over time, which is itself a "flag" for skepticism, since in general Gini coefficients evolve slowly. It is therefore worthwhile to note that the EHII volatility across time within countries is

Table 3.   Summary Measures of Divergence across Data Sets.

Data Set	Years Covered	Mean Divergence from EHII	Standard Deviation of Divergence from EHII	Volatility[a] of Gini Coefficient across Countries	Volatility of EHII Gini across Matched Countries and Years Covered
LIS	1967–2008	6.34	4.25	1.87	1.55
OECD	1983–2008	6.88	3.36	1.48	1.61
EU-SILC	1995–2008	7.57	3.75	1.56	0.92
WDI: Americas	1978–2008	−4.82	5.97	3.33	1.85
WDI: Eurasia	1978–2008	6.5	6.57	3.04	2.52
WDI: Asia and Oceania	1978–2008	8.51	9.25	3.08	2.86
WDI: Africa and Middle East	1978–2008	4.34	10.34	4.47	2.3
WDI: All EHII Countries	1978–2008	1.65	8.93	3.53	2.37

[a]Volatility is measured as the mean of country-level standard deviations of Gini coefficients.

generally lower than for any of the other data sets, except marginally in the case of the OECD.

CONCLUSION

As a general conclusion, EHII is highly consistent with LIS, OECD, and EU-SILC, notwithstanding the difference in concepts measured, or differences in tax systems and welfare states. However EHII's coverage and historical depth are far greater. We take the success in tracking the (fairly reliable) inequality measures for rich country disposable income to be a sign of the general power of the relationship between industrial pay inequality and household income inequalities, and therefore an indication that the model underlying EHII is widely applicable around the world.

While the reduction in inequality achieved by passing from gross to net income is important in the wealthy countries that predominate in LIS, OECD, and EU-SILC data sets, differences across wealthy countries in the degree of redistribution and changes through time within countries both appear to be quite small. In poorer countries, the reduction in inequality achieved by tax systems is much smaller, and may be effectively nil, and again both differences across countries and changes through time in this reduction are small. Therefore it appears that in both rich and poor countries, taken as separate groups, differences and changes in *gross* income inequality are the primary source of differences and changes in inequalities generally.[9]

EHII is much less consonant with the WDI, even though the global mean divergence is small. Rather, a major source of inconsistency appears to be the mish-mash of different concepts covered in the WDI, an apparent artifact of the Bank's deference to the reporting preferences and survey histories of its member states. The conclusion we draw is that the WDI inequality coefficients are merely erratic, and that the data set should not be used for comparative purposes. Which means, in effect, that it should not be used at all.

Finally, in our view, the case for EHII as a broadly useful comparative data set with wide geographic and deep historical coverage speaks for itself. In particular, Atkinson and Brandolini (2001, 2009) and Jenkins (2015) stress the difficulties of choosing consistent Gini values for comparative research; EHII has the advantage of providing consistent values without compromising coverage. There are of course no "true" measures of inequality and no single correct inequality concept, nor any ideal data set. All of the information in this field consists of estimates and approximations, and the compromises required for any particular study will depend on the objectives in each case. Yet consistency of the EHII data, together with its extensive coverage, can provide valuable insight in studying comparative and historical developments, and especially the relationship between the evolution of inequality and global economic phenomena.

ACKNOWLEDGMENTS

We thank the editors of *Research in Labor Economics*, three anonymous referees, and the Institute for New Economic Thinking for generous support.

---

[9]However, it remains true that for the richer countries gross income inequality will overstate the degree of inequality actually experienced in household living standards.

REFERENCES

Atkinson, A. B., & Brandolini, A. (2001). Promise and pitfalls in the use of 'secondary' datasets: Income inequality in OECD countries as a case study. *Journal of Economic Literature*, *34*(3), 771–799.

Atkinson, A. B., & Brandolini, A. (2009). On data: A case study of the evolution of income inequality across time and across countries. *Cambridge Journal of Economics*, *33*, 381–404. doi:10.1093/cje/bel013

Bourguignon, F. (2015, December). Appraising income inequality databases in Latin America. *Journal of Economic Inequality*, Special Issue on Cross-National Inequality Databases, *13*(4), 557–578.

Brandolini, A. (2014). The World Top Incomes Database – WTID: An assessment. Paper presented at the UNU-WIDER Conference "Inequality: measurement, trends, impacts and policies," in the panel. *Appraising World Income Inequality Databases*, September 5–6, 2014. Helsinki, Finland.

Conceicao, P., Galbraith, J. K., & Bradford, P. (2001). The Theil index in sequences of nested and hierarchic grouping structures. *Eastern Economic Journal*, *27*(4), 491–514.

Galbraith, J. K., Lu, J., & Darity, W. A., Jr. (1999, January). *Measuring the evolution of inequality in the global economy*. UTIP Working Paper No. 7.

Galbraith, J. K., & Kum, H. (2005). Estimating the inequality of household incomes: A statistical approach to the creation of a dense and consistent global data set. *Review of Income and Wealth*, *1*, 115–143.

Galbraith, J. K., Shams, A., Halbach, B., Malinowska, A., & Zhang, W. (2014). *The UTIP global inequality data sets 1963–2008: Updates, revisions and quality checks*. UTIP Working Paper No. 68, forthcoming, United Nations University Working Paper series.

Gasparini, L., & Tornarolli, L. (2015, December). A review of the OECD income distribution database. *Journal of Economic Inequality*, Special Issue on Cross-National Inequality Databases, *13*(4), 579–602.

Jenkins, S. (2015, December). World income inequality databases: An assessment of WIID and SWIID. *Journal of Economic Inequality*, Special Issue on Cross-National Inequality Databases, *13*(4), 629–671. doi:10.1007/s10888-015-9305-3

Kim, N. N., & Kim, J. (2013). *Re-evaluating Korea's income redistributive measures*. Naksungdae Institute of Economic Research Working Paper 2013-08.

Ravaillon, M. (2015, December). The Luxembourg income study. *Journal of Economic Inequality*, Special Issue on Cross-National Inequality Databases, *13*(4), 527–547.

Smeeding, T., & Latner, J. P. (2015, December). PovcalNet, WDI and 'All the Ginis': A critical review. *Journal of Economic Inequality*, Special Issue on Cross-National Inequality Databases, *13*(4), 603–608. doi:10.1007/s10888-015-9312-4

Solt, F. (2016). The standardized world income inequality database. *Social Science Quarterly*.

Wang, C., & Caminada, K. (2011). *Disentangling income inequality and the redistributive effect of social transfers and taxes in 36 LIS countries*. LIS Working Paper No. 567. doi:10.1111/ssqu.12295

DATA SETS

Alvaredo, F., Atkinson, T., Piketty, T., Saez, E., & Zucman, G. *The World Wealth and Income Database*. Retrieved from http://myweb.uiowa.edu/fsolt/swiid/swiid.html. Accessed on November 28, 2015.

Deininger, K., & Squire, L. (1996). A new data set measuring income inequality. *World Bank Economic Review*, *10*(3), 565−591.

Eurostat, EU Statistics on Income and Living Conditions. (1995−2013). Retrieved from http://ee.europa.eu/eurostat/web/main/home. Accessed on December 19, 2014.

Luxembourg Income Studies. *Key figures on inequality and poverty*. Retrieved from http://www.lisdatacenter.org/. Accessed on November 29, 2015.

Organization for Economic Cooperation and Development. (2015). *Income inequality indicators*. Retrieved from http://www.oecd.org. Accessed on December 22, 2014.

Solt, F. *The standardized world income inequality dataset, version 5.0*. Retrieved from http://myweb.uiowa.edu/fsolt/swiid/swiid.html. Accessed on November 28, 2015.

University of Texas Inequality Project. *Estimated household income inequality*. Retrieved from http://utip.gov.utexas.edu. Accessed on November 28, 2015.

UNU-WIDER, 'World Income Inequality Database (WIID3.3)'. (2015, September). Retrieved from https://www.wider.unu.edu/project/wiid-world-income-inequality-database

World Bank. (2007). *World development indicators online*. Retrieved from http://data.world-bank.org/data-catalog/world-development-indicators. Accessed on October 3, 2014.

APPENDIX A

Table A1. Summary of Values by Country: EHII, WDI, LIS, OECD and EU-SILC.

Region	Country	EHII			WDI			LIS			OECD			EU-SILC		
		# Obs.	Mean	Std. Dev.	# Obs.	Mean	Std. Dev.	# Obs.	Mean	Std. Dev.	# Obs.	Mean	Std. Dev.	# Obs.	Mean	Std. Dev.
Asia and Oceania	Afghanistan	22	40.9	3.9												
	American Samoa															
	Australia	36	33.2	2.2	6	33.1	1.1	8	30.9	1.8	6					
	Bangladesh	27	44.6	2.6	8	30.2	3.2									
	Bhutan				3	41.2	4.9									
	Brunei Darussalam															
	Cambodia	3	51.6	7.9	7	35.8	3.1									
	China	16	35.6	3.5	11	36.3	5.9	1	50.5							
	Fiji	32	44.1	2.9	2	44.8	2.8									
	French Polynesia															
	Guam															
	Hong Kong	36	32.9	8.4												
	India	45	50.0	1.5	6	32.7	1.7	1	49.1							
	Indonesia	36	49.5	1.9	10	31.2	2.5									
	Japan	45	37.2	3.1	1	32.1		1	30.2		6	37.0	1.4			
	Kiribati															
	Korea, Rep.	44	39.8	2.5				1	31.1		7	35.3	0.4			
	Korea, Dem. Rep.															

Country									
Lao PDR	39	41.5	2.5	5	33.9	2.4			
Macao									
Malaysia				9	46.4	3.4			
Maldives				2	50.0	17.9			
Marshall Islands									
Micronesia, Fed. Sts.				1	61.1				
Mongolia	17	49.1	2.3	4	33.2	2.6			
Myanmar (Burma)	10	46.1	3.6						
Nepal	10	49.3	2.6	4	35.5	6.0			
New Caledonia									
New Zealand	33	35.1	3.4				8	36.6	2.5
Northern Mariana Islands									
Pakistan	32	47.6	2.2	9	31.4	1.8			
Palau									
Papua New Guinea	25	50.6	1.6	1	50.9				
Philippines	41	47.4	1.1	10	43.5	1.8			
Samoa									
Singapore	46	38.5	3.9						
Solomon Islands									
Sri Lanka	26	45.9	2.2	6	36.3	3.7			
Taiwan	25	31.8	1.6				9	28.9	1.9
Thailand	23	46.3	4.2	13	43.1	2.2			
Timor-Leste				1	30.4				
Tonga	23	45.9	3.6						

Table A1. (Continued)

Region	Country	EHII			WDI			LIS			OECD			EU-SILC		
		# Obs.	Mean	Std. Dev.	# Obs.	Mean	Std. Dev.	# Obs.	Mean	Std. Dev.	# Obs.	Mean	Std. Dev.	# Obs.	Mean	Std. Dev.
	Tuvalu															
	Vanuatu															
	Vietnam	19	44.1	7.2	8	36.5	1.3									
Eurasia	Albania				6	30.4	1.3									
	Andorra															
	Armenia	5	53.0	5.0	14	33.7	4.0									
	Austria	44	34.6	1.0	6	29.2	3.1	6	26.3	1.9	8	30.3	0.7	18	26.3	1.4
	Azerbaijan	17	49.5	6.1	7	24.8	9.5									
	Belarus				17	27.3	2.1									
	Belgium	42	35.8	2.5	6	27.4	3.1	6	24.6	2.3	7	34.5	1.1	18	27.4	1.2
	Bosnia and Herzegovina	2	36.2	1.2	3	32.4	2.1									
	Bulgaria	45	31.9	6.0	11	30.2	4.2							14	30.4	4.7
	Channel Islands															
	Croatia	23	37.1	4.2	7	29.1	3.5							11	29.6	1.5
	Cyprus	46	40.2	2.5										11	29.5	1.4
	Czech Republic	44	24.5	3.9	9	25.7	2.4	6	24.8	2.2	11	29.2	1.1	10	25.1	0.4
	Denmark	42	31.3	0.9	7	25.3	1.4	7	23.6	1.3	23	26.8	1.3	15	24.5	2.7
	Estonia	9	34.8	0.4	15	33.3	3.9	4	33.7	2.1	8	35.6	1.5	14	33.5	1.9
	Faeroe Islands															
	Finland	45	32.3	1.2	7	25.7	2.7	7	23.8	2.6	27	29.5	2.8	18	25.1	1.6
	France	30	35.6	1.6	5	33.3	2.9	7	29.6	2.2	16	30.7	1.0	19	28.6	1.3

GDR	19	22.3	1.6											
Georgia	11	48.4	1.6	17	40.5	1.2	2	41.6	3.0	22	31.4	1.7	16	27.5	2.1
Germany	45	32.9	1.8	9	29.8	1.3	11	26.8	1.3	11	35.3	1.0	18	33.9	0.8
Greece	41	42.4	1.0	5	34.8	1.4	5	33.2	1.1						
Greenland															
Hungary	43	31.9	5.9	14	27.5	2.4	7	28.9	1.5	15	30.8	1.1	13	26.5	2.4
Iceland	20	33.0	1.2	3	27.8	1.5	3	25.9	1.6	8	31.3	2.3	10	25.8	2.0
Ireland	45	36.4	1.1	8	34.6	2.2	8	31.8	1.6	8	34.8	1.3	17	31.2	1.5
Isle of Man															
Italy	40	37.0	1.2	11	34.9	2.0	11	32.6	1.8	9	32.7	1.8	17	31.5	1.2
Kazakhstan	10	46.2	2.3	12	30.5	2.8									
Kosovo															
Kyrgyzstan	13	43.4	3.8	15	34.8	6.4							10	36.1	1.4
Latvia	16	37.7	2.2	12	32.5	4.1									
Liechtenstein															
Lithuania	16	38.8	2.6	14	32.9	3.4							11	34.0	2.1
Luxembourg	44	32.6	2.4				8	25.6	1.6	11	30.8	1.4	18	27.5	1.3
Macedonia	20	40.0	4.4	8	38.2	5.0									
Moldova	17	41.7	4.9	16	34.7	3.9									
Monaco															
Montenegro				7	30.0	0.8									
Netherlands	42	34.3	1.7	8	29.8	1.8	8	25.5	1.5	11	33.0	0.9	18	26.8	1.3
Norway	44	33.3	1.7	7	26.9	1.8	8	24.0	1.0	8	28.8	1.8	11	24.9	2.3
Poland	32	32.2	4.7	18	31.8	3.2	8	29.9	2.2	8	32.6	2.6	11	31.7	1.6
Portugal	39	39.7	2.1							8	37.4	1.7	17	36.1	1.3
Romania	26	34.6	4.5	17	28.6	1.9	2	28.0	0.1				14	32.6	2.6
Russia	16	40.2	1.6	13	38.6	5.8	5	36.3	3.3						

Table A1. (Continued)

Region	Country	EHII			WDI			LIS			OECD			EU-SILC		
		# Obs.	Mean	Std. Dev.	# Obs.	Mean	Std. Dev.	# Obs.	Mean	Std. Dev.	# Obs.	Mean	Std. Dev.	# Obs.	Mean	Std. Dev.
	San Marino															
	Serbia	17	36.2	1.6	9	30.8	2.1	3	33.3	1.0				1	38.0	
	Slovakia	22	31.0	4.0	10	25.8	3.6	5	24.4	3.2	8	29.7	1.5	9	25.4	1.3
	Slovenia	45	39.5	1.1	11	26.8	2.9	5	23.5	1.0	8	25.4	0.4	13	23.1	0.9
	Spain	38	28.7	0.9	7	34.3	1.7	8	32.3	1.7	8	33.9	1.3	19	33.0	1.4
	Sweden	5	32.0	0.3	6	25.3	1.5	8	22.8	2.1	9	28.5	3.5	14	23.6	1.1
	Switzerland				5	34.4	2.4	5	28.7	1.9	2	29.9	0.7	7	29.8	1.0
	Tajikistan				5	31.8	1.6									
	Turkey	43	45.7	2.3	12	40.5	1.7				7	43.9	2.9	3	45.3	0.6
	Turkmenistan				3	34.2	7.3									
	U.K.	41	33.1	3.3	7	37.3	0.8	11	32.1	3.7	16	36.9	1.2	18	32.6	1.4
	Ukraine	17	40.2	2.8	14	28.9	4.1									
	Uzbekistan				4	34.6	8.4									
	Yugoslavia	5	42.2	2.2												
Africa and Middle East	Algeria	26	39.3	1.4	2	37.8	3.4									
	Angola	6	54.0	3.5	2	50.7	11.3									
	Bahrain															
	Benin	7	50.9	1.1	2	41.1	3.5									
	Botswana	21	48.1	2.7	4	60.1	4.4									
	Burkina Faso	10	46.3	2.6	4	45.1	4.7									
	Burundi	17	49.7	2.4	3	36.3	5.2									
	Cabo Verde				2	47.2	4.7									

Country												
Cameroon	28	51.3	4.3		3	42.5	1.9					
Central African Republic	19	48.1	3.7		3	53.7	9.2					
Chad					2	41.5	2.5					
Comoros					1	64.3						
Congo	14	48.5	2.1		2	43.7	5.1					
Congo, Dem. Rep.					1	44.4						
Djibouti			1			40.0						
Egypt	39	44.5	3.7		5	31.6	1.1		1	46.4		
Equatorial Guinea												
Eritrea	42	46.7	2.2									
Ethiopia	19	46.6	1.5		5	33.2	4.1					
Gabon	8	49.8	3.4		1	42.2						
Gambia	8	42.3	1.4		2	48.8	2.1					
Ghana	26	48.8	1.1		5	38.6	3.1					
Guinea					5	41.0	5.1					
Guinea-Bissau					2	41.7	8.7					
Iran	42	44.4	4.3		5	43.3	3.3					
Iraq	27	43.4	3.3		2	29.1	0.7					
Israel	44	40.3	3.0		8	38.9	2.8		9	34.3	3.1	9	41.8	2.4
Ivory Coast	22	47.9	1.3		9	40.1	2.9					
Jordan	42	48.7	1.5		7	36.4	3.7					
Kenya	36	49.5	1.7		4	48.4	6.5					
Kuwait	32	52.4	2.2									
Lebanon												
Lesotho	11	50.7	1.7		5	56.6	4.4					

Table A1. (Continued)

Region	Country	EHII			WDI			LIS			OECD			EU-SILC		
		# Obs.	Mean	Std. Dev.	# Obs.	Mean	Std. Dev.	# Obs.	Mean	Std. Dev.	# Obs.	Mean	Std. Dev.	# Obs.	Mean	Std. Dev.
	Liberia	3	50.2	1.4	1	38.2										
	Libyan Arab Jamahiriya	17	45.8	3.5												
	Madagascar	26	45.7	3.3	7	43.0	3.7									
	Malawi	35	50.6	3.6	3	45.5	5.2									
	Mali				4	40.6	7.3									
	Malta	44	34.8	3.0										10	27.7	1.0
	Mauritania				6	42.0	4.5									
	Mauritius	40	40.9	4.3	2	35.8	0.2									
	Morocco	31	49.7	1.6	5	39.9	0.8									
	Mozambique	13	51.4	1.2	3	45.8	1.3									
	Namibia				3	66.5	6.9									
	Niger				5	37.9	6.0									
	Nigeria	28	45.8	2.6	5	42.6	3.3									
	Oman	15	51.5	1.3												
	Qatar	15	53.1	1.6												
	Rwanda	12	48.8	3.5	4	46.1	11.5									
	Sao Tome and Principe				2	42.3	12.0									
	Saudi Arabia															
	Senegal	29	45.7	4.0	5	43.3	6.1									
	Seychelles	11	36.3	2.4	2	54.3	16.3									
	Sierra Leone				2	37.4	2.9									

Somalia	12	47.2	1.4						
South Africa	41	44.3	1.5	6	61.5	4.3	3	58.4	1.2
South Sudan									
Sudan	2	48.0	0.1	1	35.3				
Swaziland	26	50.3	2.5	3	55.2	4.8			
Syrian Arab Republic	28	46.4	1.7	6	25.3	1.5			
Tanzania	34	50.1	2.5	4	36.0	2.0			
Togo	14	49.4	3.4	2	44.1	2.6			
Tunisia	29	48.3	2.8	6	39.9	2.8			
U.A.E.	4	46.4	3.1						
Uganda	19	49.0	1.9	8	43.1	2.6			
West Bank and Gaza				3	35.7	2.6			
Yemen	27	48.7	5.7	2	34.7	1.7			
Zambia	18	47.6	1.7	7	51.5	4.9			
Zimbabwe	36	45.4	1.7						
Americas									
Antigua and Barbuda									
Argentina	17	45.7	2.0	23	48.1	3.2			
Aruba									
Bahamas	3	50.1	1.2						
Barbados	28	44.5	1.5						
Belize	2	47.3	0.6	7	57.6	2.9			
Bermuda									
Bolivia	32	48.0	3.2	15	54.2	5.9			

Table A1. (*Continued*)

Region	Country	EHII			WDI			LIS			OECD			EU-SILC		
		# Obs.	Mean	Std. Dev.	# Obs.	Mean	Std. Dev.	# Obs.	Mean	Std. Dev.	# Obs.	Mean	Std. Dev.	# Obs.	Mean	Std. Dev.
	Brazil	17	48.5	0.7	28	57.8	2.7	4	46.6	1.6						
	Canada	45	36.5	1.6	10	32.7	1.1	12	30.0	1.6	29	34.2	1.5			
	Cayman Islands															
	Chile	44	46.4	2.5	11	54.5	2.1				3	52.0	0.4			
	Colombia	43	45.1	1.1	20	55.8	2.5	3	50.4	2.0						
	Costa Rica	22	42.0	1.2	26	47.3	3.2									
	Cuba	13	32.1	0.9												
	Curacao															
	Dominica															
	Dominican Republic	23	46.7	2.1	18	49.5	1.9									
	Ecuador	45	46.4	2.4	16	52.1	3.5									
	El Salvador	28	45.6	2.0	18	48.8	4.1									
	Grenada															
	Guatemala	26	47.8	3.7	9	55.3	2.8	1	49.0							
	Guyana				2	48.0	5.0									
	Haiti	21	47.0	1.9	1	59.2										
	Honduras	26	44.0	3.1	23	55.7	2.5									
	Jamaica	34	48.6	2.0	8	46.1	10.0									
	Mexico	31	43.6	1.7	14	49.2	2.1	12	46.6	1.7	7	49.3	2.4			
	Nicaragua	21	41.9	1.6	5	46.4	6.5									
	Panama	40	45.5	2.5	19	54.9	2.9									

	Gross Income			Mixed			Net Income			Net Income			Net Income		
Paraguay	2	44.6	0.2	16	52.4	4.1									
Peru	21	50.9	3.1	18	48.6	5.2	4	48.6	2.9						
Puerto Rico	12	47.8	1.9												
Sint Maarten (Dutch part)															
St. Kitts and Nevis															
St. Lucia				1	42.6										
St. Martin (French part)															
St. Vincent and the Grenadines															
Suriname	20	46.2	2.2	1	52.9										
Trinidad and Tobago	26	49.3	2.3	2	41.4	1.6									
Turks and Caicos Islands															
U.S.A.	42	36.9	1.7	8	39.7	1.7	11	35.2	2.2	30	40.7	1.8			
Uruguay	32	42.7	3.4	20	44.6	2.2	4	40.6	2.4						
Venezuela	34	43.1	2.5	13	48.0	3.6									
Virgin Islands															
Total	3,842			1,110			259			382			443		
Concept	Gross Income			Mixed			Net Income			Net Income			Net Income		

APPENDIX B

Table B1. Estimated Household Income Inequality (EHII), by Region, 1963–2008.

Years	Countries																									
	ALB	ARM	AUT	AZE	BEL	BGR	BIH	CHE	CYP	CZE	DNK	ESP	EST	FIN	FRA	GBR	GEO	GER	GRC	HRV	HUN	IRL	ISL	ITA	KAZ	KYR
														Europe and Central Asia												
1963			34.7		32.6	29.7			46.1	22.8	30.6	40.7		32.9		28.0		31.0	42.8		29.8	36.1				
1964			34.8		32.4	29.4			45.0	23.0	30.4	40.4		33.1				31.2	43.5		29.2	36.4				
1965			34.9		32.3	28.5			44.4	23.0	30.3	40.1		33.0				30.8	44.0		29.4	36.2				
1966			34.6		32.5	28.2			44.3	22.6	30.7	40.8		33.2				30.9	43.4		28.8	36.1				
1967			34.9		33.0	28.1			43.7	22.3	31.1	40.6		33.3				31.4	42.7		28.7	36.3		40.1		
1968			35.1		32.9	27.6			43.3	21.5	31.4	40.7		33.5		28.2		31.4	42.4		28.0	36.0	35.0	39.7		
1969			35.1		32.2	27.9			43.1	21.2	30.9	41.0		32.9		28.3		31.5	42.0		27.3	36.4	35.0	39.0		
1970			34.2		31.7	27.4			42.3	21.2	30.6	41.0		32.4		28.4		31.5	42.2		26.9	35.9	34.0	39.2		
1971			33.6		31.8	27.5			42.1	21.4	30.8	40.7		31.4		28.5		31.2	41.9		27.1	36.3	33.5	38.3		
1972			33.3		32.2	27.9			40.7	21.4	30.8	40.7		31.4		29.2		31.2	41.7		26.5	36.2	31.9	38.2		
1973			32.6		32.9	27.0			40.7	21.3	30.3	40.7		30.9		29.1		31.2	41.5		26.5	35.3	32.4	37.6		
1974			32.9		33.1	26.8			43.2	21.3	30.7	40.9		30.7		28.9		31.5	41.6		26.1	35.3	33.2	36.8		
1975			33.7		33.7	27.0			44.5	21.1	32.1	39.9		31.1		29.4		31.9	41.5		26.4	36.0	33.9	36.8		
1976			33.4		33.9	27.1			43.0	21.2	31.7	40.1		30.9		29.4		32.0	40.9		25.8	36.4	34.2	36.4		
1977			33.1		34.6	27.4			41.9	21.2	31.4	40.3		31.1	32.8	29.1		32.1	41.0		26.1	36.5	32.9	35.9		
1978			33.0		34.7	27.3			41.4	21.1	31.7	36.9		31.4	33.0	29.5		31.9	41.5		26.0	36.4	32.1	35.9		
1979			33.2		35.5	27.8			40.6	21.0	31.8	37.4		31.2	32.9	29.7		32.0	41.9		26.1	36.3	29.7	35.2		
1980			33.4		35.7	27.1			40.5	21.1	31.9	37.0		30.3	33.1	30.5		32.0	42.1		26.4	36.1		34.9		
1981			33.7		36.2	27.1			38.9	20.9	31.7	37.6		30.5	33.6	31.7		32.3	42.3		26.5	36.1		35.0		
1982			34.1		36.4	27.1			39.0	20.9	32.0	37.9		30.5	33.8	32.5		32.4	41.4		26.8	36.8		35.5		
1983			34.3		36.5	27.5			39.0	20.9	31.9	37.9		30.8	33.5	33.0		32.4	41.6		27.5	37.3		36.8		

Year																										
1984			34.4		36.8	27.4			38.8	20.8	31.4	38.2		31.3	33.7	33.3		32.5	41.9		27.9	38.0		37.5		39.4
1985			34.5		37.1	27.3			38.6	20.6	31.0	38.9		31.5	34.5	33.8		32.6	41.6		28.2	38.0		37.2		43.0
1986			34.4		37.0	27.4			39.0	20.7	30.6	39.3		31.8	34.7	34.0		32.5	40.8	30.6	28.0	38.5		37.9		38.0
1987			34.7		37.3	28.0			38.7	23.8	30.9	39.3		31.8	34.7	34.3		32.5	41.1	31.1	28.6	38.6		37.9		37.9
1988	32.3		34.4		37.4	27.2			38.6	23.4	31.1	39.7		31.8	34.9	34.2		32.5	41.3	32.4	30.4	38.7				38.7
1989	30.8		34.5		37.1	25.0			38.1	23.2	31.0	40.0		32.1	34.6	34.2		32.5	42.0	33.2	31.0	38.3	32.7	37.5		
1990	31.2		35.2	38.5	37.0	25.1	35.3		38.4	23.7	29.9	40.0		32.3	36.8	34.6		32.3	42.5	34.3	31.5	38.0	34.4	36.7		
1991			35.2	38.7	37.3	30.2	37.1		38.6	26.2	30.4	39.9		32.3	36.8	35.0		31.6	43.2	35.4	32.9	37.1	32.2	37.7		
1992			35.5	41.9	37.5	35.0			38.7	27.7		40.3		33.3	37.0	35.3		32.2	43.3	29.1		37.2	32.1	37.9		
1993	35.2		35.9	40.1		38.2			39.3	28.7		40.6		33.7	37.0	36.6		32.7	43.0	31.4		37.2	32.5	38.3		
1994	58.0	47.9	35.9	45.5		39.7			38.7			40.6		33.2	37.7	35.3		33.4	43.0	34.8	39.0	36.8	33.1	38.1		44.0
1995	51.9	55.3	35.0	36.9					39.1	28.5	30.7	40.0		33.1		35.7		33.5	43.3	35.9	40.1	36.8	32.5	36.8		44.7
1996	45.2	57.2		37.8		38.9			39.5	28.9	31.4	39.8		32.8	36.2	35.4		34.8	43.9	37.4	40.9	36.7	32.6	35.9		44.5
1997	42.4	57.3	35.5	38.0		40.1		31.6	39.5	29.2	29.8	39.7		33.1	36.3	35.2		35.1	43.2	37.9	41.3	36.1		37.2		46.1
1998	43.1	47.4	35.6	37.7		39.8		32.2	39.5	29.7	30.8	39.6		33.0	36.5	35.4	47.7	34.7	43.3	39.7	39.6	35.7		36.6	46.4	43.7
1999	44.1		35.6	37.7		40.2		31.7	40.4	30.3	31.0	39.4		32.5	36.6	36.4	46.4	33.8		40.4	39.6	35.0		36.6	48.5	49.0
2000	46.1		36.1	37.8		41.4		32.2	38.3	30.5	31.8	39.3	34.7	32.7	36.8	36.8	51.4	35.4		40.7	39.0	34.3		36.4	49.1	47.1
2001	44.6		35.6	38.2		40.7		32.2	38.3	30.2	31.4	38.9	35.5	33.1	36.6	36.4	49.6	35.0	44.1	41.3	39.4	34.8		36.1	48.4	47.6
2002	44.0		35.6	40.6		40.6			37.5	30.1	32.5	38.6	35.2	33.0	36.9	36.6	50.0	35.3		41.4	39.5	34.7		36.2	47.5	
2003	49.7		35.8	39.2		40.3			38.6	30.6	33.0	38.6	35.0	33.7	37.0	37.0	49.6	36.0	44.0	41.2	39.8	34.3		36.3	46.7	
2004	48.1		35.5	39.3		40.3			38.6	29.9	31.7	38.6	34.8	34.4	36.3	37.2	49.1	36.2	44.0	41.1	40.3	34.7		36.1	45.6	
2005	48.5		36.0	39.7		40.1			36.4	30.2	32.9	38.4	34.8	34.0	37.3	36.8	47.4	36.8	44.1	41.3	41.3	36.5		36.6	44.1	
2006	47.5		35.9	39.5		39.9			36.5	30.2	33.7	38.4	34.7	34.6	37.5	37.8	47.9	37.1	43.2	41.3	40.3	36.5		36.5	43.2	
2007	47.2		35.5	50.9	39.6	39.8			36.5	29.8	33.2	38.3	34.4	34.4	37.5	37.6	47.1	36.8	43.2	40.7	40.0	36.7		36.3	42.4	
2008	47.9		50.7	50.7		40.7			36.9				34.3				46.6	40.4								

Table B1. (*Continued*)

Years	LTU	LUX	LVA	MDA	MKD	NLD	NOR	POL	PRT	ROU	RUS	SVK	SVN	SWE	TUR	UKR	YUG
								Europe and Central Asia									
1963		31.8				31.2	31.5		44.1	32.7				29.3	44.9		
1964		30.6				31.2	31.6		43.4	32.1				28.8	45.6		
1965		30.7				31.3	31.7		42.1	31.5				28.5	44.8		
1966		28.7				31.3	31.6		42.6	31.8				28.5	44.4		
1967		28.9				31.8	31.8		42.7	31.9				28.5	44.0		
1968		29.2				31.7	31.6		42.8	31.6				28.5	43.9		
1969		30.0				32.8	31.7		43.5	30.1				27.8	43.5		
1970		32.0				33.2	31.4	29.5	44.0					28.0	43.0		
1971		31.1				33.3	31.5	29.2	41.1					27.9	43.9		
1972		30.5				33.5	31.4	28.9	40.4					27.7	44.7		
1973		30.1				33.4	31.2	28.7	40.2					27.8	42.8		
1974		30.7				33.2	31.5	28.8	40.3					27.5	42.5		
1975		29.7				33.3	32.3	29.2	37.5					27.4	43.4		
1976		29.4				33.3	31.8	29.2	37.9					27.5	42.5		
1977		29.5				32.8	31.4	28.7	37.5					27.6	43.2		
1978		30.5				32.8	31.9	28.8	37.8					27.6	44.2		
1979		31.7				32.8	32.1	29.0	37.5					27.6	46.9		
1980		32.0				32.8	32.1	29.1	37.3					27.6	45.5		
1981		30.9				33.8	32.3	27.5	38.0					27.9	44.9		
1982		32.1				33.8	32.7	27.6	38.3					28.5	44.2		
1983		31.9				34.9	32.7	28.0	38.3					28.9	43.7		
1984		32.0				34.9	33.0	28.7	38.7					28.9	43.8		
1985		32.8				35.4	33.2	29.4	39.5					29.1	43.7		
1986		32.7				35.3	32.9	30.0	39.5					29.2	43.6		

Year																	
1987		32.7			30.7	34.6	33.0	29.6	39.3			22.3	29.0	44.1			
1988		33.7			34.7	35.1	33.4	29.3	40.5			22.8	29.4	44.3			
1989		34.3			33.4	35.3	33.9	29.9	40.7			23.7	29.3	46.0			
1990		34.1		30.2	35.4	35.2	33.9	33.4		24.5		25.7	28.6	47.0			
1991	32.7	33.7			38.5	35.2	35.7	32.8		26.8	31.7	28.4	29.2	47.4			
1992	33.1	33.9		45.0	36.3	35.2	35.8	34.3		30.2	33.9	29.2	30.1	48.9	36.1	
1993	36.1	35.0	41.1	46.3	37.3	35.7	35.1	34.9		30.6	34.6	36.1	29.8	30.5	48.7	33.8
1994		34.9	41.2	47.3	38.3		34.1	36.1		32.2	35.8	38.2	30.3	30.5	49.5	34.0	39.3
1995		33.8	41.8	44.8	39.4	35.4	34.5	36.8		33.6	35.3	39.5	33.0	29.7	49.3	39.1	40.7
1996	39.5	34.4	40.8	42.4	41.2	35.4	34.1		37.2	34.3	36.0	40.4	32.6	29.5	48.3	41.9	42.9
1997	39.4	34.1	38.1	42.6	41.2	36.6	34.0		37.3	37.0	35.8	40.6	33.1	29.3	47.9	42.6	43.6
1998	39.6	34.1	37.1	46.5	41.7	36.4	34.2		37.6	36.4	36.1	40.7	32.8	29.3	48.4	42.5	44.6
1999	40.2		37.3	49.5	41.0	35.5	34.6		37.5	37.1	36.7	42.0	32.4	29.4	48.6	43.0	
2000	40.9	34.3	37.0	45.0	42.4	35.4	34.5		38.2	39.0	36.6	42.7	32.5	29.6	49.6	41.9	
2001	41.6	34.4	36.0	37.4	42.9	36.0	35.2		38.6	39.8	36.9	41.8	32.9		41.5	
2002	40.6	34.6	35.5	40.5		36.8	35.5	42.7	38.6	40.1	37.4	40.5	33.1		49.3	41.0	
2003	40.6	36.4	35.2	39.4	45.2	37.6	36.0	40.0	39.0	39.5	37.6	41.2	33.8		49.3	41.5	
2004	39.6	37.0	35.5	38.9	44.8	36.4	36.6	40.4	39.4	39.4	37.6	41.0	36.9		47.4	41.4	
2005	39.9	36.7	36.0	38.3	45.0	37.0	36.5	40.2	39.1	39.1	38.1	40.4	34.3		46.7	41.1	
2006	39.0	37.7	36.7	38.1	45.9		36.5	40.0	38.9	39.4	37.7	40.0	33.5		46.7	40.3	
2007	38.8	37.3	36.5	36.7	45.0			39.0	39.9	39.0	36.8	39.6	34.9			41.3	
2008	39.5		38.0							39.9		39.1	33.3			40.6	

Table B1. (Continued)

Countries — Asia

Years	AFG	AUS	BGD	CHN	FJI	HKG	IDN	IND	JPN	KHM	KOR	LKA	MMR	MNG	MYS	NPL	NZL	PAK	PHL	PNG	SGP	THA	TON	TWN
1963		30.9						47.0	36.2		43.5							45.0	47.0	51.6	44.7			
1964		31.2						47.1	36.0		43.2						33.9	43.9	46.8	48.4	45.5			
1965		31.1						47.1	35.4		43.8						33.8	44.0	46.6	52.5	46.6			
1966		30.9						47.0	35.0		43.8	51.9					33.8	44.8	46.5	51.4	46.4			
1967		31.0	41.1					47.4	34.9		43.1						33.8	44.5	49.6	51.0	46.0			
1968		31.2	41.8		42.9			48.1	34.5		44.1				46.2		33.9	46.0	47.1	49.7	45.9	49.7		
1969		31.0	42.3					48.0	34.2		43.3				46.7		33.5	44.1	47.3	51.4	45.8	50.0		
1970		31.0	40.2		40.8		51.6	48.3	34.0		43.4				46.1		33.7	44.6	48.2	51.5	45.4	48.1		
1971		31.1	41.8		43.0		52.0	48.6	34.3		44.1				46.3		33.6	48.2	46.7	50.8	44.2	50.0		
1972		31.3	42.1		42.1	27.1	50.8	48.7	33.8		44.1				45.3		33.6	48.3	45.7	51.2	42.2			
1973		31.2	44.3		42.4	29.0	49.7	49.7	33.7		41.7				44.2			47.7	47.0	50.9	40.0			33.9
1974	42.1	31.1	42.1		41.1	27.2	51.1	50.9	34.5		41.9				43.1		32.6	46.8	47.9	50.3	39.3	49.9		34.8
1975	41.8	31.1	43.0		40.9	23.6	50.9	50.7	35.0		42.0				43.0		32.1	46.2	47.0	48.6	38.9	49.9		35.4
1976	43.2	30.7	44.8	31.4	41.2	24.0	51.9	51.5	35.0		40.9				42.3		32.0	45.8	47.6	47.7	38.9	49.9		33.0
1977	44.8	30.9	45.9	32.0	42.7	23.9	51.4	51.3	35.2		40.4				42.7		32.0	47.3	48.0	48.0	38.6	51.2		32.3
1978	45.8	31.6	44.3	32.5	43.2	22.9	51.4	50.9	35.4		39.7				42.2		31.8	48.0	46.8	50.2	37.4			32.9
1979	43.7	31.8	43.1	32.4	43.1	23.1	51.2	50.7	35.5		38.8				40.8		32.2	49.1	45.4	50.1	36.2	49.9	42.4	33.3
1980	43.9	32.3	42.4	31.9	44.6	23.2	51.2	51.4	35.5		39.4	47.8			40.1		32.5	47.8	44.2	50.0	35.4		41.0	32.2
1981	43.3	32.5	43.5	33.2	45.4	25.4	50.6	51.7	35.5		40.0	49.4			39.7		32.1	47.3	45.5	47.0	35.9		41.5	31.6
1982	41.5	32.9	44.4	33.5	46.2	24.6	50.5	50.7	35.8		39.4	46.9			40.8		32.3	48.6	45.4	50.4	36.4	47.5		31.5
1983	41.4	33.5	45.1	34.1	47.4	24.6	50.4	49.8	35.7		39.9	45.8			42.0		32.3	48.8	47.6	51.7	36.6		48.8	31.0
1984	42.1	33.9	43.9	34.9	46.8	24.0	50.5	49.8	35.6		38.8	47.2			41.9		32.5	49.4	46.9	52.1	36.2	46.9	43.3	31.0
1985	45.3	34.2	45.3	34.8	46.7	25.3	50.9	49.6	35.7		38.5	47.2			43.2		33.0	48.6	47.4	53.4	37.2		45.4	30.0
1986	44.3	34.7	46.1	34.8	44.5	24.6	51.0	50.0	35.8		37.8	45.1			44.2	47.8		48.3	48.2	52.2	37.5	44.5	47.8	29.5

Year																							
1987	38.2	35.2	45.9	47.1	24.8	51.1	50.1	35.9		36.8	48.3			43.9	50.9		48.9	48.6	52.9	36.4	47.5	48.9	29.1
1988	37.1	34.9	46.4	48.7	26.0	50.0	49.8	35.9		36.6	47.1			43.6	50.7		48.4	48.5		34.8	49.3	41.1	29.7
1989		34.9	47.8	48.9	27.4	49.5	50.2	35.9		36.7	45.4	47.6		42.2	50.5		48.9	48.1		34.5	46.0	39.4	30.9
1990		35.6	47.7	48.2	29.3	47.6	49.9	35.8		37.4	46.4	46.8	49.5	40.9	52.4		49.4	48.3		34.2	46.7	43.4	31.7
1991		36.1	48.9	50.2	31.1	47.4	49.7	35.5		36.7	44.6	46.1	51.0	40.0	49.3		49.9	48.3		34.3		46.0	32.0
1992		37.0	49.2	47.8	32.2	46.9	50.0	35.5	52.4	37.3	43.0	45.2	49.9	39.3				48.6		34.3	45.4	48.2	32.2
1993					34.7	45.8	49.8	35.7		36.9	43.0	39.9	46.7	38.6	47.7			49.2		34.8	42.2	45.8	31.7
1994					36.1	46.5	50.2	39.7		37.2	43.3	46.9	48.6	38.7	45.1	38.6		49.1		34.3		44.9	31.4
1995					37.4	48.8	50.4	39.8	59.0	36.6	44.0	42.4	50.8	38.1		38.4		48.7		33.9		43.1	31.6
1996		36.2		42.1	39.1	47.2	49.9	40.1		37.2	44.2	43.4	50.2	38.9	46.1	38.8	50.8	47.2		34.4	41.6	46.5	31.9
1997		35.8		40.0	40.7		50.5	40.3		37.3	44.6	50.8	48.9	38.7		39.0		47.0		35.0		46.5	31.8
1998		36.8	50.2	43.8	41.0	50.8	50.5	40.5		38.6	46.0	51.4	45.6			39.0		46.3		36.3	42.8		
1999		36.2			41.6	49.8	50.6	40.8	43.2	37.9	46.2		47.2	39.0				46.8		37.1			
2000		36.4		42.0	41.6	47.2	51.5	41.1		38.3	46.1		43.8	38.1						37.1	40.1	52.9	
2001		36.3		44.9	43.0	51.7	51.9	42.0		38.4	46.9			40.2	52.7	37.7	52.5	47.1		37.8	39.9	49.4	
2002	43.6		41.8	41.3	43.5	46.5	51.9	42.9		38.1				40.0						37.8		48.5	
2003	36.3			40.4	43.6	49.5	52.4	43.1		38.8			48.7	40.1		37.1		47.3		37.8		48.5	
2004	36.5		40.5	41.8	44.8	47.9	51.8	43.2		39.2			52.2	40.1		36.5				37.7		52.1	
2005	34.8		39.9		45.2	48.9	51.5	43.1		39.3			49.5	39.7		42.4		48.6		37.3			
2006	31.5		39.6		44.0	46.7	51.3	43.1		38.8	42.5		48.4	39.2		42.7	50.2	47.6		37.2	35.1		
2007	40.7		38.8		45.9	45.8	51.4	42.9			47.9		52.8	39.2		43.1				37.5			
2008	36.7		37.5		44.0	44.0					43.4		51.1							37.7			

Table B1. (Continued)

Countries

North and Latin America

Years	ARG	BHS	BLZ	BOL	BRA	BRB	CAN	CHL	COL	CRI	CUB	DOM	ECU	GTM	HND	HTI	JAM	MEX	NIC	PAN	PER	PRI	PRY	SLV	SUR	TTO	URY	USA	VEN
1963							35.5	47.0	42.9	41.8		43.3	45.2		47.2		45.6			43.6				49.7				35.5	46.3
1964							35.1	45.6	43.9			40.7	48.0		44.7		46.5			45.3				47.2				35.4	
1965							34.8	45.6	44.3	44.6		42.6	49.1		43.4		45.8		42.9	44.4				46.7				35.1	46.4
1966							34.3	44.9	44.2			45.1	48.3		47.4		46.1		44.1	44.0				46.8		49.8		34.6	
1967							34.3	43.6	44.1			47.8	47.6				46.3		42.9	42.9				46.3		49.0		34.1	44.4
1968						45.3	34.7	44.9	44.4	43.6		47.2	46.2	46.6	45.8	52.7	46.2		42.4	43.4				45.1		47.6	40.3	34.0	44.2
1969							34.6	42.6	44.4			46.6	47.7		41.6	50.7	47.9		42.0	43.5				45.5				33.9	44.2
1970				42.6		44.6	34.9	44.4	44.3			47.2	46.1			47.2	49.7	42.3	40.4	43.4				44.3				34.4	43.1
1971				41.7		44.4	35.0	43.1	44.8			47.9	46.3	45.4	42.9	46.2	48.9	42.5	42.2	42.9				44.5				35.0	43.6
1972				44.6		44.9	35.1	40.7	44.9			47.1	45.7	47.6	42.8	46.7	48.4	42.4	41.5	44.6				45.3				35.2	42.7
1973				42.8		44.3	34.9	40.3	44.5			49.6	44.6	46.0	43.4	46.6	47.7	43.1	43.3	44.2				44.2				35.0	42.2
1974				43.7		45.7	34.7	41.5	44.3			49.3	43.1	45.2	42.4	48.6	49.0	42.2	41.1	45.0				44.8	51.5	45.4		35.2	40.7
1975				46.5		45.0	34.7	42.3	45.2			45.7	42.5	45.4	43.7	46.4	49.5	42.0	40.1	44.2				45.4	49.8	45.9		36.0	41.0
1976				47.1		45.5	34.9	44.4	44.6			46.2	42.2	44.9		46.1	49.0	42.1	40.3	45.4				44.2	48.6	47.4	37.9	36.3	40.2
1977				48.5		44.9	35.2	44.8	45.4		32.0	47.1	42.1	44.5		45.5	47.1	41.7	39.1	44.4				43.3	47.6	46.0	37.0	36.1	40.4
1978				45.0		43.9	34.8	44.8	44.1		31.8	47.2	40.5	43.6		46.5	47.1	42.0	39.0	43.7				43.7	46.6	47.4	37.1	35.9	39.8
1979				44.0		42.8	34.1	45.3	43.4		32.3	47.1	43.3	45.7		45.8	48.1	42.1	40.2	44.0				44.0	44.6		36.4	35.9	39.1
1980				43.5		44.5	34.3	45.7	42.9		33.5	48.2	44.4	46.5		47.0	47.8	42.2	43.3	43.1				43.0	43.0		40.0	36.3	39.2
1981				44.3		40.7	34.9	46.5	43.5		33.1	47.7	44.2	44.1	37.1	45.8		42.2	42.6	43.3				43.3	43.2	47.6	40.0	36.7	39.5
1982				45.7		41.6	36.3	47.4	43.8		33.4	46.6	45.1	45.1	39.2	45.9		41.8	42.7	43.7	48.4			43.1	42.9	47.2	41.4	37.0	41.4
1983				49.3		43.8	36.9	48.9	44.6		32.9	47.4	45.4	45.7	44.3	47.8	45.9	42.4	44.3	44.3	45.4			44.0	44.2	46.8	41.9	37.4	42.3
1984	41.9			52.8		44.0	37.0	49.5	44.8		32.0	48.3	45.8	46.1	45.8	48.0	47.2	42.6	43.7	43.4	48.7			45.4	46.0	47.0	42.2	37.3	41.9
1985	42.9			51.3		42.5	37.1	49.6	45.4	42.4	31.7	48.6	45.8	45.6	44.3	47.9		42.5	42.8	44.3	49.1			46.3	45.5	48.2	41.5	37.5	41.3
1986	43.2			50.1			37.0	50.0	45.1	42.6	31.6		46.2	47.1	41.3	45.7	50.9	42.9		45.1	47.5			46.4	46.4	49.3	41.5	37.7	42.0

Year	Values
1987	44.2 50.7 43.1 36.7 49.1 45.2 43.1 30.9 46.1 47.8 39.2 44.3 50.3 43.7 46.0 46.6 46.0 50.1 41.1 37.4 42.7
1988	44.9 48.2 43.8 36.4 48.3 44.8 41.5 30.6 46.9 48.0 41.9 45.1 52.1 44.4 47.8 47.3 46.1 51.5 41.3 37.4 42.3
1989	46.3 48.8 48.7 45.0 36.3 47.4 45.1 41.4 31.4 46.4 40.8 52.7 42.0 47.0 51.9 42.3 46.2 39.4 37.5 42.6
1990	45.8 50.4 48.5 46.2 47.3 36.9 47.1 45.4 41.1 45.5 46.7 52.3 44.5 47.6 53.2 46.4 46.1 40.3 37.7 44.5
1991	51.2 50.5 47.7 46.9 37.6 47.0 45.4 42.3 47.7 55.4 48.3 51.2 44.5 46.9 48.9 48.6 48.2 50.3 41.3 38.2 46.0
1992	46.9 50.1 48.3 46.2 37.6 46.6 46.4 41.8 48.3 54.6 46.2 51.6 45.7 50.4 48.5 48.6 49.2 46.6 49.9 41.8 38.1 43.6
1993	45.4 50.5 48.3 46.3 38.2 46.4 46.2 40.8 48.8 55.2 48.2 46.1 49.6 51.0 49.2 44.0 51.1 43.2 38.2 45.1
1994	45.5 50.7 48.7 44.6 38.2 46.3 46.1 42.5 49.9 54.3 49.1 44.3 49.5 51.0 48.4 49.9 49.8 43.7 38.4 44.3
1995	45.6 50.7 48.6 44.8 38.0 46.6 46.1 39.3 47.9 53.5 46.0 45.5 51.9 48.1 50.2 52.7 44.7 38.4 45.9
1996	46.1 50.4 48.2 45.1 37.9 46.8 46.0 42.6 50.4 46.2 50.9 50.7 47.8 48.0 45.3 47.8
1997	44.5 49.7 48.2 44.9 38.0 47.1 46.0 40.6 50.1 49.0 46.6 49.7 49.7 47.8 45.8 46.1 38.4 46.8
1998	47.3 50.3 48.9 37.8 48.8 46.3 40.4 49.5 50.0 46.5 49.6 49.6 49.1 47.2 52.3 46.6 38.0 48.4
1999	47.2 50.5 49.2 38.0 48.2 46.8 41.7 49.7 46.5 49.8 49.8 48.6 52.3 46.7 38.2
2000	47.6 51.1 49.1 38.3 47.7 46.6 41.9 48.2 46.4 49.3 49.3 48.3 52.3 46.5 38.3
2001	48.4 51.4 49.4 38.4 48.6 47.1 42.0 45.1 49.5 45.3 54.3 44.5 52.4 46.6 38.5
2002	49.2 49.0 38.4 48.9 47.1 42.8 43.7 50.0 49.9 54.6 44.8 51.8 47.4
2003	48.7 38.4 48.9 47.3 42.9 43.3 48.0 54.8 46.7
2004	48.7 38.9 49.9 46.6 47.9 48.8 42.5 54.3 47.3 39.7
2005	48.5 38.4 50.3 46.5 49.1 47.1 43.5 54.2 47.1 40.1
2006	48.5 38.3 48.0 47.2 47.7 54.2 40.1
2007	47.6 38.5 49.1 46.0 54.0 40.1
2008	

Table B1. (Continued)

Year		Countries																									
	AGO	ARE	BDI	BEN	BFA	BWA	CAF	CIV	CMR	COG	DZA	EGY	ERI	ETH	GAB	GHA	GMB	IRN	IRQ	ISR	JOR	KEN	KWT	LBR	LBY	LSO	MAR
										Middle East and Africa																	
1963																48.3		48.5	47.4	35.4	49.3	52.9					
1964												45.2				49.0		49.8	46.9	35.4	50.1	51.8			52.7		
1965												42.9	48.3			48.7		50.3	47.5	35.8	47.6	51.8			51.9		
1966								47.6				41.6	44.4	43.9		49.0		49.7	47.3	36.7	49.9	51.9			49.8		
1967								47.0		49.4	40.8	41.7	45.8			50.2		49.4	46.9	36.8	49.5	51.4	50.5		45.4		
1968								46.7		50.0	40.2	42.7	47.1			50.5		49.9	46.2	36.2	50.6	50.4	51.4		45.1		
1969	51.9							46.2	48.8	49.8	41.0	42.8	47.4			50.0		51.0	46.2	35.6	49.5	50.4	52.6		44.6		
1970	52.3							46.0	46.5	51.0	41.2	41.6	48.7			49.3		49.2	45.0	36.4		51.2	51.9		46.0		
1971	52.4		53.8					46.9	45.3	51.3	40.4	43.4	48.0			49.0		48.1	45.9	36.3	48.0	50.7	51.0		44.2		
1972	51.1		53.0					46.5		52.3	39.9	41.7	48.6			50.0		47.2	45.9	37.2		49.9	51.7		44.1		
1973			52.6				50.2	46.7			40.2	40.7	49.1			49.0		46.0	44.2	36.7	50.3	50.4	53.7		43.8		
1974			51.1		51.7		50.0	46.7			38.6	40.0	48.6			48.3		47.4	43.1	36.8	49.7	51.2	53.3		43.3		
1975			49.5	51.4	49.5		51.1	47.9	45.7		38.7	40.0	47.8			48.7	41.9	47.6	42.6	37.5	50.7	50.5	52.7		42.2		
1976			47.8	51.8	48.4		48.9	47.9	45.4		36.8	40.2	48.0			49.2	42.8	47.0	42.2	39.1	51.1	50.5	50.5		42.7		50.9
1977		48.6	47.8	51.5	45.1		50.1	48.6	47.5		37.1	40.4	46.0			48.7	41.6	47.3	39.7	38.7	51.4	49.9	50.2		42.5		50.3
1978		48.5	47.5	52.0	43.9		49.2	47.9	46.9		39.3	39.3	44.9			48.5	39.8		40.0	38.9	51.4	49.2	50.3		42.1		49.9
1979			46.2	50.6	45.1			48.1	45.3		36.5	41.6	44.5			47.3	42.0	46.2	43.4	40.5	48.0	49.9	50.2		45.9		50.2
1980			48.0	50.3	43.8		39.1	48.0	46.5		37.0	41.1	44.6		47.6	46.1	43.8	41.7	39.3	41.3	46.3	48.8	49.8		51.3		50.6
1981		41.9		48.7	44.4	48.2	44.5	48.7	46.9	49.0		42.6	43.4		46.6	47.3	44.2	39.0	38.7	40.5	48.2	49.3	50.3				50.2
1982					45.4	47.6	40.1	49.0	47.6	46.6		44.3	42.6			46.7	42.2	38.2	39.1	39.2	49.5	49.5	50.0			48.0	49.8
1983			49.7		46.2	47.6	48.8	48.7	49.1	46.4		43.9	43.4			49.9		37.8	39.9	40.1	50.1	48.7	50.0			50.0	49.7
1984						47.0			52.5	46.1	38.3	44.3	45.9			48.8		37.5	40.5	42.0	49.6	50.4	51.4	49.4			47.2
1985		46.7				47.0	48.8			46.1	37.6	42.3	45.6			49.5		36.7	40.1	41.6	49.4	50.4	51.7	51.7		48.3	47.3
1986			48.7			47.0	44.6			47.4	39.7	42.8	43.3			49.8		36.9	40.0	41.4	50.4	49.9	53.5	49.4			48.0

Year																							
1987		46.6	47.5	46.9			47.1	39.7	42.6	43.2				48.3	38.2	38.5	41.0	50.4	48.3	52.8	48.9		
1988		47.5	47.7	48.2			47.0	41.0	43.8	43.5					37.0		41.5	50.2	47.9	53.2	49.2		
1989		51.0		49.3		54.0		39.6	44.9	44.0					38.8		41.3	49.9	48.4	53.3	49.7		
1990		52.4		49.2		51.5		38.9	45.2	44.0	43.0				40.6	46.2	42.2	47.0	47.9	58.0	50.8		
1991		52.0		50.6		54.4		38.3	46.3	46.1		50.3			40.9	48.6	43.0	46.6	48.1	60.0	49.2		
1992	56.5		47.1	52.2		55.2		39.9	46.5	46.3	50.1	52.2			43.6		43.1	46.1	47.7		48.1		
1993	60.0		46.8	52.9		55.0		39.6	47.2	45.2	48.6	51.8	48.7		44.9		42.7	46.6	46.9		48.1		
1994			45.9		49.1	55.0		39.5	47.6	43.9	48.0	52.3			43.2		42.0	45.8	46.8	53.4	48.1		
1995					49.1	56.7		41.4	47.8	46.2	50.4	53.5			41.9		42.0	46.4	47.3	52.7	47.4		
1996					50.6	56.4			48.4	46.6	48.0				44.0		42.4	46.8	47.7	52.6	47.1		
1997					50.3	56.0			49.1	47.7	48.7				44.8		42.5	46.8	47.5	53.5	47.8		
1998			50.3			56.6			48.0	46.2	45.4				45.5		42.7	46.8	45.3	53.5	48.6		
1999						56.3				47.3	48.4				45.6		42.9	47.9		52.7			
2000			48.6			55.7				45.1	50.2				46.2		43.7	47.9		54.1	50.8		
2001			48.7			54.3				47.7	50.6				45.7		43.3	49.4			51.0	51.9	
2002			40.7			55.0				47.5	45.2				45.5		43.8	48.2			51.2	52.1	
2003			52.4							47.6	44.7				46.0		43.8	49.6			51.6	52.0	
2004			45.8							45.9	46.6				46.2		44.8	49.1			51.0	48.7	
2005			51.4							47.5	46.6				46.0		44.8	49.0			51.9	51.2	
2006			53.0							48.2	46.6						45.4	48.8				52.2	
2007			47.6							47.4	46.1							48.2				50.8	52.6
2008			51.5							49.2	48.6							47.9				52.5	52.2

Table B1. (Continued)

Countries

Year	MDG	MLT	MOZ	MUS	MWI	NGA	OMN	QAT	RWA	SDN	SEN	SOM	SWZ	SYC	SYR	TGO	TUN	TZA	UGA	YEM	ZAF	ZMB	ZWE
1963		41.9				45.2									47.2		47.5		47.7		43.2	49.6	46.1
1964		39.9			47.1	42.4									46.9		48.7		48.1		42.9	49.0	45.7
1965		38.7			47.6	45.3									46.9		48.0	49.6	48.7			48.8	45.6
1966		37.5			45.7	43.8									46.7		48.0	53.0	48.9		43.0	48.6	46.4
1967	46.6	37.0	52.1		42.9	45.8						49.4	55.0		46.7		46.9	52.6	48.9			47.3	45.9
1968	46.2	38.1	51.5	42.0	47.1	46.2						48.3	54.1		45.9		46.9	52.2	49.1	48.7	42.9	46.2	45.5
1969	50.2	36.3	51.2	40.8	47.1	44.8			52.0			47.6			46.5	47.2	46.5	52.5	49.6	54.4		45.2	45.6
1970	49.9	35.8	52.9	39.7	47.2	45.9			52.3			48.5	50.3		44.9	46.2	46.3	51.7		54.0	42.8	45.9	45.0
1971	48.1	36.5	51.4	42.4	46.1	46.3			51.0			47.3	50.1		44.6	43.2	46.2	51.8	50.0	54.5		46.2	45.2
1972	48.5	37.3	50.9	46.7	49.4	47.5			51.9	48.0		44.3	50.1		44.3		46.3	53.0		55.6	43.5	45.4	45.4
1973	50.6	36.0	50.6	47.3	48.1	48.3			55.1			47.1	53.3		44.0	46.6	46.6	51.9		56.6	42.4	45.8	45.1
1974	49.6	35.9		47.9	47.3	48.1			48.7		40.5	46.9			43.6	49.1	47.6	49.4		57.8	42.5	45.6	44.9
1975	47.9	33.6		48.1	47.8	46.4					39.6	47.4			43.3	48.0	47.0			57.6	42.7	46.7	44.3
1976	46.6	33.3		46.8		46.2					42.0	46.4	49.4	31.7	43.9	50.2	47.1	46.7		56.0	41.8		44.3
1977	50.2	31.5		45.7		45.7			45.1		42.3	47.7	53.7	37.4	45.2	50.8	45.5	46.7		52.9	42.2		44.7
1978	45.3	31.1		46.7		45.7			45.1		40.4	45.0	51.8	38.8	45.2	51.8	45.2	45.6		39.7	42.6		44.9
1979	42.8	31.2		46.3	49.3				46.1		40.6		48.4	35.8	45.4		44.6	46.0		40.4	43.1		45.5
1980	38.8	30.9		46.2	47.0	42.2					40.7		51.1	33.2		52.2	44.5	45.1		41.3	43.5	48.0	44.6
1981	42.0	30.7		46.7	48.7	39.7					48.2		49.5	34.7		53.4	44.3	47.9		43.5	43.3	48.3	43.0
1982	39.3	29.6		46.4	48.2	41.8					49.1		49.3	36.0		56.5		46.8		44.0	43.3	49.1	43.2
1983	43.8	30.9		45.9	49.6	45.9					48.1		50.3	39.6		49.6				42.5	43.3		43.5
1984	46.1	31.3		43.7	48.6	41.4			44.7		47.7		47.8	37.9		47.3		46.8		43.5	43.4		44.7
1985	43.4	31.9		41.8	49.9	44.0			47.8		37.4		47.6	37.3					48.6	42.7	44.3		44.1
1986	41.7	31.9		39.0	53.2			52.0	45.6		40.6		45.4	37.3				51.4		42.7	44.0		43.8
1987		31.4		37.8	56.1			52.5			43.0		51.5					51.4	51.5		44.0		43.7

Year																
1988		31.8	36.5	55.3			54.8	47.6	53.0			51.9		43.9	44.8	
1989			36.6	56.2				46.4	51.9			51.7		44.2	44.5	
1990	51.3	32.5	36.3	52.2			55.8	44.8	50.2			47.9		44.3	45.2	50.5
1991	52.4	33.2	36.7	52.6	47.3		53.8	48.9	45.1			49.2		44.6	44.8	
1992	49.4	33.1	35.5	54.5	48.0		52.4	48.3	48.7		51.6				52.5	
1993	50.7	34.0	35.9	54.5	50.0	50.8	54.6	46.4	49.6		52.8	44.8	49.7	44.9	45.3	
1994	54.0	33.8	36.3	52.3	50.1	51.6	52.9	51.0	51.8		49.0	44.5	49.7	45.4	46.8	50.0
1995		35.9	36.7	53.2	49.1	51.8		48.4	48.0		49.5	47.9	49.7	45.5	47.0	
1996		34.2	36.9	52.5	48.8	52.7		48.7			51.7	49.9	49.7	45.7	47.3	
1997		35.2	38.5	54.5		51.4		49.7			51.7	50.0	49.7	46.0	48.2	
1998		34.6	38.6	55.0		50.9		50.0		46.2	52.0	49.9	49.7	45.1	47.6	49.4
1999		36.2	37.5	54.9		50.4		48.5		46.2	52.1	50.2	49.7	45.1		48.5
2000	49.8	35.7	37.0	55.5		52.2		47.0		47.6	52.8	50.5		46.0		47.2
2001	42.5	35.6	36.8	54.1	47.9	51.8		48.7		48.1	54.0			46.8		47.1
2002	44.2	35.9	36.4			53.9		50.5		48.4				46.6		
2003	44.6	36.3	38.0			54.0	55.9			48.3	52.0			48.1		48.4
2004	46.7	36.7	39.9			49.0	50.4			48.7	50.8			47.1		49.3
2005	45.6	35.7	40.7			51.5	50.5			49.3	51.1			46.4		48.9
2006	45.5	40.7	39.3			49.9	52.2			49.0	54.5			46.6		48.9
2007		39.5	39.6			50.7				47.7	54.5			44.8		
2008										47.2				45.0		

APPENDIX C

Table C1.   Revised Coefficient Estimates Relating UTIP-UNIDO to
Deininger-Squire.

Dependent Variable		lnGiniDS		
Variable	Coefficient	Std. err.	T-statistic	$P > \text{abs}(t)$
Income/expenditure	−0.15***	0.03	−4.58	0.000
Household/personal	−0.79***	0.02	−4.63	0.000
Gross/net	−0.06***	0.02	−3.11	0.000
lnUTIPUNIDO	0.1***	0.01	8.64	0.000
Mfgpop	−2.84***	0.24	−11.73	0.000
Constant	4.2	0.04	93.53	0.000
Number of observations:		430		
F (5,424)		109.27		
R-squared		0.56		
Adj R-squared		0.56		
Root MSE		0.159		

Source: Authors.
***Significant at 0.01 level.
LnGiniDS: natural log of Deininger-Squire Gini Coefficient.
LnUTIPUNIDO: natural log of UTIP-UNIDO Theil statistic.
mfgpop: ratio of manufacturing employment to population.
The three dummy variables are constructed as binary indicators so that income, gross and household measures are set to zero; whereas expenditure, net, and personal measures are set to one. Thus in each case the coefficient estimates are (and were expected to be) negative.

DECOMPOSING CHANGES IN MALE WAGE DISTRIBUTION IN BRAZIL

Yang Wang[a], Nora Lustig[a] and Otavio Bartalotti[b]

[a]Department of Economics, Tulane University
[b]Department of Economics, Iowa State University

ABSTRACT

Between 1995 and 2012, the wage distribution of male workers in Brazil shifted to the right and became less dispersed. This paper attempts to identify the reasons for that movement in male wage distribution, focusing on the impact of education expansion on wage distribution. The Oaxaca-Blinder (OB) and Recentered Influence Function (RIF) decomposition results show that both changes in returns on skills and upgrades in the composition of work skills contribute to increases in the average wage and wages at the 10th and 50th percentiles. The shifts in returns to skills had a decreasing impact on wages at the 90th percentile and are identified as the primary force reducing wage inequality. Education expansion had an equalizing impact on wage distribution, primarily through the decline in return to education.

Income Inequality Around the World
Research in Labor Economics, Volume 44, 49–78
Copyright © 2016 by Emerald Group Publishing Limited
All rights of reproduction in any form reserved
ISSN: 0147-9121/doi:10.1108/S0147-912120160000044009

Keywords: Wage inequality; decomposition; wage structure effect; composition effect; education expansion

JEL Classifications: J31; J82; I24

INTRODUCTION

Brazil has been a country of high income inequality. It was the second most unequal country in the world in 1989 when its Gini coefficient of household per capita income equaled 0.63. Starting from 1990, especially after the end of the country's hyperinflation and the retrieve of its economic stability at around 1995, income inequality declined continuously and significantly in Brazil. Its Gini coefficient of household per capita income was 0.52 in 2012. There are two fundamental instruments of the significant decline of income inequality in Brazil: one is the high taxation and large scale of social spending (Higgins & Pereira, 2014); the other is the convergence in earnings income inequality which happened in the country since 1990. According to the existing research, the non-wage income had contributed to 35–50% of the decline of household income inequality, and the movement in the wage income distribution accounts for the other 40–55% of the change of overall income inequality (Ferreira, Firpo, & Messina, 2015).

During the period of 1995–2012, according to the Brazil National Household Survey data, the wage distribution of full-time male workers aged between 16 and 65 shifted to the right and became less dispersed. There was a decrease in the average hourly wage of male workers between 1995 and 2004, followed by an increase after 2004, which finally resulted in a 17.7% increase from 4.01 R\$[1] in 1995 to 4.72 R\$ in 2012. However, this increase did not evenly benefit the entire wage distribution. The 10th percentile of hourly wages increased by 102.3%, the 50th percentile increased by 41.3%, and there was only a 6.9% increase at the 90th percentile. Barros, de Carvalho, Franco, and Mendonça (2010) find that the changes in wage income distribution accounted for 31–46% of the decline of income inequality between 2001 and 2007. This convergence in male wage distribution indicates a decline in male wage inequality: the Gini coefficient

---

[1]All wage measures in this paper are in 1995 prices.

of 16–65-year-old male full-time workers' hourly wages decreased from 0.56 in 1995 to 0.47 in 2012.

There are two factors working simultaneously in changing a country's wage distribution. One is the changes in the distribution of workers' characteristics in the labor force, which is named the "composition effect"; the other is changes in returns on workers' various characteristics in the labor market, which is called the "wage structure effect." The Brazil National Household Survey data show shifts in the returns to workers' different characteristics and some significant changes in the composition of male workers' characteristics. This paper attempts to identify the relative importance of the wage structure effect and the composition effect in shifting the male wage distribution in Brazil between 1995 and 2012 using the Oaxaca-Blinder (Blinder, 1973; Oaxaca, 1973) and the Recentered Influence Function (Firpo, Fortin, & Lemieux, 2009) decomposition methods.

Among all factors, how the education upgrades and changes in the return to education contributed to the movements of wage distribution is of primary interest. The period of declining wage inequality coincides with education expansion, which significantly changed the composition of the labor force. The average number of years of education of male full-time workers was 5.5 in 1995, increasing to 8.3 in 2012. The proportion of workers with incomplete middle school (0–7 years) declined from 68% in 1995 to 37% in 2012 as more workers completed middle school or a higher educational level (8+ years). At the same time, not only had the relative education premium of each education group but also the absolute wages of better-educated groups (8–10, 11–14 and 15+ years of education) declined. Because of the education expansion, education inequality decreased – the Gini coefficient of the years of education declined from 0.42 in 1995 to 0.28 in 2012. Thus, it is also of interest to check the existence of the "paradox of progress" (Bourguignon, Ferreira, & Lustig, 2005) in Brazil, which refers to the notion that a more equal distribution of education increases wage income inequality because of the convexity of the return to education.

How educational advancement impacted wage distribution is an important research question. Menezes-Filho, Fernandes, and Picchetti (2006) study the impact of education expansion on male wage distribution between 1977 and 1997. Their results show that the upgrade in the education composition of the labor force increased inequality. Blom, Holm-Nielsen, and Verner (2001) study the period between 1982 and 1998 and conclude that the mild decrease in wage inequality was primarily caused by a decline in the return to education. Ferreira, Leite, and Litchfield (2008) find that education expansion in the context of a highly convex return was an important reason for the increase in inequality during the 1980s and that the decline in inequality between 1993 and 2004 was accounted for by declines in returns to education. Barros et al. (2010) find that the accelerated education expansion in Brazil during the period 2001–2007 accounted for half of the decline in wage income inequality and that the recent decline in wage income inequality was caused not only by a decline in the return differentials across education levels but also by a more equal distribution of education. Moreover, the change in the wage differential is more important than education expansion in explaining the decline.

Our decomposition analysis shows that both changes in returns on workers' various characteristics and upgrades in the composition of work characteristics contribute to increases in both the average wage and wages at the 10th and 50th percentiles. The shifts in returns on skills have a decreasing impact on wages at the 90th percentile but are dominated by the positive composition impact; thus, wages at the 90th percentile also increased from 1995 to 2012. The changes in the wage structure are also identified as the primary force reducing wage inequality. Regarding the contribution of education expansion, the decline in relative returns on different levels of education has an equalizing impact on the wage distribution and a mild decreasing effect on the wage level of male workers. The improvement in educational attainment had a small increasing impact on wage distribution thus demonstrating the existence of the "paradox of progress," and significantly increased the wage level of male workers.

This paper makes the following contributions. First, the decomposition analysis quantifies both the extent to which the change in male wage distribution is driven by changes in the composition of workers' characteristics and the extent to which it is caused by movements in the wage structure. Second, identification of the impact of education expansion on wage distribution in Brazil provides important policy perspectives on education reform. Third, this paper provides an empirical examination of the existence of the "paradox of progress" in the Brazilian context.

The policy implications of this paper are the following: first, policies aiming at supporting the labor force's educational advancement would be beneficial in terms of both reducing wage inequality and promoting economic growth; second, the convergence of the educational premium might discourage people from gaining more education; thus, education subsidies or conditional cash transfers from the government would help; third, the increased relative return to the group with lower education may cause some unemployment among these low-skilled workers; thus, the government should also pay attention and provide the appropriate support; moreover, because of the very significant decline in both overall and wage-income inequality observed since the 1990s, an investigation of the fundamental forces of the change in inequality in Brazil would provide useful policy perspectives to other countries.

The paper is organized as follows. The section "Review of Decomposition Methods" reviews the decomposition methods. The section "Data and Descriptive Analysis" describes the data and male samples under analysis. The section "Decomposition Results" presents the decomposition results, and the final section concludes.

REVIEW OF DECOMPOSITION METHODS

Decomposition analysis is generally a partial equilibrium approach and does not attempt to understand the structural relationship between factors. The key to decomposition analysis is to create a counterfactual, which is a simulated wage distribution in which workers with a particular distribution of characteristics are paid according to a different wage structure. For example, in this analysis, the counterfactual wage distribution can be constructed either by assuming that workers in 2012 are paid according to the wage structure of 1995 or by assuming that workers in 1995 are paid according to the wage structure of 2012.

Aggregate decomposition aims to quantify two main effects that work simultaneously in changing the wage distribution: one is the "wage structure effect," which refers to the effect of changes in returns on the labor force's various characteristics in moving the wage distribution, in which workers are assumed to be the same group of people; the other is the "composition effect," which refers to the effect of changes in the distributions of workers' characteristics, where returns to different characteristics are assumed to be stable. Based on the counterfactual, the contributions of different covariates to the two separate effects can be further quantified, a phenomenon that is known as "detailed decomposition."

The most widely employed decomposition approach is the Oaxaca-Blinder decomposition (Blinder, 1973; Oaxaca, 1973), which can decompose the difference in the mean values of any two groups, for example, time 0 and time 1, female and male, immigrants and natives. The key limitation of this method is that it cannot extend beyond the mean to analyze more complex changes. One may be interested in comparing measures other than the mean value, given that examining changes at different points in a distribution could enable a better understanding of the change in inequality. This interest has led to other approaches that can decompose distributional statistics other than the mean value that help to view the entire distribution and identify the reasons of changes. The existing distributional approaches include the Residual Imputation Procedure (Juhn, Murphy, & Pierce, 1993), Inverse Propensity Reweighting (DiNardo, Fortin, & Lemieux, 1996), the Quantile Regressions Method (Machado & Mata, 2005), the Recentered Influence Function Regression (Firpo et al., 2009), and the Estimation of Conditional Distribution (Chernozhukov, Fernandez-Val, & Melly, 2013). The main difference among these approaches is the methods of generating the counterfactual distribution; all of these approaches have advantages and disadvantages. One outstanding approach proposed by Firpo et al. (2009) is the Recentered Influence Function (RIF) regression method, which replaces the independent variable Y of a regression with a recentered influence function of the distributional statistics. The recentered influence function of the mean value is itself; thus, the RIF decomposition result of the mean value will be the same as that in the Oaxaca-Blinder decomposition.

In this analysis, based on the Mincer wage equation, the Oaxaca-Blinder decomposition is employed to decompose the increase in the average wage between 1995 and 2012; then, the RIF decomposition is employed to decompose the changes in distributional statistics, including 10th, 50th and 90th quantiles, 90-10, 50-10 and 90-50 differentials, variance and Gini coefficient.

Oaxaca-Blinder Decomposition

The first step of the Oaxaca-Blinder decomposition is to create a counterfactual distribution. Assume wage Y_i is a function of worker's observable characteristics X_i and unobservable characteristics ε_i and that the wage structure is $\omega(\cdot)$. Then, the wages of workers in 2012 and 1995 can be represented as $Y_{2012i} = \omega_{2012}(X_{2012i}, \varepsilon_{2012i})$ and $Y_{1995i} = \omega_{1995}(X_{1995i}, \varepsilon_{1995i})$, respectively. There are three sources of difference between the wage distributions in 2012 and 1995: the difference between the wage structures $\omega(\cdot)$, the difference between the observable characteristics X and unobservable characteristics ε. The counterfactual can be either $Y_{ci} = \omega_{1995}(X_{2012i}, \varepsilon_{2012i})$ or $Y_{ci} = \omega_{2012}(X_{1995i}, \varepsilon_{1995i})$. Being widely employed in decomposition literature, the wage structure $\omega(\cdot)$ is always assumed to take a linear form; thus, the wage equations for 1995 and 2012 should be estimated separately to obtain $\hat{Y}_{1995} = \hat{\beta}_{1995} \cdot X_{1995}$ and $\hat{Y}_{2012} = \hat{\beta}_{2012} \cdot X_{2012}$, respectively. Then, the counterfactual can be either $\hat{Y}_C = \hat{\beta}_{1995} \cdot X_{2012}$ or $\hat{Y}_C = \hat{\beta}_{2012} \cdot X_{1995}$.

The second step is to decompose the change between two years, which can be expressed by the following equation:

$$
\begin{aligned}
\hat{Y}_{2012} - \hat{Y}_{1995} &= \left(\hat{Y}_{2012} - \hat{Y}_C \right) + \left(\hat{Y}_C - \hat{Y}_{1995} \right) \\
&= \left[(\hat{\alpha}_{2012} - \hat{\alpha}_{1995}) + \sum_{i=1}^{K} \overline{X}_{2012k} \left(\hat{\beta}_{2012k} - \hat{\beta}_{1995k} \right) \right] \\
&\quad + \left[\sum_{i=1}^{K} (\overline{X}_{2012k} - \overline{X}_{1995k}) \hat{\beta}_{1995k} \right] \\
&= \left[(\hat{\alpha}_{2012} - \hat{\alpha}_{1995}) + \sum_{i=1}^{K} \overline{X}_{1995k} \left(\hat{\beta}_{2012k} - \hat{\beta}_{1995k} \right) \right] \\
&\quad + \left[\sum_{i=1}^{K} (\overline{X}_{2012k} - \overline{X}_{1995k}) \hat{\beta}_{2012k} \right]
\end{aligned}
$$

where the first term is the wage structure effect, which measures the effect of the differences in the wage structure between 1995 and 2012 in changing the mean value, where workers are assumed to be the same group of people, and the second term is the composition effect, which measures the effect of changes in the observed characteristics of workers, where returns on different characteristics are assumed to be at either the 1995 level or the 2012 level. Because of the constant term, the wage structure effect considers the returns on both the observable characteristics and the unobservable characteristics. The contributions of each covariate to the wage structure and composition effect can also be quantified. Separating the wage structure effect and the composition effect is the main goal of "aggregate decomposition," and the quantification of the contributions from each covariate is called "detailed decomposition."

Recentered Influence Function (RIF) Decomposition

The Recentered Influence Function (RIF) decomposition also involves two steps. The first step is to aggregately decompose the change in the distributional statistics of wage distributions into the wage structure effect and the composition effect, which can be achieved by a reweighting technique. Specifically, suppose that the distributional statistics in 1995 and 2012 are represented by $f(Y_{1995})$ and $f(Y_{2012})$ and that the corresponding statistics of the counterfactual distribution are represented by $f(Y_C)$; the change in the wage distribution can be decomposed according to the following equation:

$$f(Y_{2012}) - f(Y_{1995}) = [f(Y_{2012}) - f(Y_C)] + [f(Y_C) - f(Y_{1995})]$$

The counterfactual Y_C is generated by reweighting the wage distribution in 1995 by a reweighting factor. The first term in the equation is the composition effect and the second term is the wage structure effect. The reweighting factor is defined (Firpo et al., 2009) as $\varphi_i = \frac{1-P(X_i)}{P(X_i)} \cdot \frac{p}{1-p}$, where $P(X_i)$ is the probability of a worker being at time 1995 given characteristics X_i in the joint sample of 1995 and 2012; thus, $P(X_i)$ can be estimated by a discrete choice model and p denotes the sample share of 1995 in the joint sample. Here, the counterfactual wage distribution is $Y_c = \varphi_i \cdot Y_{1995}$, and the counterfactual can also be generated by reweighting the 2012 sample in a similar manner.

The second step of RIF decomposition is to measure each covariate's contributions to the wage structure effect and the composition effect by running RIF regressions on the distributional statistics of the two original wage distributions and the counterfactual distribution. The RIF regression is a regular regression in which the dependent variable Y is replaced by its recentered influence function. According to Firpo et al. (2009), it can obtain the average effects of independent variables on a distributional statistic. The recentered influence function of quantile q_τ is defined by the following equation:

$$RIF(Y; q_\tau) = q_\tau + \frac{\tau - I(Y \leq q_\tau)}{f_Y(q_\tau)}$$

where $f_Y(\cdot)$ is the probability density function of Y and $I(\cdot)$ is an indicator function. Next, the RIF quantile regression can be specified as $E[RIF(Y; q_\tau)|X] = X\beta_\tau$, where β_τ is the marginal effect of the covariates on the wage quantile q_τ.

After estimating the RIF regressions for the wage distributions of 1995, 2012 and the counterfactual, the difference in the τth quantile of the 2012 and 1995 wage distributions can be decomposed by resembling the Oaxaca-Blinder decomposition procedure, which can be represented by the following equation:

$$\hat{q}_\tau(Y_{2012}) - \hat{q}_\tau(Y_{1995}) = \overline{X}_{1995}\left(\hat{\beta}_C^\tau - \hat{\beta}_{1995}^\tau\right) + \left(\overline{X}_{2012}\cdot\hat{\beta}_{2012}^\tau - \overline{X}_{1995}\cdot\hat{\beta}_C^\tau\right)$$

$$= \sum_{i=1}^{K}\overline{X}_{1995k}\left(\hat{\beta}_{Ck}^\tau - \hat{\beta}_{1995k}^\tau\right) + \sum_{i=1}^{K}\left(\overline{X}_{2012k}\cdot\hat{\beta}_{2012k}^\tau - \overline{X}_{1995k}\cdot\hat{\beta}_{Ck}^\tau\right)$$

where the first term is the sum of the wage structure effects of each covariate and the second term is the sum of the composition effects.

DATA AND DESCRIPTIVE ANALYSIS

The data employed in this analysis are from the 1995–2012 Brazil National Household Survey (PNAD) by the Brazilian Institute of Geography and Statistics (IBGE). The PNAD survey covers the general characteristics of the population, including health, education, job characteristics, household income and housing conditions. The sample analyzed in this paper is restricted to full-time male workers between 16 and 65 years of age with positive working experience, working at least 140 hours per month, not currently a student, and not working without pay or as a domestic worker. The sample of each group defined by gender, education level and year is trimmed at the 1st and 99th percentiles. Wage income in the analysis includes both cash income and the values of the goods and products paid from the primary job. For the purpose of comparison across years, the monetary incomes of each year are deflated to real values in 1995 prices using the CPI conversion factors from the Brazilian Institute of Geography and Statistics. Data from each survey cohort between 1995 and 2012 are used to describe the evolution of male wage inequality and the characteristics of male workers; then, the decomposition analysis compares only 1995 and 2012. Moreover, five education groups are defined: workers who are illiterate or who have an incomplete primary education (0–3 years); workers with 4–7 years of education, which can be viewed as the complete primary and incomplete middle school level; workers with 8–10 years of education, which includes complete middle school and incomplete high school; workers with 11–14 years of education, which is equivalent to complete high school and incomplete college; and workers with 15 or more years of education, which includes complete college and graduate study.

Male Wage Distribution between 1995 and 2012

According to the PNAD data, the average hourly wage of male full-time workers decreased between 1995 and 2004 and then increased after 2004, resulting in a 17.7% increase over the entire period. The increase in wage income did not evenly benefit all workers across the entire distribution: comparing 2012 with 1995, the overall increase in hourly wages at the 10th percentile was 102.3%, and the 50th percentile increased by 41.3%. However, there was only a 6.9% increase at the 90th percentile, comparing 2012 with 1995. Fig. 1 depicts the evolution of hourly wages at the 10th, 50th, and 90th percentiles over the entire period. Wage income has been indexed with respect to the average of 1995 and 1997 for all three series. As depicted in the figure, the 10th percentile wage series increased over the period and the median series exhibits a similar changing pattern but increases at a lower speed. Wages at the 90th percentile decreased between 1995 and 2005 and then increased afterwards.

Indeed, comparing 1995 and 2012, the speed of the increase in real wages monotonically decreases as we move to the right of the wage distribution.

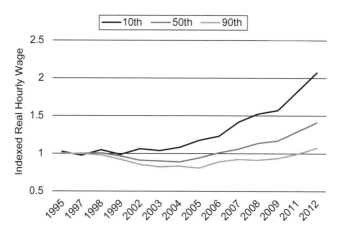

Fig. 1. Indexed Hourly Wage by Percentile: Males Aged 16–65. *Notes*: Calculated based on full-time male workers with positive working experience, working at least 140 hours per month, not currently a student, not working without pay or as domestic workers, and between 16 and 65 years of age, based on PNAD's 1995–2012 data. The sample of each group defined by gender, education level and year is trimmed at the 1st and 99th percentiles. Wage income in the analysis includes both cash income and the values of the goods and products paid from the primary job. The wage measure is in constant 1995 prices.

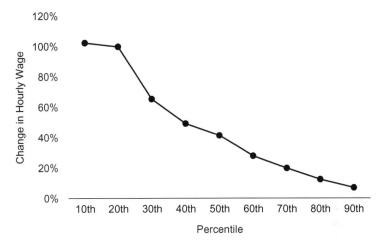

Fig. 2. Hourly Wage Change by Percentile: Males Aged 16–65. *Notes*: Calculated based on full-time male workers with positive working experience, working at least 140 hours per month, not currently a student, not working without pay or as domestic workers, and between 16 and 65 years of age, based on PNAD's 1995–2012 data. The sample of each group defined by gender, education level and year is trimmed at the 1st and 99th percentiles. Wage income in the analysis includes both cash income and the values of the goods and products paid from the primary job. The wage measure is in constant 1995 prices.

Fig. 2 shows the changes in the hourly wage between 1995 and 2012 at each 10th percentile, showing an essentially linear pattern with a negative slope. This pattern demonstrates a convergence across the entire wage distribution and is consistent with the observed decrease in wage inequality. The Gini coefficient of hourly wages was 0.56 in 1995 and 0.47 in 2012, which is a 16.2% decrease. The 90-10 log hourly wage differential decreased from 2.4 in 1995 to 1.8 in 2011, the 50-10 log hourly wage differential decreased 34.4%, and the 90-50 log hourly wage differential decreased 20%, indicating that convergence at the lower tail is more significant than it is at the upper tail.

Changes in the wage distribution exhibit different patterns within each education group. Fig. 3 depicts the evolution of hourly wages at each 10th quantile within each education category between 1995 and 2012. As shown, workers with 0–3 years of education experienced the largest relative increase in hourly wages; the wages of workers with 4–7 years of education also increased across the entire wage distribution of this educational group. However, the wages of workers with 8–10 and 11–14 years of education increased at the lower tail but declined at the upper tail of the distribution.

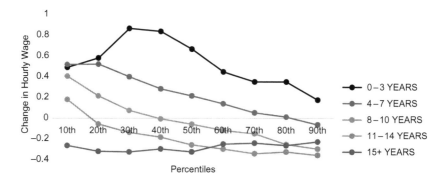

Fig. 3. Hourly Wage Change at Different Education Levels: Males Aged 16–65. *Notes*: Calculated based on full-time male workers with positive working experience, working at least 140 hours per month, not currently a student, not working without pay or as domestic workers, between 16 and 65 years of age, based on PNAD's 1995–2012 data. The sample of each group defined by gender, education level and year is trimmed at the 1st and 99th percentiles. Wage income in the analysis includes both cash income and the values of the goods and products paid from the primary job. The wage measure is in constant 1995 prices.

The wages of workers with 8–10 years of education increased by 7.5–40.4% at different quantiles up to the 30th quantile, and workers with 11–14 years of education experienced an increase in wages by 18% only up to the 20th quantile. Most of the group with 11–14 years of education and all of the workers with a complete tertiary education experienced a decline in wages between 1995 and 2012 ranging between 6% and 32%. The 20th percentile of the tertiary group experienced a 32% decline; the decline at the 90th percentile was only 23%. Generally, the increases/decreases at the lower percentiles are always higher than the increases/decreases at the higher percentiles, thus indicating a decrease in each education group's wage inequality. Table 1 shows that other than workers with 15 or more years of education, whose Gini coefficient increased from 0.42 to 0.45, the Gini coefficient and Theil index of all other educational groups declined throughout the entire period. In each year, the better-educated group always exhibited higher wage inequality.

Changes in Workers' Characteristics between 1995 and 2012

Table 2 summarizes the samples under analysis between 1995 and 2012. As the numbers show, many characteristics of full-time male workers did not

Table 1. Inequality Measures of Hourly Wage within Education Groups: Male Aged 16–65.

		1995	1997	1998	1999	2002	2003	2004	2005	2006	2007	2008	2009	2011	2012
0–3 Years	Gini	0.44	0.45	0.43	0.42	0.40	0.40	0.38	0.38	0.37	0.38	0.37	0.37	0.37	0.37
	Theil	0.37	0.41	0.38	0.34	0.33	0.34	0.28	0.28	0.28	0.28	0.28	0.26	0.28	0.28
	Obs.	20,298	19,352	17,344	17,377	17,099	15,949	16,459	15,983	14,930	14,114	13,202	12,845	11,567	9,965
4–7 Years	Gini	0.44	0.43	0.42	0.41	0.41	0.40	0.40	0.39	0.39	0.39	0.37	0.36	0.35	0.35
	Theil	0.37	0.36	0.34	0.32	0.34	0.31	0.31	0.31	0.34	0.32	0.28	0.27	0.25	0.27
	Obs.	22,269	21,953	20,908	21,208	21,764	21,126	21,619	21,946	21,477	20,138	19,228	19,429	15,260	16,291
7–10 Years	Gini	0.44	0.44	0.42	0.42	0.41	0.41	0.41	0.40	0.39	0.38	0.38	0.37	0.35	0.34
	Theil	0.36	0.40	0.35	0.34	0.33	0.37	0.33	0.31	0.30	0.33	0.30	0.30	0.27	0.23
	Obs.	8,321	9,025	9,048	9,189	10,554	10,784	11,580	11,946	12,439	12,928	13,093	12,730	12,359	12,642
11–14 Years	Gini	0.46	0.47	0.45	0.46	0.46	0.45	0.45	0.44	0.44	0.42	0.42	0.41	0.39	0.40
	Theil	0.39	0.44	0.38	0.40	0.40	0.39	0.38	0.38	0.38	0.34	0.37	0.33	0.30	0.35
	Obs.	8,848	10,058	10,451	11,041	15,073	16,052	17,847	19,756	20,846	21,066	22,498	23,901	22,637	23,870
15 + Years	Gini	0.42	0.42	0.43	0.41	0.43	0.43	0.43	0.45	0.44	0.45	0.45	0.47	0.46	0.45
	Theil	0.30	0.30	0.33	0.28	0.32	0.32	0.32	0.37	0.35	0.37	0.37	0.45	0.38	0.36
	Obs.	3,302	3,570	3,659	3,732	4,164	4,214	4,468	4,748	5,137	5,443	5,846	6,454	6,047	6,561

Notes: Author's calculation based on PNAD 1995 to 2012 data, wage is adjusted to 1995 price using CPI conversion factors. Samples include full-time male workers aged between 16 and 65 with positive working experience, worked at least 140 hours per month, not currently in school, not working without pay or domestic workers.

Table 2. Characteristics of Labor Market: Male Aged 16–65.

Variable	1995 Mean	1997 Mean	1998 Mean	1999 Mean	2002 Mean	2003 Mean	2004 Mean	2005 Mean	2006 Mean	2007 Mean	2008 Mean	2009 Mean	2011 Mean	2012 Mean
Years of education	5.52	5.79	6.02	6.07	6.56	6.78	6.89	7.07	7.29	7.44	7.65	7.82	7.98	8.25
0–3 Years education	33.00%	31.00%	29.13%	28.57%	24.88%	23.18%	22.65%	21.40%	19.80%	18.90%	17.81%	17.00%	16.62%	14.08%
4–7 Years education	35.34%	34.34%	33.83%	33.90%	31.86%	30.99%	30.11%	29.43%	28.73%	27.26%	25.97%	25.65%	22.43%	23.53%
8–10 Years education	13.13%	13.88%	14.58%	14.55%	15.20%	15.85%	15.97%	15.96%	16.39%	17.46%	17.55%	16.78%	18.25%	17.99%
11–14 Years education	13.36%	15.23%	16.56%	17.15%	21.92%	23.52%	24.84%	26.69%	28.02%	28.83%	30.63%	31.82%	33.56%	34.78%
>= 15 Years education	5.18%	5.55%	5.89%	5.83%	6.15%	6.46%	6.43%	6.53%	7.05%	7.55%	8.05%	8.76%	9.15%	9.61%
White	56.26%	55.74%	56.16%	56.08%	54.43%	53.68%	52.75%	50.99%	50.78%	49.91%	49.16%	48.75%	48.23%	46.60%
Non-white	43.74%	44.26%	43.84%	43.92%	45.57%	46.32%	47.25%	49.01%	49.22%	50.09%	50.84%	51.25%	51.77%	53.40%
Tenure	7.64%	7.85%	7.79%	7.90%	7.80%	7.96%	7.92%	7.89%	7.91%	8.07%	7.89%	8.07%	8.05%	7.99%
Experience	23.82%	23.89%	23.86%	23.99%	23.65%	23.50%	23.49%	23.19%	23.17%	23.21%	23.10%	23.19%	23.26%	23.14%
Union	20.72%	19.65%	19.02%	19.11%	19.49%	19.93%	20.38%	20.54%	20.95%	19.62%	20.09%	19.75%	18.36%	17.54%
Formal employee	44.34%	43.22%	43.26%	42.38%	43.77%	44.67%	45.69%	46.22%	47.46%	49.70%	51.75%	51.99%	54.21%	54.70%
Informal employee	20.99%	21.33%	21.50%	21.57%	22.16%	21.32%	21.51%	21.16%	20.63%	19.50%	18.73%	18.25%	16.37%	16.09%
Self-employed	28.56%	29.23%	29.19%	29.81%	27.85%	27.73%	26.83%	26.40%	25.47%	25.31%	23.23%	23.41%	24.84%	24.18%
Employer	6.11%	6.21%	6.06%	6.24%	6.21%	6.28%	5.97%	6.22%	6.45%	5.49%	6.30%	6.35%	4.58%	5.03%
Age	36.34	36.68	36.88	37.07	37.21	37.28	37.38	37.26	37.46	37.66	37.75	38.01	38.25	38.39
Monthly wage	817.36	814.72	817.68	754.15	730.20	691.53	681.79	700.78	746.88	778.75	795.64	824.19	873.24	921.61
Monthly hours	209.94	211.13	212.32	210.20	210.25	209.38	207.79	206.55	205.56	204.70	202.90	202.00	199.92	198.74
Hourly wage	4.01	3.97	3.97	3.70	3.58	3.40	3.37	3.49	3.73	3.90	4.02	4.18	4.46	4.72
Log hourly wage	0.82	0.81	0.83	0.78	0.75	0.72	0.73	0.77	0.84	0.91	0.96	1.00	1.10	1.17
HH PC Inc.	392.35	392.35	402.86	378.67	389.46	374.90	375.90	396.57	432.16	450.83	467.96	489.63	523.21	564.26
Obs.	63,038	63,958	61,410	62,547	68,654	68,125	71,973	74,379	74,829	73,689	73,867	75,359	67,870	69,329

Notes: PNAD 1995–2012 Survey data, wage is adjusted to 1995 price using CPI conversion factor. Samples include full-time male works aged between 16 and 65 with positive working experience, worked at least 140 hours per month, not currently schooling, not working without pay or domestic workers.

change much during the period: the average age of the male samples was always approximately 36–38; the proportion of white workers changed from 56.3% in 1995 to 46.6% in 2012; the average years of experience in the current job and the average years of overall working experience[2] were always approximately 8 and 23, respectively, during the period; and there were fewer workers with union status in 2012, although that change is small. Given the relatively stable composition of male workers' characteristics, the effects of these characteristics on changing the wage distribution would be small in terms of the composition effect and would mainly work through the wage structure effect.

The most significant changes in the composition of male workers' characteristics over the period under analysis are the improvement of educational attainment. For full-time male workers, the average years of education increased from 5.52 to 8.25, and the Gini coefficient of the years of education decreased from 0.42 to 0.28, indicating educational expansion and a less-dispersed distribution of education within the male workforce. The proportions of workers with 0–3 years and 4–7 years of education decreased from 33% to 14% and from 35% to 24%, respectively. Simultaneously, workers with 8–10 years of education increased from 13% in 1995 to 18% in 2012, workers with complete high school and incomplete college increased from 13% to 35%, and 10% of workers had completed a college education in 2012 compared to 5% in 1995. Moreover, the allocation of workers between employers and employees and between formal workers and informal workers also changed. Fifty-five percent of workers were formal employees in 2012 compared to 44% in 1995, and informal employees, employers and self-employed workers all showed proportional decreases. These changes in the composition of workers' characteristics could affect the wage distribution through both the wage structure effect and the composition effect.

DECOMPOSITION RESULTS

The kernel density estimation of log hourly wages of 1995 and 2012 are depicted in Fig. 4. The 2012 wage distribution became less dispersed and moved to the right compared to the 1995 wage distribution, indicating

---

[2]Here, experience is defined as physical age minus 7 minus number of years of education.

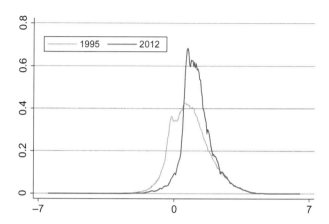

Fig. 4. Kernel Density Estimation of Log Hourly Wage: Males Aged 16–65. *Note:* Calculated based on full-time male workers between 16 and 65 years of age based on PNAD's 1995–2012 data.

growth in average wages and a decline in inequality. Moreover, the long right tail in both years indicates the existence of very high-wage earners; the right tail also extended further in 2012.

Change in Wage Structure

Table 3, which reports the ordinary least squares (OLS) estimates of the Mincer wage equations for 1995, 2012 and the pooled samples, documents the wage structure change among Brazilian male workers. For the Mincer regressions, the log hourly wage is the dependent variable, and the omitted education category is workers with 0–3 years of education. The results show that male wages experienced a significant increase, given that the estimated coefficient of the year 1995 dummy in the pooled regression is both negative and significant. The estimated coefficients of the education dummies are all positive and significant, which indicates that workers with better education normally earn more than workers who are illiterate or who have an incomplete primary education. Moreover, a comparison of the estimates associated with the education dummies in the 1995 results with those in the 2012 results shows a decline in relative returns at all education levels in 2012; the better-educated group experienced a greater decline, which is also depicted in Fig. 5. Fig. 6 shows the evolution of

Table 3. OLS Regression Results: Male Aged 16−65.

	Year 2012 Coef.	Year 1995 Coef.	Pooled Coef.
	Dependent Variable: Log Hourly Wages		
Time = 1995			−0.09***
			(0.005)
4−7 Years education	0.306***	0.469***	0.425***
	(0.01)	(0.008)	(0.006)
8−10 Years education	0.501***	0.835***	0.698***
	(0.01)	(0.011)	(0.007)
11−14 Years education	0.748***	1.232***	0.966***
	(0.01)	(0.012)	(0.008)
> = 15 Years education	1.590***	2.096***	1.824***
	(0.015)	(0.018)	(0.011)
Experience	0.032***	0.05***	0.039***
	(0.0008)	(0.001)	(0.0006)
Experience^2	−0.0004***	−0.0007***	−0.0005***
	(0.00001)	(0.00002)	(0.00001)
Tenure	0.005***	0.002***	0.004***
	(0.0004)	(0.0005)	(0.0003)
White	0.179***	0.256***	0.216***
	(0.005)	(0.007)	(0.004)
Self-employed	−0.631***	−0.698***	−0.678***
	(0.017)	(0.018)	(0.012)
Formal employee	−0.433***	−0.492***	−0.480***
	(0.016)	(0.017)	(0.012)
Informal employee	−0.710***	−0.878***	−0.814***
	(0.018)	(0.018)	(0.013)
Union	0.03***	0.081***	0.065***
	(0.007)	(0.009)	(0.006)
Constant	0.540***	0.041*	0.333***
	(0.021)	(0.022)	(0.016)
Observations	69,329	63,038	132,367
R-squared	0.397	0.48	0.449

Notes: PNAD 1995−2012 Survey data, wage is adjusted to 1995 price using CPI conversion factor. Samples include full-time male workers aged between 16 and 65 with positive working experience, worked at least 140 hours per month, not currently schooling, not working without pay or domestic workers. Standard errors in parentheses.
***$p < 0.01$, *$p < 0.1$.

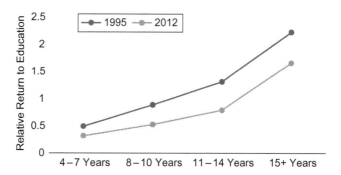

Fig. 5. Relative Return to Education: Males Aged 16–65. *Notes*: Calculated based on full-time male workers with positive working experience, working at least 140 hours per month, not currently a student, not working without pay or as domestic workers, between 16 and 65 years of age, based on PNAD's 1995–2012 data. The sample of each group defined by gender, education level and year is trimmed at the 1st and 99th percentiles. Wage income in the analysis includes both cash income and the values of the goods and products paid from the primary job. The wage measure is in constant 1995 prices.

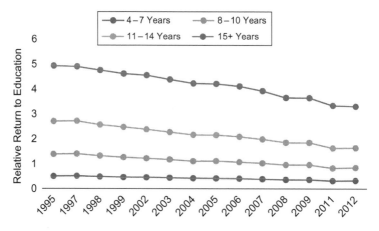

Fig. 6. Change in Relative Return to Education: Males Aged 16–65. *Notes*: Calculated based on full-time male workers with positive working experience, working at least 140 hours per month, not currently a student, not working without pay or as domestic workers, between 16 and 65 years of age, based on PNAD's 1995–2012 data. The sample of each group defined by gender, education level and year is trimmed at the 1st and 99th percentiles. Wage income in the analysis includes both cash income and the values of the goods and products paid from the primary job. The wage measure is in constant 1995 prices.

the relative returns for each education group, generated based on the Mincer regression results for each year between 1995 and 2012.

As shown in Tables 2 and 3, both the composition of male workers' characteristics and the wage structure experienced significant changes between 1995 and 2012, which supports the application of the decomposition approaches. The decomposition results of the changes in average value, the values at the 10th, 50th, and 90th quantiles and the inequality measures are reported below.

Decomposition of Increase in Average Wage

The Oaxaca-Blinder decomposition results of the increase in average wages between 1995 and 2012 are reported in Table 3 for the counterfactuals generated using the OLS estimates for the 1995, 2012 and pooled samples. When using the OLS estimates of the pooled regression as the reference, an underlying assumption is that the wage structure change can be completely captured by the year-fixed effect. There was an approximately 0.35 log unit increase in the average hourly wage between 1995 and 2012. The estimated wage structure effect is positive, which means that changes in the returns on workers' different characteristics had an increasing impact on average wages, assuming the composition of workers' characteristics is fixed. The changes in the composition of workers' characteristics also had an increasing impact on average wages, which means that the average wage would increase because of changes in the composition of the male labor force, assuming no change in the wage structure. Moreover, the wage structure effects always account for a larger proportion of the increase than the composition effects, regardless of how the counterfactual is generated.

The contribution of educational expansion to the increase in average wages is also reported in Table 4. For the 4–7 years of education group, the wage structure effect and the composition effect are both negative, which means both that the decline in the relative return to those with 4–7 years of education, as reported in Table 3, had a decreasing effect on average wages and that the decrease in the proportion of workers in this education group, as reported in Table 2, also decreased average wages. Similarly, the composition effects of the 8–10, 11–14, and 15 + education groups are all positive and based on Table 3, we know that the proportions of workers in these three groups increased, which means that the educational improvement of the male labor force had an increasing effect on average wages. The negative wage structure effects of these three education

Table 4. Oaxaca-Blinder Decomposition Results: Male Aged 16–65.

Reference Group:	Using 1995 Coef:		Using 2012 Coef:		Using Pooled Coef:	
Decomposition Method:	Overall change = 0.346		Overall change = 0.346		Overall change = 0.346	
Oaxaca-Blinder	Composition effect = 0.321***	Wage structure effect = 0.0244***	Composition effect = 0.208***	Wage structure effect = 0.137***	Composition effect = 0.256***	Wage structure effect = 0.0896***
4–7 Years education	−0.055***	−0.038***	−0.036***	−0.058***	−0.05***	−0.04***
8–10 Years education	0.041***	−0.06***	0.024***	−0.044***	0.034***	−0.05***
11–14 Years education	0.264***	−0.168***	0.160***	−0.065***	0.207***	−0.111***
>=15 Years education	0.093***	−0.049***	0.071***	−0.026***	0.081***	−0.037***
Exp	−0.034***	−0.417***	−0.022***	−0.430***	−0.027***	−0.425***
Exp^2	0.017***	0.204***	0.011***	0.211***	0.013***	0.209***
Tenure	0.0007***	0.022***	0.002***	0.022***	0.001***	0.022***
White	−0.025***	−0.036***	−0.017***	−0.043***	−0.021***	−0.04***
Self-employed	0.031***	0.016***	0.028***	0.019***	0.03***	0.017***
Formal employee	−0.051***	0.032**	−0.045***	0.026**	−0.05***	0.031***
Informal employee	0.043***	0.027***	0.035***	0.035***	0.04***	0.03***
Union	−0.003***	−0.009***	−0.001***	−0.01***	−0.002***	−0.009***
Constant		0.500***		0.5***		0.500***

Notes: PNAD 1995–2012 Survey data, wage is adjusted to 1995 price using CPI conversion factor. Samples include full-time male workers aged between 16 and 65 with positive working experience, worked at least 140 hours per month, not currently schooling, not working without pay or domestic workers.
***$p < 0.01$, **$p < 0.05$.

groups show that decreased relative returns on education had a decreasing effect on average wages. The negative wage structure effects are dominated by the positive composition effect; thus, the overall impact of educational improvement on average wages is positive.

In brief, both the changes in the composition of male workers' characteristics and the changes in the wage structure between 1995 and 2012 in Brazil contributed to the increase in average wages. For each education group, the decline in relative returns had a negative impact on average wages that was dominated by the positive impact of the educational improvement of male workers. These findings are robust for different counterfactuals.

Decomposition of Changes across the Wage Distribution

The RIF method is employed to decompose the changes at the 10th, 50th, and 90th quantiles and the changes in the inequality measures, including the 90-10, 50-10, and 90-50 differentials, variances, and Gini coefficients. The counterfactual is generated by reweighting the wage distribution of 1995, which means that the difference between the actual 2012 distribution and the counterfactual distribution represents the "composition effect" and the difference between the actual 1995 distribution and the counterfactual is the "wage structure effect."

The unconditional quantile regression results for the 10th, 50th, and 90th quantiles in both years are reported in Table 5, which shows the wage structure at different income levels in both years. The results show that the relative return at each education level becomes higher as it moves to a higher quantile in both years. The reason for this result is the positive relationship between education and unobservable skill, according to Arias, Azuara, Bernal, Heckman, and Villarreal (2010), in which more skilled workers, who are more likely to be at the top of the wage distribution, would benefit more from educational investment. Additionally, each estimate associated with education in the 1995 results is higher than the corresponding estimate in the 2012 results, which demonstrates the decline in relative returns to each education group. Returns on experience and tenure also exhibit declining patterns similar to the returns on education. Workers who are white and have a union affiliation are always paid better at each quantile. Wage differences between employers versus employees and the self-employed increase when moving to higher quantiles.

Table 5. Quantile Regression Results: Male Aged 16–65.

Year:	1995			2012		
Quantile:	10th	50th	90th	10th	50th	90th
4–7 Years education	0.351***	0.428***	0.427***	0.311***	0.233***	0.254***
	(0.011)	(0.008)	(0.013)	(0.01)	(0.007)	(0.014)
8–10 Years education	0.637***	0.784***	0.845***	0.440***	0.391***	0.440***
	(0.016)	(0.011)	(0.018)	(0.011)	(0.008)	(0.016)
11–14 Years education	0.930***	1.223***	1.339***	0.547***	0.596***	0.815***
	(0.016)	(0.012)	(0.018)	(0.011)	(0.008)	(0.015)
>=15 Years education	1.825***	2.151***	2.212***	1.132***	1.541***	1.943***
	(0.023)	(0.016)	(0.026)	(0.014)	(0.01)	(0.019)
Experience	0.040***	0.05***	0.055***	0.019***	0.028***	0.04***
	(0.001)	(0.001)	(0.002)	(0.0009)	(0.0006)	(0.001)
Experience^2	-0.0006***	-0.0007***	-0.0008***	-0.0003***	-0.0004***	-0.0006***
	(0.00002)	(0.00002)	(0.00003)	(0.00002)	(0.00001)	(0.00002)
Tenure	-0.0006	0.005***	0.011***	0.00006	0.008***	0.013***
	(0.0006)	(0.0004)	(0.0006)	(0.0004)	(0.0003)	(0.0005)
White	0.194***	0.232***	0.249***	0.128***	0.164***	0.161***
	(0.009)	(0.007)	(0.01)	(0.006)	(0.004)	(0.008)
Self-employed	-0.742***	-0.683***	-0.701***	-0.681***	-0.638***	-0.684***
	(0.02)	(0.015)	(0.023)	(0.015)	(0.011)	(0.021)
Formal employee	-0.271***	-0.548***	-0.825***	-0.161***	-0.498***	-0.780***
	(0.02)	(0.014)	(0.022)	(0.015)	(0.01)	(0.02)
Informal employee	-0.637***	-0.901***	-1.094***	-0.602***	-0.717***	-0.906***
	(0.021)	(0.015)	(0.025)	(0.016)	(0.011)	(0.022)

Union	0.09***	0.127***	0.135***	0.006	0.061***	0.099***
	(0.012)	(0.008)	(0.013)	(0.008)	(0.006)	(0.011)
Constant	−0.642***	0.0691***	0.956***	0.042***	0.697***	1.305***
	(0.028)	(0.021)	(0.033)	(0.021)	(0.014)	(0.029)
Observations	63,038	63,038	63,038	69,329	69,329	69,329
R-squared	0.198	0.288	0.360	0.194	0.220	0.334

Notes: PNAD1995–2012 Survey data, wage is adjusted to 1995 price using CPI conversion factor. Samples include full-time male workers aged between 16 and 65 with positive working experience, worked at least 140 hours per month, not currently schooling, not working without pay or domestic workers. Standard errors in parentheses.
*** $p < 0.01$, ** $p < 0.05$, * $p < 0.1$.

The quantile decomposition results of changes at the 10th, 50th, and 90th quantiles are documented in Table 6. The log hourly wage increased at all three quantiles in 2012: the 10th quantile increased the most, and the 90th quantile increased the least, as shown in panel A of Table 6. Panel B reports decomposition results based on the RIF regressions. The changes in the wage structure had an increasing effect on the 10th and 50th quantiles but a decreasing effect on the 90th quantile. The composition effects are positive for all three quantiles. At the 50th and 90th quantiles, the composition effects account for most of the change, and the wage structure effects are much smaller.

Moreover, the contributions of each education group to the wage structure effects at the 50th and 90th quantiles are all negative, which means that the decline in the relative returns on education had decreasing effects on wages at the 50th and 90th quantiles. Additionally, the impacts are larger at the 90th quantile. However, the wage structure effects of each education group at the 10th quantile are positive. The composition effects of each education group are similar to the mean decomposition results shown in Table 4: the decrease in the proportion of workers with 4−7 years of education decreased wages at each quantile and the expansion of better-educated groups increased wages throughout the distribution.

In brief, the quantile decomposition results show that changes in workers' characteristics increased wage income at the 10th, 50th, and 90th quantiles. The changes in returns to different characteristics had an increasing impact on the 10th and 50th quantiles, but the wage structure effect decreased wages at the 90th quantile. The expansion of better education groups had an increasing impact at each quantile. The decrease in the relative returns of each education group had an increasing impact on the 10th quantile and a declining impact on the 50th and 90th quantiles.

The RIF decomposition is also applied to decompose the decrease on inequality between 1995 and 2012. The results, reported in Table 7, show that movements in the wage structure during this period had an equalizing impact on the wage distribution and that changes in workers' characteristics had an unequalizing impact on the wage distribution. Moreover, the unequalizing composition effects are always offset by the equalizing wage structure effect; thus, the degree of inequality decreased. In terms of education, a positive composition effect of education expansion demonstrates the existence of the "paradox of progress" (Bourguignon et al., 2005), which means that a more equal distribution of education increases wage income inequality because of the convexity of returns to education. However, the negative wage structure effect dominates the positive composition effect,

Table 6. Quantile Decomposition Results: Male Aged 16–65.

Reference Group: 1995 Coef.	10th Percentile		50th Percentile		90th Percentile	
A. Raw log hourly wage gap:	0.704		0.345		0.067	
B. Decomposition method: RIF						
Mean RIF Gap	0.683		0.333		0.049	
	Composition effect = 0.124	Wage structure effect = 0.559	Composition effect = 0.293	Wage structure effect = 0.0397	Composition effect = 0.506	Wage structure effect = 0.457
4–7 Years education	−0.045	0.019	−0.061	−0.062	−0.026	−0.019
8–10 Years education	0.025	0.027	0.048	−0.0928	0.032	−0.058
11–14 Years education	0.108	0.074	0.266	−0.207	0.349	−0.340
>= 15 Years education	0.0220	0.0291	0.0629	−0.0328	0.2110	−0.1550
Exp	−0.010	−0.058	−0.023	−0.4690	−0.030	−0.571
Exp^2	0.0028	0.0552	0.0070	0.228	0.0094	0.3010
Tenure	−0.0030	−0.0077	0.0017	00.016	0.0082	0.0249
White	−0.012	0.004	−0.027	−0.037	−0.023	−0.021
Self-employed	0.010	−0.040	0.017	0.022	0.051	0.039
Formal employee	0.003	0.046	−0.036	0.036	−0.145	0.098
Informal employee	0.022	−0.013	0.042	0.040	0.074	0.028
Union	0.002	−0.011	−0.004	−0.012	−0.006	−0.004
Constant		0.434		0.611		0.219

Notes: PNAD 1995–2012 Survey data, wage is adjusted to 1995 price using CPI conversion factor. Samples include full-time male workers aged between 16 and 65 with positive working experience worked at least 140 hours per month, not currently schooling, not working without pay or domestic workers.

Table 7. RIF Decomposition of Changes in Wage Inequality: 1995–2012, 16–65 Years Old Male Sample.

	90–10		90–50		50–10		Variance	
Overall Changes:	−0.635		−0.285		−0.35		−0.323	
	Composition effect = 0.382	Wage structure effect = 1.016	Composition effect = 0.213	Wage structure effect = 0.497	Composition effect = 0.169	Wage structure effect = 0.519	Composition effect = 0.184	Wage structure effect = 0.506
4–7 Years education	0.019	−0.038	0.035	0.043	−0.016	−0.081	0.028	−0.017
8–10 Years education	0.007	−0.084	−0.016	0.035	0.023	−0.120	−0.006	−0.038
11–14 Years education	0.241	−0.414	0.083	−0.133	0.158	−0.281	0.084	−0.213
>= 15 Years education	0.189	−0.184	0.148	−0.122	0.041	−0.062	0.118	−0.150
Exp	−0.020	−0.513	−0.007	−0.102	−0.013	−0.411	−0.007	−0.227
Exp^2	0.007	0.246	0.002	0.073	0.004	0.173	0.003	0.118
Tenure	0.011	0.033	0.006	0.009	0.005	0.023	0.009	−0.016
White	−0.011	−0.024	0.004	0.016	−0.014	−0.041	0.002	0.016
Self-employed	0.041	0.079	0.034	0.018	0.007	0.061	0.023	0.027
Formal employee	−0.148	0.052	−0.109	0.062	−0.039	−0.010	−0.094	0.036
Informal employee	0.052	0.041	0.032	−0.013	0.020	0.053	0.029	−0.001
Union	−0.008	0.007	−0.002	0.008	−0.006	−0.001	−0.005	0.007
Constant		−0.215		−0.392		0.177		−0.048

Notes: Author's calculation based on PNAD 1995 and 2012 data, wage is adjusted to 1995 price using CPI conversion factor. Samples include full-time male workers aged between 16 and 65 with positive working experience, worked at least 140 hours per month, not currently schooling, not working without pay or domestic workers.

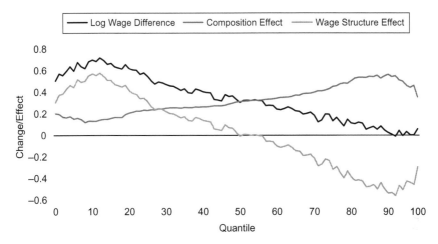

Fig. 7. RIF Decomposition: Males Aged 16–65, 1995 versus 2012. *Notes*: Calculated based on full-time male workers with positive working experience, working at least 140 hours per month, not currently a student, not working without pay or as domestic workers, between 16 and 65 years of age, based on PNAD's 1995–2012 data. The sample of each group defined by gender, education level and year is trimmed at the 1st and 99th percentiles.

which means that the overall impact of education was equalizing. The results are also depicted in Figs. 7 and 8.[3]

CONCLUSION

This paper investigates the changes in the male wage distribution of Brazil from 1995 to 2012 using PNAD data. The Oaxaca-Blinder decomposition is used to decompose the change in average wages between 1995 and 2012. The RIF decomposition is applied to decompose changes in other distributional statistics. The shift in the wage distribution coincides with education expansion; thus, the contribution of education is particularly interesting.

---

[3]All results reported in this section are robust when alternative decomposition methods are applied, which include the Residual Imputation Procedure (Juhn et al., 1993), Inverse Propensity Reweighting (DiNardo et al., 1996), the Quantile Regressions Method (Machado & Mata, 2005) and the Estimation of Conditional Distribution (Chernozhukov et al., 2013).

YANG WANG ET AL.

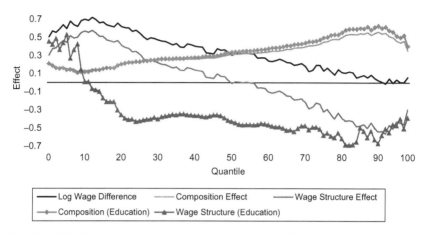

Fig. 8. RIF Decomposition: Males Aged 16−65, 1995 versus 2012. *Notes:* Calculated based on full-time male workers with positive working experience, working at least 140 hours per month, not currently a student, not working without pay or as domestic workers, between 16 and 65 years of age, based on PNAD's 1995−2012 data. The sample of each group defined by gender, education level and year is trimmed at the 1st and 99th percentiles.

The wage structure in Brazil changed during the period under analysis; however, the composition of male workers' characteristics also changed. The results show that although both changes in the wage structure and changes in the composition of workers' characteristics increased both average wages and the wages at the 10th and 50th quantiles, the wage structure effect decreased wages at the 90th quantile. Regarding the decline in wage inequality, the wage structure effect was the main force in decreasing male wage inequality, and the composition effect was actually working in the opposite direction but was much smaller compared to the wage structure effect. The detailed decomposition results show that the decline in relative returns on different education groups had a decreasing effect on average wages and wages at different quantiles, in addition to decreased inequality. The improvement in the education composition of the male labor force had an increasing impact on wage income and wage inequality, which demonstrates the existence of the "paradox of progress."

The coincidence of education expansion and the decline in the educational premium warrants further exploration given its contribution to the evolution of the entire wage distribution. The identification of the causes of the decline in the educational premium would also provide useful policy perspectives for education reform. Moreover, as noted in the previous section, the lower tail inequality declined more significantly than the upper tail inequality over the entire period under analysis; it would also be interesting to observe how institutions have different impacts on the lower and upper tails of the wage distribution.

ACKNOWLEDGMENT

We thank two anonymous referees for their comments and suggestions on an earlier draft of this paper.

REFERENCES

Arias, J., Azuara, O., Bernal, P., Heckman, J., & Villarreal, C. (2010). *Policies to promote growth and economic efficiency in Mexico.* IZA Discussion Papers No. 4740.

Barros, R., de Carvalho, M., Franco, S., & Mendonça, R. (2010). Markets, the state and the dynamics of inequality: Brazil's case study. In L. F. López Calva & N. Lustig (Eds.), *Declining inequality in Latin America: A decade of progress?* (ch. 6). Washington, DC: Brookings Institution.

Blinder, A. (1973). Wage discrimination: Reduced form and structural estimates. *Journal of Human Resources, 8*, 436–455.

Blom, A., Holm-Nielsen, L., & Verner, D. (2001). Education, earnings, and inequality in Brazil, 1982–1998: Implications for education policy. *Peabody Journal of Education, 76*, 180–221.

Bourguignon, F., Ferreira, F., & Lustig, N. (Eds.). (2005). *The microeconomics of income distribution dynamics in East Asia and Latin America.* Washington, DC: The World Bank/Oxford University Press.

Chernozhukov, V., Fernandez-Val, I., & Melly, B. (2013). Inference on counterfactual distributions. *Econometrica., 81*(6), 2205–2268.

DiNardo, J., Fortin, N. M., & Lemieux, T. (1996). Labor market institutions and the distribution of wages, 1973–1992: A semiparametric approach. *Econometrica, 64*, 1001–1044.

Ferreira, F. H. G., Firpo, S. P., & Messina, J. (2015). *A more level playing field? Explaining the decline in earnings inequality in Brazil, 1995–2012.* Brooks World Poverty Institute Working Paper Series iriba_wp12.

Ferreira, F. H. G., Leite, P. G., & Litchfield, J. A. (2008). The rise and fall of Brazilian inequality: 1981–2004. *Macroeconomic Dynamics, 12*, 199–230.

Firpo, S., Fortin, N. M., & Lemieux, T. (2009). Unconditional quantile regressions. *Econometrica, 77*(3), 953–973.

Higgins, S., & Pereira, C. (2014). The effects of Brazil's taxation and social spending on the distribution of household income. *Public Finance Review, 42*(3), 346–367.

Juhn, C., Murphy, K. M., & Pierce, B. (1993). Wage inequality and the rise in returns to skill. *Journal of Political Economy, 101*, 410–442.

Machado, J. F., & Mata, J. (2005). Counterfactual decomposition of changes in wage distributions using quantile regression. *Journal of Applied Econometrics, 20*, 445–465.

Menezes-Filho, N. A., Fernandes, R., & Picchetti, P. (2006). Rising human capital but constant inequality: The education composition effect in Brazil. *Rio de Janeiro, 60*(4), 407–424.

Oaxaca, R. (1973). Male-female wage differentials in urban labor markets. *International Economic Review, 14*, 693–709.

CHANGES IN WELFARE WITH A HETEROGENEOUS WORKFORCE: THE CASE OF PERU

Adrian Robles[a] and Marcos Robles[b]

[a]Johns Hopkins University, Washington, DC
[b]Inter-American Development Bank Washington, DC

ABSTRACT

This paper argues that the assumption of a homogeneous workforce, which is implicitly invoked in the decomposition analysis of changes in welfare indicators, hides the role that schooling and its returns may have on the understanding of these changes. Using Peruvian cross-sectional data for a period of 10 years (2004–2013) and counterfactual simulations, this paper finds that the main factor contributing to poverty reduction has been individuals' changes in labor earnings, and the role of these changes has been less important in reducing income inequality. The main driving force of reduced income inequality has been the fall in returns to education, which at the same time has been one of the important factors to constraining the period's remarkable progress in poverty reduction and expansion of the middle class.

Income Inequality Around the World
Research in Labor Economics, Volume 44, 79–107
ISSN: 0147-9121/doi:10.1108/S0147-912120160000044010

Keywords: Poverty; middle class; inequality; decomposition; labor; Peru

JEL Classifications: C83; E24; D63; I24; I32

INTRODUCTION

The period from 2003 to 2013 was one of Latin America's most notable in terms of economic progress. Both the sustained economic growth (the GDP per capita grew at an average annual rate of 5.2 percent)[1] and the substantial fall in income inequality (the Gini coefficient for per capita income decreased from 0.56 to 0.49; Inter-American Development Bank [IDB], 2015) implied significant increases in purchasing power – both in absolute and relative terms – at the bottom of the income distribution, with considerable upward mobility along this distribution. The percentage of people with income below USD 4.00 a day decreased by 20 percentage points, from 43 percent to 23 percent; extreme poverty (people with income below USD 2.50 a day) was cut in half, from 26 percent to 11 percent; and the size of the middle class (people with income between USD 10.00 and USD 50.00 a day) increased from 21 percent to 33 percent. In this period, Peru – with 31 million inhabitants, the fifth-most populous country in Latin America, after Brazil, Mexico, Colombia, and Argentina – showed some of the most significant changes. Compared to the Latin American (18 countries) average, the annual per capita product of Peru grew faster than a 36 percent pace, and its Gini coefficient decreased nearly 3 additional percentage points between 2003 and 2013. Also, the headcount poverty ratio, at the USD 4-a-day line, fell 16 percent faster than the regional average, and the middle class grew 50 percent faster. Peru also showed greater resilience to shocks of the recent global financial crisis (Grosh, Bussolo, & Freije, 2014). (The changes observed in Peru are described in detail in the Stylized Facts section.)

The region's dramatic changes have been detailed in a number of recent studies, which have also provided plausible explanations of how

---

[1]Gross Domestic Product in USD based on 2011 purchasing power parity (International Monetary Fund [IMF], 2014).

the changes came about and described the challenges to maintain and deepen the progress achieved (Ferreira et al., 2012; Gasparini & Lustig, 2011; Levy & Schady, 2013; Lustig, Lopez-Calva, & Ortiz-Juarez, 2013). Several studies have focused more closely on the factors that have contributed to changes in poverty and inequality based on a non-parametric decomposition approach (Azevedo, Davalos, Diaz-Bonilla, Atuesta, & Castañeda, 2013; Azevedo, Inchauste, & Sanfelice, 2013; Freije, 2014; Inchauste et al., 2014). We follow this approach, but we concentrate exclusively on Peru and, in doing so, we use decomposition techniques enriched in terms of analytical scope and empirical application. Specifically, this paper aims to quantify the contribution of the forces behind the changes in Peru's welfare indicators based on counterfactual simulations.

The methods for counterfactual decompositions developed by Ravallion and Huppi (1991), Datt and Ravallion (1992), and Kolenikov and Shorrocks (2005) explain variations in poverty based on changes in aggregated components that have limited usefulness to define specific policies that fight against it. Unlike these works, the methods proposed more recently (Azevedo, Inchauste, Olivieri, Saavedra, & Winkler, 2013; Azevedo, Nguyen, & Sanfelice, 2012; de Barros, de Carvalho, Franco, & Mendoca, 2006, 2007, 2010) generate entire counterfactual distributions, allowing us to quantify the contribution of changes in a greater number of factors to the observed distributional change in poverty and inequality. On this basis, we explicitly consider the educational dimension in the income identity equation. By using an indicator of human capital stock, utilized extensively in the literature on economic growth for aggregate production functions, the assumption that all units of the labor force are homogeneous and possess equal capacities is relaxed.

Using data gathered from the National Household Survey of Peru (ENAHO, for its Spanish acronym) collected over 10 years, our results show that while the changes in labor income are one of the main factors contributing to poverty reduction in recent years, their role — in contrast to previous estimates — is less important to inequality reduction if the analysis takes into account that the working-age population's human capital is not homogeneous. Instead, the main driving force of the reduction in poverty was the fall in returns to education. Both unequalizing and equalizing effects of this fall occurred, that is, returns were larger for higher levels of education and the fall was smaller for higher levels of education (convexities in returns increased), but returns were also proportionately higher for graduates of each education level, particularly among those with the lowest levels (sheepskin effects in the returns[2]). At the same time, the fall in returns to education was one of the most important factors that limited the achievement of more effective progress in reducing poverty and increasing the size of the middle class.

This paper provides three key contributions to the existing literature and sheds some light from a policy perspective. First, an indicator of human capital stock for the working-age population, associated with schooling and its returns, is incorporated into the income identity equation. This allows for a more appropriate identification of the forces behind the movements of population groups over the income distribution and improves the depth in the decomposition analysis. Second, consistent with the values of international lines, we define multiples of the national poverty lines that may be appropriate in the case studies at country level to define and analyze poor, vulnerable, middle class, and rich groups in the population. The lines thus defined consider the geographical price differences within countries, an aspect that is treated poorly in cross-country studies using international lines. Third, we provide detailed evidence on Peruvian population movements along the income distribution over the last decade and contributions of monetary and non-monetary income components on changes in poverty, inequality, and the middle class. The revision of the Peruvian experience can provide lessons to other countries in the region, given the tremendous distributive changes over the last decade.

This paper is organized in five sections. After the Introduction, the section "Empirical Methodology" describes three methodological aspects: the procedure used to include the educational dimension in the income identity equation, the strategy used to estimate returns to education by identifying convexities and sheepskin effects, and the decomposition method based on counterfactual simulations. The section "Data Characteristics" shows the characteristics of data sources and the values of the poverty lines used. The section "Distributional Changes of Household Income Sources" reports distributional changes observed in Peru and the changes of more immediate determinants that have contributed to the recent increase in household income. Decomposition results and final remarks are presented in the last two sections.

---

[2]Larger returns to diploma years (or complete level years) than to other years of education, indicating that individuals with more schooling tend to earn more not because (or, at least, not solely because) schooling makes them more productive, but rather because it certifies them as more productive (Hungerford & Solon, 1987).

EMPIRICAL METHODOLOGY

Income Identity

In order to decompose the observed changes in monetary welfare indicators (poverty, middle class, or inequality), the household per capita income (Y_{pc}) is disaggregated by monetary and non-monetary components as follows:

$$Y_{pc} = \frac{Y}{n} = \frac{Y^L + Y^{NL}}{n} = \frac{n_a}{n} * h * \left(\frac{n_o}{n_a} * n_h * \frac{Y^L}{n_o * h * n_h} + \frac{Y^{NL}}{n_a * h} \right) \qquad (1)$$

where n is the number of household members, Y^L is the household's labor income (sum of each occupied adult member's labor income), Y^{NL} is the household's non-labor income (sum of each adult member's non-labor income), n_a is the number of adults in the household, n_o represents the number of occupied adults, n_h the number of hours worked, $h = e^{\phi(s)}$ is the adults' stock of human capital defined as a function of the years of education completed (s) (following Bils & Klenow, 2000; Hall & Jones, 1999; Mankiw, Romer, & Weil, 1992), and ($n_a * h$) and ($n_o * h$) are the units of adult and employed human capital, respectively.

The function $\phi(s)$ reflects the efficiency of an individual with s years of education regarding the efficiency of an individual with no schooling, $\phi(0) = 0$. For example, if an individual has completed tertiary education (16 years of schooling) and the average return per year of education is 0.08, the person's stock of human capital (h) in this formulation is 3.6 ($= e^{0.08*16}$) times the stock of a worker with 0 years of education. The derivative of $\phi(s)$ is the return to schooling (r) estimated in a Mincerian wage regression: an additional year of schooling raises a worker's efficiency proportionally by $\phi'(s)$. The next section discusses the suggestion that $\phi(s)$ can be approximated by a piecewise linear function if returns are estimated for each education level. Note that if $\phi(0) = 0$ is always true, that is, $h = 1$ for all individuals, the per capita income equation to be decomposed will therefore be the same as the one used so far, that is, assuming an undifferentiated workforce.

Returns to Education

Given the evidence of convexities and sheepskin effects in estimating returns to education in Peru (Yamada, 2007; Yamada & Castro, 2010), we use a specification of labor income equation that allows obtaining the return to an additional year of schooling at each education level:

$$\ln W = \alpha + \sum_i \sum_j r_{ij}s_{ij} + \gamma_1 X + \gamma_2 X2 + \gamma_3 Z + \mu \tag{2}$$

where $\ln W$ is the natural logarithm of real hourly labor income; r_{ij} are the returns to an i = incomplete or complete additional year of education for j = primary, secondary, tertiary, and postgraduate, and s_{ij} are years of education completed;[3] X is the potential experience measures as the age minus years of completed schooling and six years (the mandatory starting age for school), and $X2$ is its squared divided by 100; Z is a vector of controls that includes dummies for sex, urban-rural residence area, and parent education (at least incomplete secondary and otherwise);[4] and μ is the error term in the regression.[5]

Eq. (2) was estimated using the Heckman sample selection correction procedure due to the presence of sample selection bias in this type of specification (non-random selection to be in or out of the sample associated with people's decisions to work or not work). The procedure corrects this problem in two stages. First a probit model for the probability of working is estimated in order to predict the employment probability for each individual, and then a labor-income ordinary least squares model is estimated by incorporating a transformation of predicted individual probabilities as an additional explanatory variable. The selection model considers marital status (married/cohabiting and otherwise), the number of children in the home aged 0−11 years (both variables strongly affect the chances of labor participation, but not our outcome), and, implicitly, the individual's salary income via the inclusion of its predictors (age, years of education, urban-rural, and sex).

---

[3]For the graduate level, returns are estimated without discriminating between incomplete and complete.

[4]Given that demand for education is endogenous to ability (individuals with greater learning ability are more likely to consume greater amounts of education), the variable "parent education" is included to reduce the effect of this endogeneity on estimating returns.

[5]A specification based on dummies for education levels produces the same results if estimated coefficients are then divided by the average years of education at each level.

After estimating returns to education, the function $\phi(s)$ can be approximated by a piecewise linear function breaking years of education (s) in splines and taking into account the education levels of individuals:

$$\phi(s) = \begin{cases} r_{ip}^t*(s-0), & 0 \le s \le 5 \\ r_{ip}^t*5+r_{cp}^t*(s-5), & s=6 \\ r_{ip}^t*5+r_{cp}^t*1+r_{is}^t*(s-6), & 7 \le s \le 10 \\ r_{ip}^t*5+r_{cp}^t*1+r_{is}^t*4+r_{cs}^t*(s-10), & s=11 \\ r_{ip}^t*5+r_{cp}^t*1+r_{is}^t*4+r_{cs}^t*1+r_{it}^t*(s-11), & 12 \le s \le 15 \\ r_{ip}^t*5+r_{cp}^t*1+r_{is}^t*4+r_{cs}^t*1+r_{it}^t*4+r_{ct}^t*(s-15), & s=16 \\ r_{ip}^t*5+r_{cp}^t*1+r_{is}^t*4+r_{cs}^t*1+r_{it}^t*4+r_{ct}^t*1+r_{po}^t*(s-16), & s \ge 17 \end{cases}$$

(3)

where r_{ij}^t are the returns to an additional year of education for the level ij (as detailed above) in each period t.[6] If $\bar{r} = \phi(s)/s$ is the average return to education, Eq. (1) can be rewritten as:

$$Y_{pc} = \frac{n_a}{n} * (e^s)\bar{r} * \left(\frac{n_o}{n_a} * n_h * \frac{Y^L}{n_o * h * n_h} + \frac{Y^{NL}}{n_a * h} \right)$$

(4)

This is the equation we use to decompose the observed change in poverty, the middle class, and inequality. Note that in this specification, although labor and non-labor income are estimated at the household level (aggregating income from its members), the heterogeneity of human capital is not altered because the decomposition is estimated at individual level and, therefore, the adults' stock of human capital does not need to be aggregated because $(e^s)\bar{r} = e^{\phi(s)} = h$.

Decomposition Method

The decomposition of observed changes in welfare measures into contributions of each component (and of its interactions with all other components)

---

[6] The approximation proposed is an extension of the function $\phi(s)$ from the simplest formulation of the earnings equation, when the schooling variable is not broken into splines, $\phi(s) = r * s$, as described by Hall and Jones (1999).

in two points in time ($t = 0, 1$) can be estimated in a straightforward manner. According to de Barros et al. (2006) and Azevedo et al. (2013), counterfactual distributions of the welfare aggregate for t_1 can be constructed by replacing the observed values of components in t_0. Thus, poverty, middle-class, or inequality rates could be computed for each cumulative counterfactual distribution, that is, measures that would have prevailed in absence of the change in that component. For example, if p_j is the contribution of the component j on change in the Gini (G), this contribution and its interactions with all other components can be calculated as the difference between the observed Gini in t_1 and its estimated cumulative counterfactual for t_1 by substituting the observed value of the component j (c_j) in t_0 to the observed distribution in t_1:

$$p_j = G\left(f\left(c_1^{t1}, ..., c_j^{t1}, ..., c_n^{t1}\right)\right) - G\left(f\left(c_1^{t1}, ..., c_j^{t0}, ..., c_n^{t1}\right)\right) \quad (5)$$

where $f(\cdot)$ is a cumulative density function of household income per capita, which depends on each of its components. However, this procedure has two problems. Shorrocks (1982, 2013) argues that this kind of decompositions (by factor components) does not guarantee that the final sum of all contributions is equal to the total change, in our example in G from t_0 to t_1, because the sum depends on the order in which the component cumulative effects are calculated. An additional problem is the way to assign to households the value c_j from the period t_0 to the period t_1 in the context of cross-sectional data.

Following the example of the Gini, for the first problem, Shorrocks (1982, 2013) shows that marginal effects of the sequential elimination of each component contributing to the change in Gini, considering all the possible sequences, and assigning to each component the average of its marginal contributions, produces an exact additive decomposition of the Gini into n contributions. This means that if the exercise is done starting from the left and then from the right, the averages are the result of $n!$ elimination sequences, where $n!$ is the factorial of the number of income components. Formally, this is the equivalent to the Shapley value allocation method in game theory, and is therefore referred to as the Shapley decomposition (Sastre & Trannoy, 2002).

We follow Azevedo et al. (2012) to address the second problem. They propose to match individuals or households based on their observed income rank in each period, that is, assuming a distributional dynamic in which each individual keeps his or her rank across the periods. Thus, the entire trajectory of the observed income distribution and its components are tracked by assigning the average value of each component for each percentile in t_0 to each individual or household in the same percentile in t_1.

It should be noted that this kind of decomposition has some analytical limitations: It does not identify causal effects; counterfactuals are generated by modifying one income component at a time keeping everything else constant; and the decomposition procedure does not ensure aggregation consistency.[7] Despite these limitations, the procedure provides relevant empirical evidence on the immediate determinants behind the distributional changes.

DATA CHARACTERISTICS

In order to estimate the contributions of monetary and non-monetary per capita household income components (Eq. (4)) in reducing poverty and inequality, we use the 2004−2013 rounds of the ENAHO, conducted by the National Institute of Statistics and Informatics (INEI for its acronym in Spanish). The survey's data is collected annually from a sample of about 90,000 people in 22,000 households in urban and rural areas of all regions. It provides detailed information on demographics, employment, education, housing, and income and expenditure of households and their members. Although the labor and non-labor income as well as employment characteristics data are collected from the members aged 14 and over, non-monetary income components (adults, employed, schooling, and returns) used for the decomposition were constructed in terms of the population aged 18 and over. Since the decomposition is estimated at the individual level, we avoid data loss by estimating household income per adult member or member employed, that is, after aggregating income of all household members.

We also take advantage of the detailed information offered in the ENAHO to use more comprehensive measures of labor and non-labor income than those from harmonized databases used for cross-country analysis. The ENAHO includes labor income from primary and secondary

---

[7]That is, results may be different depending on the level of disaggregation of a component, for example if non-labor income is expressed in two or four variables (Shorrocks, 2013). We show (Table 4) that the disaggregation generates minimal differences in the results.

activity, in cash and in-kind (including those used for self-consumption),[8] and the non-labor income includes the following subgroups: property income, imputed rent of the owned or occupied home, public transfers (including transfers from social program and living allowance), private transfers (including domestic and overseas remittances), and other income. The sum of all these components corresponds to the concept of total net household income, that is, excluding deductions for taxes, retirement pension, and others. Our measure of economic welfare is then obtained dividing this income by the household's size. We do not use any adjustment by economies of scale and equivalence scales because in Peru there is no standard procedure for this measurement. However, below we use the scale of a Latin America country in order to check the robustness of our decomposition results.

The values of the monetary income components were expressed at 2013 prices using the National Consumer Price Index, which is constructed monthly by the INEI based on the price indexes of the country's most important cities. In addition, we use national poverty lines to decompose the observed changes in poverty, which are a set of 83 lines corresponding to the same number of subregions, a combination of consumption baskets for seven geographic domains, and median prices in the cities (3 or 4 lines for each of 25 regions). In other words, we use a variable that takes 83 different values corresponding to the same number of subregions where the Peruvian population lives. The value of these lines is equal to the cost of a basic basket of food and non-food items and, and on average, very close to the value of a poverty line of $5.0 per capita a day at 2005 purchasing power parity (PPP) for the period analyzed. With this line we measure what is known as "moderate poverty."[9]

In this paper we propose using multiples of the national moderate poverty line in order to measure the size of other population groups. Given that the national poverty line is close on average to USD 5 per capita a day at 2005 purchasing power parity (Table 1), the resultant values (USD 10 and 50) are similar to those used in comparative studies between countries

---

[8]The self-consumption measure is calculated using the survey question: "At how much do you estimate the value of the goods used for consumption that are produced by the household or are purchased to sell?"

[9]To calculate the share of extreme and moderate poverty, countries generally use the "cost of basic needs" approach to drawing consumption-based poverty lines. According to the World Bank's handbook on poverty (Haughton & Khandker, 2009), first the cost of acquiring enough food for adequate nutrition is estimated (extreme poverty line) and then the cost of other essentials such as clothing and shelter are added (moderate poverty line).

Table 1. Per Capita Poverty Lines, 2004–2013.

Year	2005 PPP[a]	2005 CPI[b]	Poverty Lines			
			National (S/. per month)	\$ a day (2005 PPP)		
				1	2	10
2004	1.653	0.984	237.9	5.7	11.4	57.0
2005	1.653	1.000	235.9	5.6	11.1	55.7
2006	1.653	1.020	235.1	5.4	10.9	54.4
2007	1.653	1.038	238.2	5.4	10.8	54.1
2008	1.653	1.098	250.3	5.4	10.8	53.8
2009	1.653	1.130	251.6	5.3	10.5	52.5
2010	1.653	1.148	259.9	5.3	10.7	53.4
2011	1.653	1.186	272.3	5.4	10.8	54.1
2012	1.653	1.230	283.9	5.4	10.9	54.5
2013	1.653	1.264	292.2	5.5	10.9	54.5

Source: Authors' calculation based on data from the INEI and the World Bank.
[a]2005 PPP conversion factor, private consumption (local currency unit (LCU) per international \$).
[b]National Consumer Price Index.

based on suggestions from Lopez-Calva and Ortiz-Juarez (2011). These authors use an empirical methodology to analyze the middle class based on the notion of vulnerability to poverty. They found that USD 10 a day, associated with a low (0.10) probability of falling into poverty, depicts the beginning of the middle class (lower threshold). Also, they established the upper threshold at USD 50 a day, an income amount that it is observed in the upper tail of the income distribution of the countries studied. Based on these thresholds, we define three groups that, in turn, reflect different probabilities of falling into poverty. Thus, the *vulnerable* are defined as those who live in households with per capita income between one and two times the national poverty line, the *middle class* are those with income between 2 and 10 times the national poverty line,[10] and the *rich* are those with income more than 10 times the national poverty line.

---

[10]In addition to income, other definitions of the middle class have been considered in the literature. Atkinson and Brandolini (2013) consider, for example, roles of property and wealth, and labor-market status. They analyze the interrelationships of these different notions and assess the extent of overlapping in the resultant classifications.

DISTRIBUTIONAL CHANGES OF HOUSEHOLD INCOME SOURCES

Peru experienced enormous distributional changes in recent years, much broader than the average changes experienced in Latin America, as described above. Based on income measures, national poverty lines, and data from the ENAHOs, the moderate poverty rate declined from 54 percent in 2004 to 24 percent in 2013, the size of middle class was multiplied by 2.4 over the same period (from 16 to 39 percent), becoming the largest group of the four considered in the analysis since 2012 (Fig. 1), and the income inequality (Gini coefficient) decreased 6.6 percentage points (from 0.513 to 0.447).[11] The economic growth that accompanied this process was also substantial. The GDP and per capita GDP accumulated 80 and 62 percent of real growth, respectively, during the same period (BCRP, 2014), despite negative effects in 2008 and 2009 from the global economic crisis.

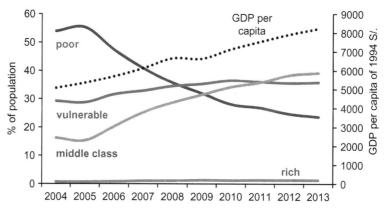

Fig. 1. Percentage of Poor, Vulnerable, Middle-Class, and Rich People, 2004–2013. *Notes*: The *poor* are those living in households with per capita income below the national poverty line, the *vulnerable* with per capita income between 1 and 2 times the poverty line, the *middle class* with per capita income between 2 and 10 times the poverty line, and the *rich* with per capita income above 10 times the poverty line. *Source*: Authors' calculation based on data from the INEI and the BCRP.

---

[11]If per capita income is expressed at 2013 prices of the Lima Metropolitan Area using the values of the poverty line (as proxies for regional deflators), the Gini coefficient falls 5.1 percentage points.

The growth-inequality decomposition introduced by Datt and Ravallion (1992) quantifies the relative contributions of economic growth and redistribution to changes in poverty. We follow Azevedo, Castaneda, and Sanfelice (2012), who implemented the Shapley value of this decomposition and extended it to changes in the middle class. The results show that 70 percent of the reduction in poverty and 75 percent of the increase in the size of the middle class is due to the increase in per capita household income (Table 2). This evidence also shows that, with respect to growth, the size of the middle class is more sensitive than the incidence of poverty. Our estimates indicate that on average, for each point of per capita GDP growth, poverty fell by 1.6 percent, while the size of the middle class grew by 1.9 percent between 2004 and 2013. In addition, disaggregated data from the ENAHOs shows that regions with low initial levels of income inequality (Gini coefficient lower than 0.45 in 2004) are associated with higher poverty reductions. These regions experienced falls of 11.4 percent a year between 2004 and 2013 versus 8.6 percent in regions with higher initial inequality (Gini above 0.45). This coincides with the cross-country literature that argues that the higher initial inequality in a country, the higher the growth rate required for a given amount of poverty reduction (Fosu, 2009; World Bank, 2005).

These growth and redistribution components of changes in a welfare indicator are the results of several monetary and non-monetary forces

Table 2. Shapley Value of Growth and Distribution Components of Changes in Poverty and Middle Class, 2004−2013.

	Percentage Points			%		
	FGT0	FGT1	FGT2	FGT0	FGT1	FGT2
Poverty						
Growth	−21.04	−10.15	−5.99	70	67	65
Distribution	−9.18	−5.11	−3.21	30	34	35
Total change	−30.22	−15.25	−9.20	100	100	100
Middle-class size						
Growth	17.30	10.73	7.15	75	73	72
Distribution	5.69	3.92	2.77	25	27	28
Total change	22.98	14.65	9.91	100	100	100

Source: Authors' calculation based on data from the 2004−2013 ENAHOs.
Notes: The poor are those living in households with per capita income below the national poverty line, and the middle class with per capita income between 2 and 10 times the poverty line; FGT0 = poverty headcount, FGT1 = poverty gap, FGT2 = poverty gap squared.

that determine population movements along different segments of income distribution. Before quantifying the contribution of each of these forces on changes in indicators of poverty, the middle class, and inequality, we describe some associations between the annual growth of some of these forces with annual growth in per capita income between 2004 and 2013 by income deciles. Our purpose is to observe how such forces might have influenced in distributive changes. Fig. 2 summarizes this dynamic for per capita income and each of its components defined in Eq. (4). Monetary components include labor income and non-labor income (public transfers, private transfers, property income, imputed rent, and other income) and non-monetary components at the adult level: number, schooling, and returns to education of adults, and number, and hours worked of adult employed.

Among the monetary components, a couple of facts stand out owing to their clearly defined trends and relatively high increases. Pro-poor growth in per capita income was associated with a shrinking of the labor earnings gap between poor and non-poor workers. Although the increase in earnings was shared by all population groups, the annual growth of this variable was almost three times higher among the poorest deciles than among the richest deciles. As the labor earnings are calculated per hour worked and per unit of the adults' stock of human capital (defined as a function of the years of education completed),[12] it can be deduced that closing the earning gaps was partly associated with changes in the type of employment − according to the ENAHOs, formal employment increased 4 percentage points for the poorest 40 percent of the population between 2004 and 2013 − than with the increase in working hours or number of jobs (see corresponding panels in Fig. 2).

The equalizing influence of government transfers is also remarkable − two-thirds of growth in this source was concentrated in the four poorest deciles. This trend began to be more pronounced in 2007 when the conditional cash transfers program (*Juntos*) significantly increased its coverage, and again with the implementation of *Pension 65*, *Beca 18*, and *Bono Gas*, all with well-established pro-poor targeting strategies. It should be noted that this change also meant the poorest deciles were more dependent on government transfers (10 percentage points of total household income, from 7 percent to 17 percent) and less dependent on labor earnings (6 points, from 65 percent to 59 percent) between 2004 and 2013. The increase in private transfers (remittances, child support, alimony, and so on), income from property

---

[12]Fig. 3 shows the values of this stock in 2004 and 2013 by years of education.

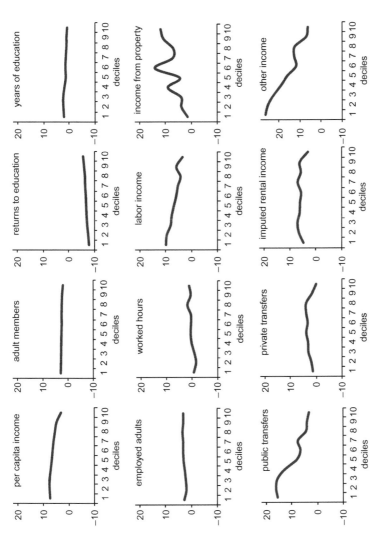

Fig. 2. Annual Change in per Capita Income and Its Components by Deciles (%), 2004–2013. *Source:* Authors' calculation based on data from the 2004–2013 ENAHOs.

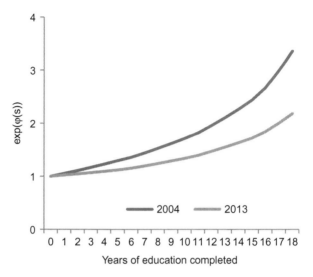

Fig. 3. Human Capital Stock of Adult Population [$h = \exp(\phi(s))$], 2004 and 2013. *Note*: After estimating returns to education, the function $\phi(s)$ is approximated by a piecewise linear function breaking years of education in splines and taking into account the education levels of individuals (see Eq. (3)). *Source*: Authors' calculation based on data from the 2004–2013 ENAHOs.

(interest, rents, profits), and imputed income from owner-occupied housing were generally more favorable for vulnerable and middle class groups.[13]

Among the non-monetary components, changes in returns to education should show important influences on movements along different segments of the income distribution because of the magnitude and heterogeneity of changes across the adult population (third panel of Fig. 2). The average return per additional year of education fell at an annual rate of 6.7 percent between 2004 and 2013, and the rate was higher among the poorest population (7.9 percent in the poorest decile vs. 5.7 in the richest decile). In addition, as has been shown in several studies with disaggregated estimates (e.g., Castro & Yamada, 2012), Table 3 shows that the returns were not only greater for higher levels of education (i.e., there were convexities in returns or increasing marginal returns), but they also fell less for

---

[13]Note that the population classification based on the national poverty lines described above identifies the poor in percentiles 0–24 and the middle class in percentiles 59–98 in 2013 (0–54 and 83–99 in 2004, respectively).

Table 3. Returns to Education, 2004–2013.

	Heckman Estimation										Annual Growth 2004–13
	2004	2005	2006	2007	2008	2009	2010	2011	2012	2013	
Incomplete primary	0.052	0.055	0.067	0.036	0.057	0.036	0.027	0.025	0.025	0.023	−8.8
Complete primary	0.048	0.057	0.064	0.040	0.047	0.042	0.028	0.031	0.035	0.029	−5.6
Incomplete secondary	0.058	0.061	0.062	0.050	0.055	0.045	0.037	0.037	0.041	0.037	−4.7
Complete secondary	0.059	0.061	0.063	0.051	0.057	0.046	0.041	0.041	0.043	0.041	−3.8
Incomplete tertiary	0.073	0.071	0.076	0.066	0.068	0.059	0.054	0.052	0.054	0.052	−3.7
Complete tertiary	0.090	0.089	0.094	0.086	0.088	0.079	0.069	0.069	0.071	0.070	−2.8
Postgraduate	0.116	0.110	0.115	0.098	0.101	0.096	0.084	0.085	0.085	0.085	−3.4
Sheepskin effects: Complete/incomplete level											
Primary	0.94	1.02	0.96	1.13	0.82	1.17	1.04	1.23	1.39	1.27	3.5
Secondary	1.01	1.01	1.02	1.03	1.04	1.04	1.10	1.11	1.18	1.30	2.8
Tertiary	1.23	1.26	1.23	1.30	1.30	1.33	1.28	1.33	1.04	1.11	−1.2

Source: Authors' calculation based on data from the 2004–2013 ENAHOs.
Note: Returns correspond to an additional year of schooling at each education level based on estimating the natural logarithm of real hourly labor income model (Eq. (2)).

individuals with higher levels of education. For example, the returns for each additional incomplete primary year decreased three times more than complete tertiary: 8.8 versus 2.8 percent per year between 2004 and 2013. But as well as changes in returns showing unequalizing effects on per capita income growth, they also showed equalizing effects for those that complete levels of education (lower part of Table 3). The returns per additional year of education were proportionately higher for those who completed the last year of each education level (sheepskin effects[14]), particularly for those who completed only the lowest levels, as discussed in Fig. 4.

---

[14]In other words, workers are not rewarded for the contributions of schooling that improve productivity, but rather for obtaining the certificate that comes with completing the level of schooling.

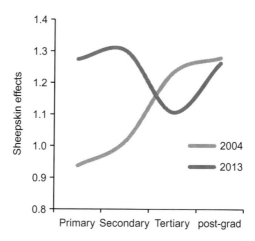

Fig. 4. Sheepskin Effects in Returns to Education. *Note*: Sheepskin effects: ratio between returns to complete/incomplete level. *Source*: Authors' calculation based on data from the 2004–2013 ENAHOs.

Also, the second and fourth panels of Fig. 2 consistently show that the fall in returns is associated with an increase in the labor supply, which is somewhat more marked among the lowest deciles. According to information from ENAHOs, this would happen for size of the working-age population (adults) and their levels of schooling. The years of education completed in adults increased by 1.3 percent annually between 2004 and 2013 (2 percent in the poorest decile versus 0.7 in the richest), and the numbers of adults rose on average by 2.4 percent annually in the last nine years (2.8 percent in the poorest decile versus 1.9 in the richest). These increases are, in turn, associated with what is known as the demographic bonus or demographic window[15] that the country and most of Latin

---

[15]Defined as a period in which the proportion of the working-age population is particularly prominent. More precisely, it occurs when the population under 15 years of age falls below 30 percent of the total population and the proportion of population 65 years and older is still below 15 percent of the total (United Nations [UN], 2004). According to CELADE-CEPAL (2013), Peru started one such period in 2010 and will finish it in 2043. The working-age population per dependent person increased from 1.59 at the beginning of the 2000s to 1.87 in 2014 (16 percent) and will reach its highest figure (2.03) in 2030. As such, the window of opportunity or bonus means, for example, a lower spending in children aged 0–14 between 1990 and 2015 (when the size of this group of the population decreased from 38 percent to 28 percent) and the possibility to use this saving in education for the secondary-age population.

America is currently experiencing, which tends to benefit the lowest deciles or poorest members of the population. Below we show that this situation of educational expansion and heterogeneous falling returns (and their influences on income inequality) is also associated with the phenomenon labeled by Bourguignon, Ferreira, and Lustig (2005) as the "paradox of progress."

DECOMPOSITION RESULTS

The four panels of Table 4 summarize the estimates on decomposing changes in poverty, size of the middle class, and income distribution (Gini coefficient) between 2004 and 2013. The first panel shows the changes in each indicator (described in detail in the previous section), and the following three panels show sequentially disaggregated decompositions. The most disaggregated panel includes 11 income components, six monetary and five non-monetary (second panel).[16] The following decomposition compresses the four non-labor income components (third panel), and the last one excludes education, return, and hour components (fourth panel). In all cases, the estimates include measures of incidence, income gap and squared income gap. We focus on the incidence measures.

The second panel suggests that the most important contributor to poverty reduction and the rise of the middle class was growth in labor earnings (per hour worked of one unit of human capital stock). This factor explained almost 60 percent of movements observed in both population groups between 2004 and 2013.[17] Although the increase in labor earnings was also important to reducing income inequality, it was not the main driving force. The fall in returns to education played this role. The third part of the Gini coefficient reduction was due to this fall, which is in line with the findings of several authors that assign a relevant role to changes in returns to education (Azevedo et al., 2013; Gasparini & Lustig, 2011; Lopez-Calva & Lustig, 2010). Unlike those other papers, our evidence on the role of returns to education in the reduction of inequality was obtained by introducing indicators of the adults' stock of human capital in the equation of household income (compare the results of the panels 2 and 4 of Table 4). The fall in returns to education was also an important factor that

---

[16]Observed values in this panel are the average of 39.9 million (11!) possible sequences.

[17]If an indicator declines over period, a negative sign denotes contribution to the decline, while a positive sign indicates the opposite effect.

Table 4. Decomposition of Observed Changes in Poverty, the Middle Class, and Inequality, 2004–2013.

	Poor			Middle Class			Gini Coeff. (%)
	FGT0 (%)	FGT1 (%)	FGT2 (%)	FGT0 (%)	FGT1 (%)	FGT2 (%)	
2004	53.9	23.1	12.9	16.2	10.7	7.5	51.3
2013	23.7	7.9	3.7	39.2	25.4	17.4	44.7
Total change (percentage points)	−30.2	−15.3	−9.2	23.0	14.7	9.9	−6.6
Disaggregated decomposition							
Adult population	18.8	19.2	19.1	16.2	16.6	16.9	18.2
Years of education	6.3	4.7	3.9	9.7	9.2	8.8	−3.0
Returns to education	−21.0	−21.1	−21.8	−25.5	−21.3	−19.2	33.3
Employed adults	6.0	2.7	0.3	6.9	7.1	7.2	−1.5
Hours worked	11.6	5.5	1.2	14.6	15.9	16.5	7.6
Labor income	58.0	62.7	66.1	57.3	52.8	50.5	18.2
Income from property	1.2	1.1	1.1	1.9	1.4	1.2	−7.6
Public transfers[a]	6.1	11.8	16.6	5.0	4.7	4.6	15.2
Private transfers[a]	4.2	3.0	1.6	4.5	4.5	4.6	6.1
Imputed rental income[b]	6.9	7.9	8.5	7.5	7.1	6.8	7.6
Other non-labor income	1.8	2.6	3.2	1.9	2.0	2.0	6.1
Total change	100.0	100.0	100.0	100.0	100.0	100.0	100.0
Decomposition with aggregate non-labor income							
Adult population	18.9	19.5	19.5	16.3	16.8	17.1	21.2
Years of education	6.5	5.0	4.2	9.9	9.3	9.0	−1.5
Returns to education	−20.8	−20.9	−21.5	−25.1	−20.8	−18.6	36.4
Employed adults	6.0	2.6	0.2	7.1	7.3	7.5	0.0
Hours worked	11.6	5.3	0.6	14.9	16.3	17.0	9.1
Labor income	58.1	63.2	67.0	57.4	52.9	50.6	22.7
Non-labor income	19.7	25.3	29.9	19.5	18.2	17.5	13.6
Total change	100.0	100.0	100.0	100.0	100.0	100.0	100.0
Decomposition with aggregate non-labor income; without education, returns, and hours							
Adult population	20.7	20.5	19.9	17.7	18.9	19.6	27.3
Employed adults	6.7	2.5	−0.1	8.0	8.6	9.0	3.0
Labor income	57.1	58.6	59.6	58.1	56.4	55.5	51.5

Table 4. (*Continued*)

	Poor			Middle Class			Gini Coeff. (%)
	FGT0 (%)	FGT1 (%)	FGT2 (%)	FGT0 (%)	FGT1 (%)	FGT2 (%)	
Non-labor income	15.6	18.4	20.6	16.2	16.1	15.9	19.7
Total change	100.0	100.0	100.0	100.0	100.0	100.0	100.0

Source: Authors' calculation based on data from the 2004−2013 ENAHOs.
Notes: The poor are those living in households with per capita income below the national poverty line, and the middle class with per capita income between 2 and 10 times the poverty line; FGT0 = incidence, FGT1 = income gap regarding poverty line, FGT2 = FGT1 squared.
[a]Cash and in-kind.
[b]From owner-occupied housing.

explained the changes in poverty incidence and size of the middle class. It was the second driving force after labor earnings, although in both cases the decline in returns to education restricted progress toward a situation with less poverty (in 21 percent) and more middle class (in 26 percent).

The positive influence of the fall in returns to education on income inequality − unlike the negative impact on poverty reduction and rise of the middle class associated with changes in labor supply − would be largely connected with the differentiated increase in sheepskin effects in the returns at all education levels during the period analyzed. Table 3 shows that the last grade of schooling in each level is disproportionately rewarded in terms of higher hourly labor earnings, that is, returns higher associated with graduation from primary school, secondary school, and university (as has been detected several times in the literature, e.g., Hungerford & Solon, 1987; Schady, 2003), and, interestingly, they changed favorably for the first two levels of education. The ratio between returns to complete and incomplete primary education and the ratio between complete and incomplete secondary education substantially increased 3.5 and 2.8 percent per year between 2004 and 2013, respectively, while the ratio for tertiary education decreased 1.2 percent per year. This implied income redistributions within all groups (poor, vulnerable, middle class) that primarily benefited the workforce with lower levels of education. It should be noted that the volume of graduates at all levels was equivalent to 35 percent of the labor force in 2013, a group that since 2004 grew almost three times more than non-graduates. Consequently, the unequalizing effect of the convexities in the returns to education (i.e., increasing returns with the levels of education) would have been more than exceeded by the equalizing effect of the observed changes in sheepskin effects (i.e., important increases of returns for graduates of primary and secondary). This does not mean that the paradox of progress (a situation, as cited above, where an equalizing increase in schooling generates an initial unequalizing change in the income distribution due to the convexities of returns) has been overcome – that will only occur when the dispersion of years of schooling becomes smaller and smaller (Lustig et al., 2013).

Changes in returns to education, as noted above, were associated with an increased supply of educated workers happened by increasing the proportion of the working-age population (given de demographic transition) and investments made in previous decades to improve the coverage of education. The decomposition results in Table 4 indicate that a greater share of working-age adults was as important as changes in labor earnings (around 18 percent) to understand the fall of the Gini coefficient. This factor explained similar percentages of poverty reduction and increases in the size of the middle class. The second panel also suggests that a larger proportion of this workforce was able to participate in the labor market with extended workdays. The increase of hours worked contributed to a 12 and 15 percent in poverty reduction and rise of the middle class, respectively – almost double the contribution from increased employment.

Moreover, despite the substantial change of government transfers in favor of the poorest members of the population, these transfers had a relatively small role in explaining declines in poverty and income inequality. Their impact only accounted for 6 and 15 percent of reduction in poverty and the Gini coefficient, respectively. According to data from the 2013 ENAHO, despite public transfers representing about a quarter of net income for poor people who receive such transfers, 69 percent beneficiaries were not poor and 7 percent of the extreme poor did not receive them. The same source shows that even the conditional cash transfer program (*Juntos*), the best targeted of all existing programs, has room to improve its distributional impact: 29 percent of beneficiaries are not poor and 56 percent of the extreme poor do not receive transfers. The room for improving the impact of public transfers is much broader if we consider that *Juntos* is only a small part of the budget for transfers.

The contrast between the second to fourth panels confirms that the understanding of the fall in income inequality is more complex than poverty reduction and the rise of the middle class. The contribution of forces to changes in the Gini coefficient is less clear. In general, it can be noted in both panels that despite the decomposition methodology used does not ensure the principle of aggregation consistency (Shorrocks, 2013), the findings on the main factors that led to changes in the size of poverty and middle class in the last decade are not altered. It may also be noted that contributions of labor income, the size of the working-age population and the employment rate, and interactions of each with all other components remain almost unchanged in the three panels. We can also see that the effects of changes in non-labor income may have reduced interactions with all other components. The sum of effects of these subcomponents for incomes represented in the second panel is similar to the aggregate of such incomes in the third panel. The numbers are significantly different when the same comparisons are made for the Gini coefficient.

Finally, in order to observe in detail the importance of the factors associated with changes in the economic status of a larger number of groups, Fig. 5 shows the decomposition of changes in per capita income by decile between 2004 and 2013. For this purpose, we use the same Eq. (4) utilized to decompose poverty, middle class, and inequality. In general, the trends are observed more clearly in Table 4. Note the important role of labor earnings and returns to education in reducing income (second panel), the equalizing effects of public transfers (third panel), the share of working-age population in the household, and the hours worked by adults (first panel).

The robustness of the results described above is observed when the information in the first two panels of Tables 4 and 5 are compared. Table 5 was built considering equivalence scales. Among the scales for Mexico, Jamaica, and Argentina, the only Latin American countries that have this instrument for measuring poverty levels, we use Mexico's[18] because its GDP per capita is most similar to Peru's. Despite the significant changes in the incidence of poverty and the middle class due to the application of equivalence scales (panel 1 in both tables), the contributions of forces behind the changes in both indicators are practically the same.

SUMMARY AND FINAL REMARKS

Peru experienced significant distributional changes from 2004 to 2013. Poverty incidence was reduced to less than half (from 54 to 24 percent), the size of the middle class more than doubled (from 16 to 39 percent) – it has

---

[18]The weights range between 0.7 and 1, according to the age of individuals (CONEVAL, 2014).

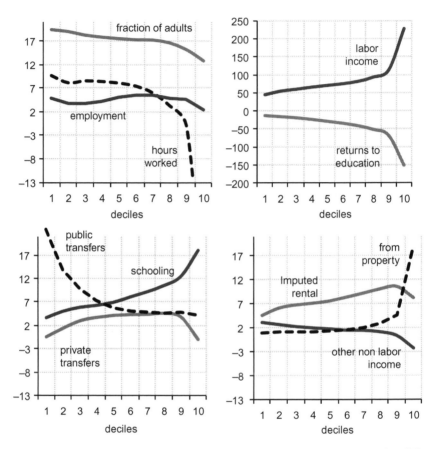

Fig. 5. Decomposition of Observed Changes in per Capita Income by Deciles (%), 2004–2013. *Source*: Authors' calculation based on data from the 2004–2013 ENAHOs.

been the predominant group since 2012 – and the income inequality figure fell by almost 7 percentage points. With a series of counterfactual simulations, we identified and quantified the contribution of the more immediate determinants of these changes. We modified the assumption of a homogenous working-age population and introduce additional dimensions to the income identity equation. This allowed a more accurate identification of the forces behind the changes in welfare indicators and a more comprehensive analysis of decomposition.

Table 5. Decomposition of Observed Changes in Poverty, the Middle Class, and Inequality using Equivalence Scales, 2004–2013.

	Poor			Middle Class			Gini Coeff.
	FGT0 (%)	FGT1 (%)	FGT2 (%)	FGT0 (%)	FGT1 (%)	FGT2 (%)	(%)
% of population in 2004	46.8	18.7	10.1	19.8	13.1	9.1	50.4
% of population in 2013	18.8	5.9	2.7	45.7	29.3	19.9	43.8
Total change (percentage points)	−28.0	−12.8	−7.3	25.8	16.3	10.9	−6.6
Adult population	16.7	17.6	17.7	14.0	14.8	15.3	18.4
Years of education	6.0	4.4	3.6	9.0	8.3	7.9	−4.2
Returns to education	−21.7	−22.7	−23.8	−22.8	−18.9	−16.8	28.4
Employed adults	5.9	1.9	−0.8	7.9	8.3	8.6	−2.6
Hours worked	11.1	4.0	−1.0	16.3	17.2	17.6	8.8
Labor income	60.0	65.6	69.4	55.2	50.9	48.8	20.1
Income from property	1.3	1.2	1.2	1.9	1.4	1.1	−5.2
Public transfers[a]	7.5	14.4	20.0	5.1	4.9	4.7	15.9
Private transfers[a]	3.9	2.3	0.6	4.3	4.3	4.2	5.4
Imputed rental income[b]	7.3	8.5	9.4	7.3	6.8	6.5	8.8
Other non-labor income	2.1	3.0	3.7	2.0	2.0	2.0	6.1
Total change	100.0	100.0	100.0	100.0	100.0	100.0	100.0

Source: Authors' calculation based on data from the 2004–2013 ENAHOs.
Notes: Equivalence scales are those from Mexico with a range between 0.7 and 1 according to the age of individuals. The poor are those living in households with per capita income below the national poverty line, and the middle class with per capita income between 2 and 10 times the poverty line; FGT0 = incidence, FGT1 = income gap regarding poverty line, FGT2 = FGT1 squared.
[a]Cash and in-kind.
[b]From owner-occupied housing.

We found that the favorable performance of the labor market, mainly from labor earnings, accounts for slightly above three-quarters of the percentage rise in both poverty reduction and the rise of the middle class. We also found that a greater number of factors (compared to other economic mobility indicators used in this paper) affect the reduction of income inequality, revealing a more complex understanding of its changes over time and how to fight against it. The labor earnings increase was not the main factor in reducing the Gini coefficient, as it was for changes in the poverty rate and the size of the middle class. The earnings increase explained only about half of what the decline in returns to education added to the lowered Gini coefficient. We also found that the fall of returns, at the same time, was one of the important factors constraining the most effective period of progress in reducing poverty and increasing mobility into the middle class. Finally, we saw how differences in the demographic trajectories inside the country are associated with what is known as the demographic bonus or demographic window, which played a key role in understanding the distributional changes observed.

Learning about the causes of these changes can be very useful for the design of future interventions. Emphasis should be placed on the factors that led to falling poverty and inequality and rising numbers of the middle class, particularly to enhance their effects to increase their role in the generation of expected changes. The decomposition analysis used in the paper has provided evidence on the efficacy of such factors. Given the demographic transition that the country is experiencing (similar to most countries in the region), investments that aim to close schooling gaps can allow the working-age population – particularly young people from poor areas – to continue expanding their opportunities for improved labor-market participation, through employment and higher wages. Additionally, improvements in levels of learning, particularly among the lowest deciles of the population, will allow the distributional effects of returns to education promote both an upward mobility and a more equitable income distribution. The literature has showed that returns to education are sensitive to improvements in learning (Card & Krueger, 1990; Hanushek & Wossmann, 2007). Finally, although social programs introduced since the mid-2000s have had substantial consequences on the welfare of the poor, an important proportion of government transfers benefits households that are not necessarily at the bottom of the income distribution. Consequently, there is significant room for improving the targeting of these programs to reduce poverty and inequality.

ACKNOWLEDGMENTS

We wish to thank two anonymous referees for very helpful suggestions and comments on an earlier version of this paper. The views expressed here are those of the authors and should not be attributed to Johns Hopkins University or the Inter-American Development Bank or its affiliates.

REFERENCES

Atkinson, A. B., & Brandolini, A. (2013). On the identification of the middle class. In J. C. Gornick & M. Jäntti (Eds.), *Income inequality: Economic disparities and the middle class in affluent countries*. Social Inequality Series. Redwood City, CA: Stanford University Press.

Azevedo, J. P., Castaneda, A., & Sanfelice, V. (2012). DRDECOMP: Stata module to estimate Shapley value of growth and distribution components of changes in poverty indicators. In *Statistical software components*. S457563. Boston, MA: Department of Economics, Boston College.

Azevedo, J. P., Davalos, M. E., Diaz-Bonilla, C., Atuesta, B., & Castañeda, R. A. (2013). *Fifteen years of inequality in Latin America: How have labor markets helped?* World Bank Policy Research Working Paper No. 6384. World Bank, Washington, DC.

Azevedo, J. P., Inchauste, G., Olivieri, S., Saavedra, J., & Winkler, H. (2013). *Is labor income responsible for poverty reduction?* A decomposition approach. World Bank Policy Research Working Paper No. 6414. World Bank, Washington, DC.

Azevedo, J. P., Inchauste, G., & Sanfelice, V. (2013). *Decomposing the recent inequality decline in Latin America*. World Bank Policy Research Working Paper No. 6715. World Bank, Washington, DC.

Azevedo, J. P., Nguyen, M. C., & Sanfelice, V. (2012). *Shapley decomposition by components of a welfare aggregate*. Washington, DC. Mimeo.

BCRP (Banco Central de Reserva de Peru). (2014). *Annual economic statistics*. Retrieved from www.bcrp.gob.pe/statistics.html

Bils, M., & Klenow, P. J. (2000). Does schooling cause growth? *American Economic Review*, *90*(5), 1160–1183. Retrieved from http://klenow.com/BKHK.pdf

Bourguignon, F., Ferreira, F. H., & Lustig, N. (Eds.). (2005). *The microeconomics of income distribution dynamics in East Asia and Latin America*. Washington, DC: World Bank.

Card, D., & Krueger, A. (1990). *Does school quality matter? Returns to education and the characteristics of public schools in the United States*. Working Paper No. 3358. National Bureau of Economic Research, Cambridge, MA.

Castro, J. F., & Yamada, G. (2012). *Convexification and deconvexification of the Peruvian wage profile: A tale of declining education quality*. Documento de Discusión DD/12/02. Centro de Investigación de la Universidad del Pacífico, Lima, Peru.

CELADE (Centro Latinoamericano y Caribeño de Demografía)-CEPAL (Comisión Económica para América Latina). (2013). *Estimaciones y Proyecciones de Población a Largo Plazo 1950–2100*. Revisión 2013. Retrieved from http://www.cepal.org/celade/proyecciones/basedatos_BD.htm

CONEVAL (Consejo Nacional de Evaluación de la Política de Desarrollo Social). (2014). *Methodology for multidimensional poverty measurement in Mexico* (2nd ed.). Mexico City: CONEVAL.

Datt, G., & Ravallion, M. (1992). Growth and redistribution components of changes in poverty measures: A decomposition with applications to Brazil and India in the 1980s. *Journal of Development Economics*, *38*, 275–295.

de Barros, R. P., de Carvalho, M., Franco, S., & Mendoca, R. (2006). Uma Análise das Principais Causas da Queda Recente na Desigualdade de Renda Brasileira. *Revista Econômica*, *8*(1), 117–147.

de Barros, R. P., de Carvalho, M., Franco, S., & Mendoca, R. (2007). *Determinantes Imediatos da Queda da Desigualdade de Renda Brasileira.* Texto para Discussão No. 1253. IPEA, Rio de Janeiro. Retrieved from http://repositorio.ipea.gov.br/bitstream/11058/2161/1/TD_1253.pdf

de Barros, R. P., de Carvalho, M., Franco, S., & Mendoca, R. (2010). *Determinantes da Queda na Desigualdade de Renda no Brasil.* Texto para Discussão, No. 1460. Instituto de Pesquisa Econômica Aplicada, Rio de Janeiro. Retrieved from www.econstor.eu/dspace/bitstream/10419/91343/1/617127948.pdf

Ferreira, F. H., Messina, J., Rigolini, J., López-Calva, L.-F., Lugo, M. A., & Vakis, R. (2012). *Economic mobility and the rise of the Latin American middle class.* Washington, DC: World Bank.

Fosu, A. K. (2009). Inequality and the impact of growth on poverty: Comparative evidence for sub-Saharan Africa. *Journal of Development Studies, 45*(5), 726−745.

Freije, S. (2014). Changes in poverty and inequality in Latin America during the great recession. In M. Grosh, M. Bussolo, & S. Freije (Eds.), *Understanding the poverty impact of the global financial crisis in Latin America and the Caribbean.* Washington, DC: World Bank.

Gasparini, L., & Lustig, N. (2011). The rise and fall of income inequality in Latin America. In J. A. Ocampo & J. Ros (Eds.), *The Oxford handbook of Latin American economics* (pp. 691−714). Oxford: Oxford University Press.

Grosh, M., Bussolo, M., & Freije, S. (Eds.). (2014). *Understanding the poverty impact of the global financial crisis in Latin America and the Caribbean.* Washington, DC: World Bank.

Hall, R. E., & Jones, C. I. (1999). Why do some countries produce so much more output per worker than others? *Quarterly Journal of Economics, 114*(1), 83−116.

Hanushek, E., & Wossmann, L. (2007). *The role of education quality in economic growth.* World Bank Policy Research Working Paper No. 4122. World Bank, Washington, DC.

Haughton, J., & Khandker, S. (2009). *Handbook on Poverty + Inequality.* World Bank Training Series. Washington, DC: World Bank.

Hungerford, T., & Solon, G. (1987). Sheepskin effects in the returns to education. *Review of Economics and Statistics, 69*, 175−177.

Inchauste, G., Azevedo, J. P., & Essama-Nssah, B., Olivieri, S., Nguyen, T. V., Saavedra-Chanduvi, J., & Winkler, H. (2014). *Understanding changes in poverty.* Washington, DC: World Bank.

Inter-American Development Bank. (2015). *Sociometro-BID.* Database. Retrieved from www.iadb.org/en/research-and-data//poverty,7526.html

International Monetary Fund. (2014). *World economic outlook database.* Retrieved from www.imf.org/external/ns/cs.aspx?id=28. Accessed on October 2014.

Kolenikov, S., & Shorrocks, A. (2005). A decomposition analysis of regional poverty in Russia. *Review of Development Economics, 9*(1), 25−46.

Levy, S., & Schady, N. (2013). Latin America's social policy challenge: Education, social insurance, redistribution. *The Journal of Economic Perspectives, 27*(2), 193−218.

Lopez-Calva, L. F., & Lustig, N. (Eds.). (2010). *Declining inequality in Latin America: A decade of progress?* Washington, DC: Brookings Institution Press.

Lopez-Calva, L. F., & Ortiz-Juarez, E. (2011). *A vulnerability approach to the definition of the middle class.* Policy Research Working Paper No. 5902. World Bank, Washington, DC.

Lustig, N., Lopez-Calva, L. F., & Ortiz-Juarez, E. (2013). *Deconstructing the decline in inequality in Latin America.* World Bank Policy Research Working Paper No. 6552. World Bank, Washington, DC.

Mankiw, N. G., Romer, D., & Weil, D. N. (1992). A contribution to the empirics of economic growth. *Quarterly Journal of Economics, 107,* 407−437.

Ravallion, M., & Huppi, M. (1991). Measuring changes in poverty: A methodological case study of Indonesia during an adjustment period. *The World Bank Economic Review, 5*(5), 57−82.

Sastre, M., & Trannoy, A. (2002). Shapley inequality decomposition by factor components: Some methodological issues. *Journal of Economics, 77*(Suppl. 1), 51−89.

Schady, N. (2003). Convexity and sheepskin effects in the human capital earnings function: Recent evidence for Filipino Men. *Oxford Bulletin of Economics and Statistics, 65*(2), 171−196, 205.

Shorrocks, A. (1982). Inequality decomposition by factor components. *Econometrica, 50*(1), 193−211. Retrieved from www.jstor.org/stable/1912537

Shorrocks, A. F. (2013). Decomposition procedures for distributional analysis: A unified framework based on the Shapley value. *The Journal of Economic Inequality, 11*(1), 99−126.

United Nations. (2004). *World population to 2300.* New York, NY: Population Division, Economic and Social Affairs, United Nations. Retrieved from www.un.org/esa/population/publications/longrange2/WorldPop2300final.pdf

World Bank. (2005). *World development report 2006: Equity and development.* Washington, DC: World Bank.

Yamada, G. (2007). *Retornos a la Educación Superior en el Mercado Laboral: ¿Vale la Pena el Esfuerzo?* Documento de Trabajo No. 78. Centro de Investigación de la Universidad del Pacífico, Lima.

Yamada, G., & Castro, J. (2010). *Educación Superior e Ingresos Laborales: Estimaciones Paramétricas y No Paramétricas de la Rentabilidad por Niveles y Carreras en el Perú.* Documento de Discusión No. DD/10/06. Centro de Investigación de la Universidad del Pacífico, Lima.

WHY IS INCOME INEQUALITY SO HIGH IN SPAIN?

Carlos Gradín

ECOBAS – Universidade de Vigo and EQUALITAS; Facultade de CC. Económicas e Empresariais, Universidade de Vigo

ABSTRACT

We investigate the reasons why income inequality is so high in Spain in the EU context. We first show that the differential in inequality with Germany and other countries is driven by inequality among households who participate in the labor market. Then, we conduct an analysis of different household income aggregates. We also decompose the inter-country gap in inequality into characteristics and coefficients effects using regressions of the Recentered Influence Function for the Gini index. Our results show that the higher inequality observed in Spain is largely associated with lower employment rates, higher incidence of self-employment, lower attained education, as well as the recent increase in the immigration of economically active households. However, the prevalence of extended families in Spain contributes to reducing inequality by diversifying income sources, with retirement pensions playing an important role. Finally, by comparing the situations in 2008 and 2012, we separate the direct effects of the Great Recession on employment and unemployment benefits, from other more permanent factors (such as the weak redistributive effect of

Income Inequality Around the World
Research in Labor Economics, Volume 44, 109–177
Copyright © 2016 by Emerald Group Publishing Limited
ISSN: 0147-9121/doi:10.1108/S0147-912120160000044011

taxes and family or housing allowances, or the roles of education and the extended family).

Keywords: Income inequality; employment; Spain; Gini; RIF; decomposition

JEL classifications: D63; I32; J21; J82

INTRODUCTION

Right before the recent Great Recession started, Spain already exhibited a relatively high level of inequality within the EU, but its level has increased after the collapse of the labor market, as recent studies have already documented (Ayala, 2014; ILO, 2015). In this paper, we follow a comparative approach to investigate why inequality is so high in Spain using EU-SILC data in 2012 and in 2008. For that, we exploit existing inter-country differences in the level and nature of inequality between Spain and Germany (and other countries), as well as changes over time.

Although Germany is not the champion of low inequality in Europe, it is the leading European economy and exhibits a level of inequality below the EU average and the level of other large economies in the area.[1] Furthermore, Germany went through the financial crisis with better records in terms of income distribution, and functioning of the economy, especially in keeping its employment levels. Many of the recent economic reforms implemented in Spain regarding labor market flexibility, fiscal consolidation, retirement age, dual vocational training, etc. go in the direction of the German model.

Any comparative analysis will be influenced by the particularities of the reference country. Germany lived several structural transformations after the reunification that, for example, implied a large process of decentralization in wage setting. These had a large influence on the ability of the country to cope with the current recession but might not be easily reproduced in countries with more centralized settings such as Spain or Italy

---

[1] Inequality, measured by the Gini index with EU-SILC 2014 statistics, is actually lowest in the Nordic countries, in Belgium, the Netherlands, Slovenia, Czech Republic, or Slovakia. However, Germany displays the lowest level of inequality amongst the largest EU countries (after France), followed by Poland, the United Kingdom, and Italy, with Spain standing out with the highest level.

(Dustmannn, Fitzenberger, Schönberg, & Spitz-Oener, 2014). In order to provide a more precise view of the situation of Spain within the EU, we extend the comparison with other countries (i.e., France, Italy, Sweden, and the United Kingdom). We thus compare Spain with five countries exhibiting diverse situations regarding the composition of the labor force (e.g., by education), the structure of the economy (e.g., employment rates, economic sectors, and non-standard jobs), family size and structure, immigration profile, tax-benefit models, or other institutional settings (e.g., labor relations). Exploiting all these inter-country differences will allow us to assess the importance of each of these factors in explaining higher inequality in Spain, but with lessons that might apply to other EU countries as well.

In order to assess the particular nature of inequality in Spain, we first analyze the role of different sources of income, like the labor market and the tax-benefit system, in shaping inequality. We then concentrate on people living in economically active households (i.e., with at least one member in the labor market during the reference year). It is for this group that we observe an inter-country gap in inequality which increased between 2008 and 2012. We also analyze the role on household income inequality of different socioeconomic factors such as location, household composition by age, gender, or immigration status, as well as education or employment level and characteristics. For that, we use a Blinder-Oaxaca-type decomposition of the inter-country gap in inequality based on the Recentered Influence Function (RIF) of the Gini index (Firpo, Fortin, & Lemieux, 2007, 2009). This approach allows us to assess how inequality in each country and period is determined by households' characteristics using a linear approximation of the relationship they have with inequality. For the analysis, we estimate a counterfactual distribution in which we give Spanish households the same average characteristics of German households, while keeping constant how these characteristics affect inequality. Using this counterfactual distribution, we are able to decompose the inter-country difference in inequality into characteristics (explained) and coefficients (unexplained) effects.

In this context, the characteristics effect is the differential in inequality that can be explained by the lower employment levels, the lower attained education, higher recent immigration, or the particular sectorial composition of Spanish workers, among other things. This compositional effect is evaluated using the Spanish returns to characteristics, the specific association between characteristics and inequality prevailing in Spain, as if nothing else changed, other than the average composition of households. The coefficients effect is the remaining unexplained inequality differential (evaluated using the average characteristics of German households) that could be attributed to differences in the way these characteristics differentially affect incomes at different points of the income distribution. This distributional pattern is influenced by the local institutional framework, such as wage setting and other labor market regulations, the tax-benefit system, and living arrangements.

The same exercise is used to decompose the gap with other countries, as well as the change in inequality over time in Spain. In the last case, we take 2008 as the reference distribution to assess the impact of the deep recession that affected the EU, but with particular disastrous consequences in the Spanish economy, especially on employment levels. Combining these comparisons between countries and over time will allow us to discriminate between more structural factors of high inequality and the direct effects of the Great Recession.

In what follows, the next section describes the data, then "Inequality in Spain" section discusses the level and trend of inequality in Spain, while "Inequality and Income Sources: The Labor Market and the Tax-Benefit System" section analyzes the role of the labor market and the tax-benefit system. After that, "Methodology: Decomposing the Gap in Inequality Using the Recentered Influence Function" section presents the decomposition methodology and the following two sections discuss the results. The last section provides some final remarks.

DATA AND VARIABLES

Data

For our analysis, we use the 2008 and 2012 waves of Eurostat's cross-sectional microdata from the *EU Statistics on Income and Living Conditions.*[2] The original sources of this database are the Living Conditions Survey (*Encuesta de Condiciones de Vida base 2004*) from the National Statistical Institute in Spain and microdata based on an access panel (*Dauerstichprobe*) to the Microcensus from the German Federal Statistical Office. The former

---

[2]We use the March 2014 version of EU-SILC. Other recently released revised versions break the series for Spain regarding how income was collected (using register data instead of the survey answers as the main source), and regarding the construction of sampling weights. They do not allow to properly compare 2008, right before inequality abruptly started to raise, and 2012.

is the main source for the analysis of income distribution in Spain since it started in 2004, the latter is used here for the sake of comparability within the EU-SILC project.[3] The Spanish 2012 sample is made of 33,573 (12,714) individual (household) unweighted observations. Out of them, 27,751 individuals live in 9,170 economically active households (those with at least one adult, 16 years or older, in the labor force), the main focus of our analysis. In the case of Germany, the figures of individuals (households) are 27,938 (13,145), 20,893 (8,758) in active households.[4] EU-SILC provides rich information about households' characteristics, including income and demographic, educational, and labor market-related variables that are needed in our study. We also use the 2012 EU-SILC samples for France, Italy, Sweden, and the United Kingdom.

Our main variable of interest is *disposable income*, that is, total income obtained by the household over the income reference period (calendar year previous to the interview, i.e., 2007 and 2011, respectively) from any source (earnings, cash social transfers, and capital income), after subtracting taxes and social contributions.[5] Equivalized household income is obtained after dividing the total amount by the number of equivalent adults to consider differences in household needs. We use the standard modified OECD scale that assigns a weight of 1 to the first adult, .5 to consecutive adults, and .3 to each child (13 years old or younger), which is also the scale used by Eurostat in its reported statistics.

In our analysis, we keep a few observations reporting zero or negative household disposable income in both countries because these are also used in all Eurostat reported statistics on income distribution. This imposes a limit on the indices of inequality that can be used because some measures based on logarithms (members of the Generalized Entropy and Atkinson families) are not defined for zero or negative incomes. This does not represent a problem for the Gini index, the one used here. The inclusion or not of these incomes does not significantly affect the results or the interpretation of the

---

[3]There are some concerns about how some particular groups are represented in this panel in Germany. In particular, Frick and Krell (2010) report differences with respect to the other main longitudinal source in the country (German Socio-Economic Panel Study, SOEP) in terms of the level and trends of measured inequality and poverty in 2005–2007.

[4]The Spanish 2008 sample is made of 35,970 (13,014) individual (household) unweighted observations, with 30,339 individuals living in 9,677 active households. In the case of Germany: 28,904 (13,312) individuals (households), 21,549 (8,770) in active households.

[5]In the German case, household income is inflated by a within-household non-response inflation factor.

numbers of the Gini index.[6] Furthermore, the results about the higher inequality level in Spain are shown to be quite robust to the choice of a specific inequality index.

Households' Characteristics

We include in the regression model explanatory variables that might affect the equivalized household disposable income, and thus inequality, because they either affect the opportunities of the household to obtain income, or its needs. We define most of these characteristics as continuous variables (within-household proportions) in order to take into account the situation of all household members and not only the household head or the spouse. These characteristics of economically active households are defined as follows. Location is approximated using categorical variables for the degree of urbanization: densely populated areas (omitted), intermediate areas, and thinly populated areas. We measure household size (the number of members in the household) and household composition by different dimensions. Household composition by age is accounted for by measuring the number of 0–15-year-old children as a proportion of all household members, as well as the proportion of adults (aged 16 or older) falling in each interval: 16–24, 25–34, 35–44 (omitted), 45–54, 55–64, 65, or older. Other demographical variables are defined as the proportion of adults who are married or in consensual union, women, immigrants with less/more than 10 years of residence, and experiencing limitations from health problems.[7] Similarly, education is accounted for by the proportion of adults with primary (omitted), lower secondary, upper secondary or non-tertiary postsecondary, and tertiary education.

Regarding labor-related variables of household members we consider the activity and employment rates, the level of experience, and job

---

[6]Although the Gini index does not have an upper bound in the presence of negative incomes, this does not significantly alter its interpretation in our context because only a few incomes are negative. Thus, we do not apply any correction, such as the one proposed by Chen, Tsaur, and Rhai (1982). The number of individual observations with zero/negative disposable income in active households in 2012 is 26 in Germany and 467 in Spain (representing 0.12 percent and 1.82 percent of the corresponding populations). In 2008: 87 (0.40 percent) in Germany and 209 (0.76 percent) in Spain.

[7]In 2008, there is no information about immigration by time of residence, so the variable for this sample (as well as for 2012 when compared with 2008) refers to the proportion of foreign citizens instead.

characteristics, such as occupation, industry, and type of contract. The activity rate is constructed as the proportion of months during the income reference year spent by household members in the labor market out of household's potential (the number of adults multiplied by 12). Employment rates are obtained by computing the number of months worked by household members (separately as full-time and part-time, and in each case distinguishing if as employee or self-employed), as a proportion of the total number of months in the labor force.[8] We measure the proportion of active household members falling in each interval of paid work experience (none −omitted-, up to 1 year, 1−2 years, 3−5 years, 6−9 years, 10 or more years), as well as reporting each occupation (ISCO 2008 classification at 1 digit), industry (Eurostat compact classification based on NACE groups), or having a temporary contract.[9] The size of the working unit is considered using the proportion of active members falling in each interval of the number of workers at the local unit: 1−2 (omitted), 3−5, 6−10, 11−49, 50, or more.

The calendar year previous to the interview is the reference period for income, as well as for other variables such as age and months spent in activity or in each type of employment. The rest of variables refer to the current situation (at the time of the interview, first months of 2008/2012), such as the degree of urbanization, household size, civil status, health limitations, and worker's characteristics, such as experience, working unit size, and industry; or they refer to the current/last situation (e.g., temporary contract and occupation).[10,11]

---

[8]In 2008, there is no distinction between months worked as self-employed and as employees. In this year and in the comparison over time, self-employment is measured as the proportion of active adults reporting that status as the current/last situation at the time of the interview (distinguishing whether with or without employees).

[9]The omitted categories are Elementary occupations (ISCO group 9) and Manufacturing and other activities such as fishing, mining, or energy (NACE groups B-E).

[10]The use of longitudinal information to link two consecutive samples would partially correct this problem as it would allow the date of the interview to fall within the income reference year. However, this would not imply a great advantage in this case because we would still ignore the relevant information (e.g., job characteristics) month by month. And this would be obtained at the price of losing at least a quarter of the sample because of the rotating nature of the survey.

[11]A particular implication of this is that we do not have information regarding the industry and the size of the working unit for those who reported to be unemployed at the time of the interview but worked during the previous calendar year. For that reason we also include a new variable that reports the proportion of active people in this particular situation (labeled as labor unknown).

INEQUALITY IN SPAIN

General Trend

The discontinuity in the data surveys used to measure households living conditions in Spain during the last decades makes it a difficult task to trace the long-term trend in inequality of disposable income across households. Cantó, Gradín, and Del Río (2000) have reviewed the early literature of inequality in Spain. Ayala (2014) and Ferrer-i-Carbonell, Ramos, and Oviedo (2014) are examples of more recent reviews. There is a certain consensus, however, that points to a reduction of inequality during the transition to democracy and the consolidation of the welfare state that started in the mid-1970s and ended with the recession in the early 1990s.[12] This particular trend made Spain a special case in the context of generalized long-term increases in inequality among most OECD countries (OECD, 2008, 2011). Regarding the most recent period, according to EU-SILC statistics, the Gini index of disposable income increased from 0.310 in 2004 to 0.319 in 2006–2008. Right after the break of the current Great Recession, inequality substantially increased again to 0.350 in 2012, with much of the increase accounted for by changes in the distribution of wages and job losses (ILO, 2015).[13]

What is clear, is that right before the recession, Spain was a country with high levels of inequality compared with other EU countries. This was so even after a long-lasting economic boom between 1995 and 2007 that brought a strong reduction in unemployment and a massive expansion of sectors, such as construction and services, which significantly increased the economic opportunities of low-skilled workers and brought to the country an unprecedented number of immigrants. With the outbreak of the Great Recession, inequality could only be aggravated as the precarious situation of the labor market and an ineffective redistribution of the tax-benefit

---

[12]Torregrosa-Hetland (2016) has recently challenged this consensus, claiming that it was the result of the bias of underreported income not being homogeneous across income levels. After performing a two-step correction procedure, identifying under-reporting first with an Engel's curve approach and then with an aggregate adjustment to National Accounts, income inequality turned out to be higher and more persistent during the 1973–1990 period than previously reported.

[13]These data correspond with the EU-SILC data version of March 2014. The new updated EU-SILC data recently reported by Eurostat website broke the previous series for Spain since 2009 (based on the new *Encuesta de Condiciones de Vida*, base 2013). According to this, inequality in Spain was 0.329 in 2009 and picked up to 0.347 in 2014.

system were dramatically deteriorated. The labor market suddenly collapsed, unemployment rocketed to above 20 percent, with much larger rates among young people, unskilled workers, and immigrants (Gradín & Del Río, 2013). The unemployment spells, typically very short, significantly increased in duration, and a larger share of households faced severe employment deprivation (Gradín, Cantó, & Del Río, 2015a, 2015b).

The response of many households was an intensification of family support, an increase in the number of hours available for work (the added-worker effect, especially from women), and a radical change in the direction of migration flows.[14] The successive labor market reforms made firing easier and cheaper, but the chronic duality between temporary and permanent workers was essentially preserved with a more intensive use of short-term and (unwanted) part-time contracts.[15] This was combined with several budget cuts and tax raises to achieve fiscal consolidation constrained by the sovereign debt crisis, the restructuring of the financial sector, and the Euro membership. As a result, Spain is now one of the countries with the largest inequality across households in the EU, jointly with other countries strongly affected by the recession like the Baltics, Portugal, and Greece.

Many other developed countries were affected by the recession, but the reaction of unemployment to the contraction of the GDP was larger in countries like Spain (or the United States) in which the recession was caused by a boom-bust pattern in the housing market, while was much

---

[14]Some symptoms point to the added-worker effect having affected both the extensive and intensive margin, such as an increase in women's activity rate, a reduction in the proportion of women inactive because of family reasons, or an increase in the proportion of women involuntarily working part-time. The presence of the added-worker effect during the recession was confirmed for Spain by Addabbo, Rodríguez-Modroño, and Gálvez-Muñoz (2013), for the Mediterranean countries in general (characterized by relatively low women activity rates and a weaker welfare state) by Bredtmann, Otten, and Rulff (2014), or for the United States (Starr, 2014).

[15]Spain followed since 1984 a strategy of relaxing employment protection using flexibility-at-the-margin reforms by expanding fixed-term contracts, exhibiting the highest incidence among EU countries, with strong implications on the functioning of the labor market (Dolado, García-Serrano, & Jimeno, 2002). Right before the recession, about a third of workers had a temporary job in Spain, more than twice the EU average. This percentage was later reduced to its minimum of 23 percent in 2013 because these workers were the first to be laid off in the recession. However, the great majority of contracts signed during the last years are temporary and with an increasingly shorter duration. Part-time workers were 15 percent of all workers in the second quarter of 2015 (8 percent of men; 25 percent of women), of which 63 percent wished a full-time job, but could not find any (1,785 thousands, compared with only 744 in 2007).

smaller in countries like Germany where the downturn was driven by
a sharp decline in exports (OECD, 2010). This produced a wide range
of unemployment rates in the EU (European Commission, 2010; Gradín
et al., 2015a, 2015b; OECD, 2010). In some countries, especially
Germany, the number of hours of work was widely reduced, thus avoid-
ing a deeper reduction of employment (Brenke, Rinne, & Zimmermann,
2013; Gradín et al., 2015a; OECD, 2010). Indeed, the income distribution
in Germany had shown growing inequality since the reunification. But
it exhibited a more stable picture after the second half of the 2000s,
despite the strong initial shock produced by the recession. The role of the
expansion of part-time jobs on this trend is still controversial (Rehm,
Schmid, & Wang, 2014). Eurostat data show that Germany, after increasing inequality from 0.261 in 2005 to around 0.304 in 2007, had a small
decrease until 2012, 0.283 (later increasing to 0.297 in 2013 and 0.307 in
2014). As a result, the Gini gap between Spain and Germany increased
from 0.017 in 2008 to 0.067 in 2012 (the period under analysis here). As
for the other countries considered in our study, the short-term impact of
the recession in GDP (at market prices in euros) was even deeper in the
United Kingdom or Sweden than in Spain, but the recovery was also
much faster, with a more limited fall in employment rates. While France,
Italy, and Sweden show a stable pattern (or with small increases) in
inequality after the start of the recession, the United Kingdom reduced its
level since 2008.

Trends in Earnings Inequality

Inequality in disposable income is inherently linked to the functioning of
the labor market, although also affected by the formation of households,
and by the redistributive effect of the tax-benefit system (OECD, 2011).[16]
Earnings inequality in Spain has been extensively analyzed during the last
years using different methodologies and different datasets (see a survey in

---

[16]A recent detailed analysis of how the labor market influences income inequality in Spain can
be found in Davia (2013). The weak redistributive impact of the Spanish tax-benefit system
has already been stressed in recent studies (Ayala, Martínez, & Ruiz-Huerta, 2013; Cantó,
2014; Ruiz-Huerta, 2014).

García-Serrano & Arranz, 2014). A certain consensus emerged stating that earnings inequality in Spain has shown a clear counter-cyclical trend.

Earnings inequality was declining in the years previous to the recession mostly driven by changes in the returns to worker's characteristics, although there were also important changes in the composition of the labor force and industries. For example, using the Structural Earnings Survey Lacuesta and Izquierdo (2012) found that changes in the composition of the workforce, such as the increase in the proportion of women, the increase in university degree-holders, the aging of the population, and the reduction in accumulated experience, would have generated a significant increase in wage inequality between 1995 and 2002. If inequality indeed decreased was due to a major decrease in wage differentials between different ages and educational levels that was not compensated for by a higher value on seniority over time. As a possible factor behind this trend, the authors point to the large coverage of centralized collective agreements that do not allow much differentiation within demographic groups.

Earnings inequality abruptly increased after the start of the recession as different studies have shown using the structural wage surveys and administrative records before and after the recession started (with coverage until 2010). Among them, Arranz and García-Serrano (2012, 2014), García-Serrano and Arranz (2013), and Bonhomme and Hospido (2013a) using Social Security records; Bonhomme and Hospido (2013b) using tax files; and Casado and Simón (2013) using the Structural Earnings Survey. All these studies consistently point out that this trend was the result of a large compositional effect following the massive destruction of jobs. For example, Bonhomme and Hospido (2013a) found that age and occupation, immigrant status, and type of contract explain a relatively small part of the evolution, while when accounting for changes in sectoral composition, changes explain up to half of the increase in inequality during the beginning of the recession for males (slightly less for females).

INEQUALITY AND INCOME SOURCES: THE LABOR MARKET AND THE TAX-BENEFIT SYSTEM

We first analyze the extent to which the higher level of income inequality in Spain is related with earnings inequality, the low employment rates, or the tax-benefit model.

Inequality among Active and Inactive Households

If we classify households according to whether they have any member engaged in the labor force (active households) or not (inactive households), we can easily check that the gap in inequality of disposable income between Spain and Germany is concentrated in economically active households (making up 85 and 76 percent of the total population in 2012, respectively). Figs. 1(a)–(c) display the density and Lorenz curves of disposable income for people in all households (a) and separately for individuals in inactive and active households (b and c) in 2012. The corresponding Gini indices are reported in Table 1. The densities and Lorenz curves of disposable income among inactive households in both countries are almost undistinguishable and inequality is slightly lower in Spain (0.276 vs. 0.286).[17] It is when we focus on inequality within active households that the level of inequality in disposable income stands above in Spain (0.358 vs. 0.276, a gap of 0.083), with the Lorenz curve always falling below that of Germany (except at the very top).[18]

Figs. 2(a)–(f) display the Lorenz curves comparing Spain and Germany in 2008, and Spain in 2012 and 2008, with the corresponding Gini indices reported in Table 1. It becomes clear that the increase in inequality in Spain was driven by the labor market (the 2008 Lorenz curve dominates that of 2012 for active but not for inactive households, except for very low incomes). This pushed the inter-country gap in inequality among active households from 0.014 to 0.083. Its impact on overall inequality (the gap went from 0.017 to 0.067) was partially offset by the decline in inequality among inactive households.

The Contribution of Income Sources to Inequality

The analysis of inequality for different income aggregates among economically active households and employed or economically active workers,

---

[17]The level of inequality between active and inactive households (when each person is given the average income of her type) is also lower in Spain in 2012: 0.018 versus 0.037 in Germany (Gini). It was, however, larger in 2008: 0.047 versus 0.034.

[18]This means that the result is robust to the use of other Lorenz-consistent inequality indices such as Generalized Entropy or Atkinson families – most of them defined only for positive incomes – except when they are extremely sensitive to inequality at the top of the income distribution. Other usual inequality indices based on specific quantiles (e.g., S80/S20, p90/p10, etc.) also generally imply higher inequality across active households in Spain than in Germany.

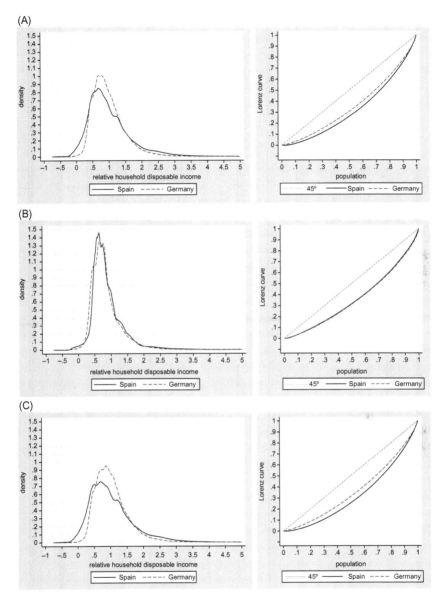

Fig. 1. Household Disposable Income in Spain and Germany: Densities and Lorenz Curves, 2012. (a) All. (b) Population in Inactive Households. (c) Population in Active Households. *Notes*: Relative household disposable income (equivalized using the OECD-modified scale) divided by country's average. A household is considered to be active (inactive) if it has at least one member (none) in the labor force in income reference year. Adaptive kernels with variable optimal bandwidth using a Gaussian kernel function. *Source*: Own construction using EU-SILC 2012 (2011 income).

Table 1. Income Inequality (Gini) in Spain and Germany.

		2008			2012			
		Spain (ES)	Germany (DE)	Gap (ES08-DE08)	Spain (ES)	Germany (DE)	Gap (ES12-DE12)	Gap (ES12-ES08)
Individual income								
Employed workers	Labor income	0.384	0.426	−0.042	0.407	0.409	−0.002	0.023
		(0.004)	(0.004)	(0.006)	(0.004)	(0.004)	(0.006)	(0.006)
Labor force	Labor income	0.424	0.478	−0.054	0.518	0.450	0.068	0.094
		(0.004)	(0.004)	(0.006)	(0.005)	(0.004)	(0.006)	(0.006)
Equivalized household income								
Inactive households	Disposable income	0.290	0.277	0.013	0.276	0.286	−0.009	−0.013
		(0.006)	(0.005)	(0.008)	(0.007)	(0.006)	(0.010)	(0.009)
Active households	Labor income	0.390	0.407	−0.018	0.459	0.380	0.080	0.070
		(0.004)	(0.004)	(0.006)	(0.004)	(0.004)	(0.006)	(0.006)
	+ Capital income (market income)	0.387	0.402	−0.015	0.455	0.375	0.080	0.067
		(0.004)	(0.005)	(0.006)	(0.004)	(0.004)	(0.006)	(0.006)
	+ Pensions	0.354	0.386	−0.032	0.415	0.360	0.054	0.060
		(0.004)	(0.004)	(0.006)	(0.004)	(0.004)	(0.006)	(0.006)
	+ Unempl. benefits	0.343	0.364	−0.021	0.385	0.346	0.039	0.042
		(0.004)	(0.005)	(0.006)	(0.004)	(0.004)	(0.006)	(0.005)
	+ Other social benef. (gross income)	0.332	0.333	−0.001	0.370	0.312	0.057	0.037
		(0.004)	(0.004)	(0.006)	(0.004)	(0.004)	(0.005)	(0.005)
	− Taxes (disposable income)	0.315	0.301	0.014	0.358	0.276	0.083	0.043
		(0.004)	(0.004)	(0.006)	(0.004)	(0.004)	(0.005)	(0.005)

All population							
Labor income	0.472	0.544	−0.072	0.538	0.525	0.013	0.067
	(0.004)	(0.004)	(0.006)	(0.004)	(0.004)	(0.006)	(0.006)
+ Capital income (market income)	0.462	0.520	−0.058	0.527	0.504	0.024	0.065
	(0.004)	(0.004)	(0.006)	(0.004)	(0.004)	(0.006)	(0.006)
+ Pensions	0.363	0.391	−0.028	0.409	0.372	0.037	0.046
	(0.003)	(0.004)	(0.005)	(0.004)	(0.004)	(0.005)	(0.005)
+ Unempl. benefits	0.353	0.372	−0.019	0.384	0.360	0.023	0.030
	(0.003)	(0.004)	(0.005)	(0.004)	(0.004)	(0.005)	(0.005)
+ Other social benef. (gross income)	0.340	0.342	−0.002	0.365	0.326	0.040	0.025
	(0.003)	(0.004)	(0.005)	(0.003)	(0.003)	(0.005)	(0.005)
− Taxes (disposable income)	0.319	0.302	0.017	0.350	0.283	0.067	0.031
	(0.003)	(0.004)	(0.005)	(0.003)	(0.003)	(0.005)	(0.005)

Source: Own construction using EU-SILC 2008, 2012 (2007, 2011 income).

Notes:
– Bootstraps standard errors (1,000 replications) in parentheses (individuals clustered within households).
– A household is active (inactive) if any (none) member was in the labor force in the income reference year.
– Household income has been divided by the number of equivalent adults (OECD-modified scale).
– Income aggregates as defined in "Data" section.
– Employed individuals are those who ever worked during 2011. Individuals in the labor force, also include those that were ever unemployed in 2011.

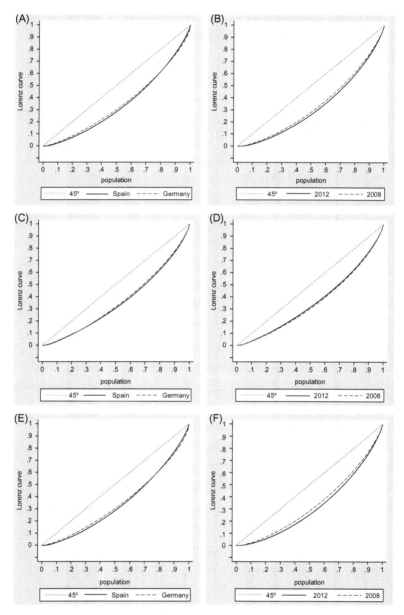

Fig. 2. Household Disposable Income in Spain and Germany in 2008 and Spain 2008–2012. (a) All, 2008. (b) All, Spain 2008–2012. (c) Inactive Households, 2008. (d) Inactive Households, Spain 2008–2012. (e) Active Households, 2008. (f) Active Households, Spain 2008–2012. *Notes*: Relative household disposable income (equivalized using the OECD-modified scale) divided by country's average. A household is considered to be active (inactive) if it has at least one member (none) in the labor force in income reference year. Adaptive kernels with variable optimal bandwidth using a Gaussian kernel function. *Source*: Own construction using EU-SILC 2008, 2012 (2007, 2011 income).

reported in Table 1, helps to separate the role of the labor market and the tax-benefit system in shaping higher inequality in Spain in comparison with Germany. Let us first analyze the situation in 2012 and then see the changes over time.

We start by checking that inequality in the distribution of individual (annual) gross earnings among employed workers is similar in both countries (first row of Table 1).[19] The gap significantly increases to 0.068 after we extend the sample to the entire labor force. This suggests that after including the population with no labor income the inequality gap arises because of massive unemployment in Spain. The gap increases to 0.080 when we measure (equivalized) household gross earnings after pooling income within households and including household members out of the labor force. The addition of capital income to obtain (equivalized) market income does not affect the inter-country Gini gap.[20] We now sequentially add social benefits and subtract taxes to obtain our main aggregate, disposable income.

The inter-country gap is substantially reduced (from 0.080 to 0.054) after adding old-age and survivors' pensions to market income, because the resulting reduction in inequality among active households is much larger in Spain (0.040) than in Germany (0.014). These pensions are known to be providing a substantial relief in families shocked by unemployment, indeed they reduce the relative inter-country gap in income by 3.4 percentage points − see average income values in Table B1 in the appendix. This is the result of extended families being more common in Spain, with a higher proportion of elderly people cohabiting with younger generations.

Although social benefits as a whole do not affect the inter-country income inequality gap, their composition is different in each case: Spain devotes much more resources to unemployment, and less to protect children and disable people, or to promote affordable housing.[21] Thus, the addition of

---

[19]This refers to annual income from wages and self-employment before taxes and social contributions, for people who reported at least one month of employment during the reference year.

[20]It is a well-known fact that households surveys tend to underestimate income from capital.

[21]According to our data, but consistently with Eurostat statistics about social benefits by function, Spain devotes most of its resources to unemployment (57 percent of the total amount), and then to disability (22 percent), social exclusion (10 percent), with small amounts to child (6 percent), and housing (1 percent) benefits. In Germany, the largest amounts are for child allowances (57 percent), unemployment (20 percent), disability (11 percent), and housing (7 percent). More detailed data about the redistributive effect of benefits by type can be found in EUROMOD's website for statistics on the Distribution and Decomposition of Disposable Income.

unemployment and other social benefits reduces further income inequality in
Spain by 0.030 and 0.015, respectively, while the impact of these benefits is
reversed in Germany (0.014 and 0.034). Finally, after subtracting taxes and
social contributions from gross income, the reduction in inequality among
economically active households in Spain (0.011) is much smaller than in
Germany (0.037). As a consequence, the inter-country gap in inequality
raises from 0.057 to its final level of 0.083.

The main conclusions discussed here do not vary much if we change
the reference country to France, Italy, Sweden, or the United Kingdom
(Table 2). Higher income inequality in Spain is explained by the inequality
among active households. This is larger in Spain because it starts with a

Table 2. Income Inequality (Gini) and Marginal Change by Income
Sources in Selected Countries, 2012.

	Spain	Germany	France	Italy	Sweden	UK
All households						
Earnings	0.538	0.525	0.513	0.516	0.453	0.585
	(0.004)	(0.004)	(0.005)	(0.004)	(0.005)	(0.007)
Market income	0.527	0.504	0.492	0.503	0.437	0.567
	(0.004)	(0.004)	(0.006)	(0.004)	(0.005)	(0.007)
Marginal change in Gini:						
+ Pensions	−0.118	−0.131	−0.115	−0.124	−0.099	−0.099
	(0.005)	(0.005)	(0.008)	(0.005)	(0.007)	(0.010)
+ Unemployment benefits	−0.025	−0.012	−0.013	−0.008	−0.009	−0.005
	(0.005)	(0.005)	(0.008)	(0.005)	(0.006)	(0.010)
+ Other social benefits	−0.018	−0.035	−0.034	−0.012	−0.046	−0.071
	(0.005)	(0.005)	(0.008)	(0.004)	(0.006)	(0.010)
− Taxes	−0.016	−0.043	−0.026	−0.040	−0.034	−0.064
	(0.005)	(0.004)	(0.007)	(0.004)	(0.005)	(0.009)
+/− Total taxes/benefits	−0.178	−0.221	−0.188	−0.184	−0.188	−0.238
	(0.005)	(0.005)	(0.008)	(0.005)	(0.006)	(0.009)
Disposable income	0.350	0.283	0.305	0.319	0.249	0.328
	(0.003)	(0.003)	(0.005)	(0.003)	(0.003)	(0.006)
Inter-country gap		0.067	0.045	0.031	0.101	0.022
(Spain-country)		(0.005)	(0.006)	(0.004)	(0.005)	(0.007)

Table 2. (*Continued*)

	Spain	Germany	France	Italy	Sweden	UK
Inactive households						
Disposable income	0.276	0.286	0.319	0.302	0.258	0.270
	(0.007)	(0.007)	(0.008)	(0.005)	(0.006)	(0.006)
Inter-country gap		−0.009	−0.042	−0.026	0.018	0.007
(Spain-country)		(0.010)	(0.011)	(0.008)	(0.009)	(0.009)
Active households						
Earnings	0.459	0.380	0.380	0.403	0.329	0.487
	(0.004)	(0.004)	(0.005)	(0.004)	(0.005)	(0.008)
Market income	0.455	0.375	0.397	0.404	0.330	0.479
	(0.004)	(0.004)	(0.007)	(0.004)	(0.005)	(0.008)
Marginal change in Gini:						
+ Pensions	−0.040	−0.014	−0.020	−0.026	−0.005	−0.032
	(0.006)	(0.006)	(0.009)	(0.005)	(0.008)	(0.011)
+ Unemployment benefits	−0.030	−0.014	−0.016	−0.010	−0.010	−0.005
	(0.006)	(0.006)	(0.009)	(0.005)	(0.007)	(0.011)
+ Other social benefits	−0.015	−0.034	−0.036	−0.011	−0.044	−0.053
	(0.005)	(0.005)	(0.009)	(0.005)	(0.007)	(0.011)
− Taxes	−0.011	−0.037	−0.025	−0.036	−0.034	−0.061
	(0.005)	(0.005)	(0.009)	(0.005)	(0.006)	(0.010)
+/− Total taxes/benefits	−0.097	−0.099	−0.097	−0.083	−0.094	−0.151
	(0.006)	(0.005)	(0.009)	(0.005)	(0.007)	(0.010)
Disposable income	0.358	0.276	0.300	0.320	0.236	0.328
	(0.004)	(0.004)	(0.006)	(0.003)	(0.004)	(0.007)
Inter-country gap		0.083	0.058	0.038	0.122	0.030
(Spain-country)		(0.005)	(0.007)	(0.005)	(0.006)	(0.008)

Source: Own construction using EU-SILC 2012 (2011 income).

Notes:

− Starting from equivalized gross market income, we sequentially add pensions, other social
  benefits, and subtract taxes to obtain disposable income.

− A household is active if any member was in the labor force in the income reference year.

− Household income has been divided by the number of equivalent adults (OECD-
  modified scale).

− Income aggregates as defined in "Data" section.

higher level of households' earnings inequality. The redistributive effect of the tax-benefit system among active households is similar to that in the other countries, but with a different composition. Spain exhibits the largest impact of pensions and unemployment benefits in reducing inequality, but the shortest impact of other social benefits (after Italy) and taxes. However, it is important to note that the weaker redistributive effect of the tax-benefit model does help to explain higher inequality across all households in Spain. Indeed, the redistributive effect is the lowest among the selected countries. We only find that the redistributive effect is the largest in Spain for unemployment benefits, intermediate in the case of pensions (after Germany and Italy), but the lowest for taxes and the second lowest for other social benefits (after Italy).

How much of this picture changed during the recession? Table 1 also shows that inequality in disposable income was higher in 2012, compared with 2008, because inequality in gross earnings largely increased, while the equalizing effect of taxes was reduced. This trend was only partially compensated by an increase in the equalizing effect of pensions and benefits, especially those for unemployment.

METHODOLOGY: DECOMPOSING THE GAP IN INEQUALITY USING THE RECENTERED INFLUENCE FUNCTION

RIF Decomposition

To obtain a decomposition of the gap in inequality between Spain and Germany (or Spain in 2008 and 2012) we use a generalization of the well-known Blinder (1973) and Oaxaca (1973) approach, proposed by Firpo et al. (2007, 2009), based on the Recentered Influence Function.[22] This method applies the conventional Blinder-Oaxaca decomposition when the dependent variable in the regression (e.g., log income) is replaced by the Recentered Influence function (RIF) of the target statistic (e.g., a quantile, or an inequality measure). The advantage of this approach is that it allows

---

[22]A throughout discussion of this methodology, comparing its econometric properties with other regression-based decomposition methods available in the literature, can be found in Fortin, Lemieux, and Firpo (2011a).

the decomposition of any distributional statistic for which the RIF exists, and becomes the conventional Blinder-Oaxaca approach when this statistic is the mean (whose RIF is the income variable). Most applications of this approach referred so far to quantiles of the income distribution, but some also have decomposed the differential of Gini indices between two distributions (Becchetti, Massari, & Naticchioni, 2014; Ferreira, Firpo, & Messina, 2014; Firpo et al., 2007, Fortin, Lemieux, & Firpo, 2011b; Groisman, 2014). We devote this section to discuss the details of the implementation of this approach.

The decomposition for the inter-distributional gap in the Gini index is done using a linear approximation based on its influence function. The influence function IF (or Gâteaux or directional derivative, Gâteaux, 1913) is a tool used for robustness analysis in Statistics (introduced by Hampel, 1974) and measures the influence that a small contamination in y has on a particular statistic. By construction it has zero expectation, and by adding the value of the target statistics we obtain the recentered influence function RIF. The RIF of the Gini index for income y, RIF(y; G), is discussed in detail in Appendix A, where we show that it is a non-monotonic transformation of incomes, in which extremely high/low incomes will have a disproportionally large influence in the Gini coefficient.

The simplest version of the RIF decomposition approach assumes that the conditional expectation of RIF(y; G) can be modeled as a linear function of the explanatory variables, given by matrix X, such that the β coefficients can be estimated by OLS

$$E(\text{RIF}(y; G)|X) = X'\beta \qquad (1)$$

Then, by the law of iterative expectations

$$G = E(\text{RIF}(y; G)) = E_X[E(\text{RIF}(y; G)|X)] = E(X)'\beta \qquad (2)$$

Thus, the β coefficients can be interpreted as the marginal impact of a small change in $E(X)$ on the Gini index. These coefficients indicate, on average, how characteristics impact on income, taking into account the distributional pattern of what incomes are affected most.

Given that income and explanatory variables — described in the data section — are defined at the household level but observations are individuals, we obtained the estimations and standard errors allowing (perfect) correlation within households (clusters), which in this context is equivalent to use household observations weighted by their household size.

Based on Eq. (2), we can produce a linear decomposition of the Gini index into the total contribution W_k of each characteristic (including the intercept) x_k, $k = 0, 1, \ldots, K$, on inequality

$$G = \overline{X}'\beta = \sum_{k=0}^{K} W_k = \beta_0 + \sum_{k=1}^{K} \overline{x}_k \beta_k \tag{3}$$

where the total contribution of the kth characteristic is the product of its average value ($\overline{x}_k$) and the marginal impact of this characteristic on overall inequality (β_k).

From Eq. (3), we can write the difference between the Gini of the reference and target distributions (with superscripts 0 and 1) as the sum of the total contributions of characteristics ($W_k^{\Delta X \beta}, k = 0, \ldots, K$):

$$G^1 - G^0 = \overline{X}^{1'}\beta^1 - \overline{X}^{0'}\beta^0 = \sum_{k=0}^{K} W_k^{\Delta X \beta} = (\beta_1 - \beta_0) + \sum_{k=1}^{K} \left(\overline{x}_k^1 \beta_k^1 - \overline{x}_k^0 \beta_k^0\right) \tag{4}$$

However, these total contributions do not separate the impact of differences in average characteristics from the impact of differences in coefficients, which is the main purpose of this paper. For that, we necessarily have to follow a comparative approach in which we compare the target distribution with a counterfactual in which either average characteristics or the coefficients are kept constant.

Let us consider the counterfactual situation in which we give households in the target distribution the average characteristics of the reference, while keeping their own coefficients. By adding and subtracting the inequality level in this counterfactual, $G^{01} = \overline{X}^{0'}\beta^1$, and re-arranging terms, we can rewrite the inter-distributional differential in income inequality as

$$G^1 - G^0 = \left(G^1 - G^{01}\right) + \left(G^{01} - G^0\right) = \left(\overline{X}^{1'} - \overline{X}^{0'}\right)\beta^1 + \overline{X}^{0'}\left(\beta^1 - \beta^0\right) \tag{5}$$

That is, the gap is the sum of $W^{\Delta X} = \left(\overline{X}^{1'} - \overline{X}^{0'}\right)\beta^1$ that represents the *aggregate characteristics effect* (inequality gap explained by shifting characteristics valued at the coefficients of the target distribution), and

$W^{\Delta\beta} = \overline{X}^{0'}(\beta^1 - \beta^0)$, the *aggregate coefficients effect* (unexplained gap due to characteristics having a different impact on inequality for each distribution, valued at the characteristics of the reference distribution).[23]

Therefore, the evaluation of the individual contribution of each variable x_k to the characteristics and coefficients effects can be measured as $W_k^{\Delta X} = (\overline{x}_k^1 - \overline{x}_k^0)\beta_k^1$ and $W_k^{\Delta\beta} = \overline{x}_k^0(\beta_k^1 - \beta_k^0)$, so that the individual effects sum up the corresponding aggregate effects. Similarly, the sum of the characteristic and coefficient effect of each characteristic add up to the total contribution of that same characteristic, $W_k^{\Delta X\beta} = W_k^{\Delta X} + W_k^{\Delta\beta}$.

We can find alternative regression-based decompositions of inequality measures in the literature.[24] Different approaches have assumed (log-)linear conditional incomes and proposed a decomposition of the total effect of characteristics on inequality using different decomposition rules. Fields (2003) used the "natural" decomposition of the variance of logs, arguing that it applied to other indices of inequality under a number of axioms (following Shorrocks, 1982). Morduch and Sicular (2002) also used the "natural" decomposition rules of inequality measures, including the Gini index, while Wan (2002) applied the Shapley decomposition (Shorrocks, 2007). These approaches, however, have not separated the characteristics and coefficients effects. In that line, Yun (2006), following Juhn, Murphy, and Pierce (1993), extended the Fields' (2003) approach. However, this is valid only for the case of the variance of logs, an index of inequality that does not verify the main inequality property (the Pigou-Dalton principle of transfers, saying that a small progressive transfer always reduces inequality).

---

[23]Our approach is slightly different to the conventional Blinder-Oaxaca decomposition of the gender wage inequality in which women are typically given the wage structure of men (or equivalently, men are given the characteristics of women). This is done because in that case the convention is to believe that, under the no-discrimination scenario, those would be the returns that would prevail. Although it is also possible the alternative counterfactual, $G^{10} = \overline{X}^{1'}\beta^0$, that takes average characteristics in the target distribution and the coefficients of the reference one (Spanish households keep their characteristics but we change how they impact inequality), we believe that using the reference's (German households) characteristics provide us with a more transparent counterfactual. This alternative counterfactual, however, is shown to provide similar qualitative results in our robustness checks.

[24]Classical decompositions of inequality measures by subpopulations into between-group and within-group components do not require the use of regressions, but only allow to control for one single factor. Regression-based techniques can be viewed as a generalization of those decompositions in which we control for several factors at the same time.

In this context, the RIF decomposition is quite general, valid for any measure of inequality for which the RIF exists, including the most popular Gini index. Given the linearity assumption, it is path-independent, it is straightforward to compute (including the standard errors), and invariant to the level of aggregation of explanatory factors. Furthermore, it can be seen as a generalization of the conventional Oaxaca-Blinder decomposition which is the particular case in which the target statistic is the mean.

Some Limitations of the Approach

Fortin et al. (2011a) already stressed that most aggregate decompositions like this one assume the invariance of the conditional income distribution. This requires two main conditions: the simple counterfactual treatment and ignorability. The first condition implies that there are no general equilibrium effects. The second one, that there is no selection of individuals based on unobservables. Detailed decompositions usually require stronger assumptions, such as linearity in the relationship between RIF and characteristics, or exogeneity of household characteristics.

In our context, we are mostly interested in the detailed characteristics effects valued at the coefficients estimated for Spain in 2012 (although we also look at the coefficients effects). This means that we look at the immediate expected effect on inequality of increasing the level of employment or education of households, for example, before they could possibly affect wages. It means also that we treat the many household outcomes, such as their level of working intensity, their composition by occupation or industry, or the number of children they have, among other things, as if they were independent of the distribution of unobservables. For example, part of the equalizing effect that we attribute to attained education could be in fact the effect of people with different levels of education differing in other abilities or effort. This is also problematic in the case of the coefficients' effects if the distribution of conditional unobservables differs across countries or over time (otherwise they cancel out).

Thus, we are looking at the observed statistical association of households characteristics with inequality, ceteris paribus, in a reduced form, and cannot claim causality or aim at producing a realistic prediction of how inequality would change with specific changes in the characteristics. We, however, still believe that this type of exercise allows us to identify which are the main drivers of inequality in Spain and how they changed during the recession. This global picture does not preclude the need for more detailed analysis of the specific mechanisms of transmission of this inequality, in which dealing with general equilibrium effects or endogeneity issues would be more viable.

Furthermore, another specific caution must be considered regarding the detailed coefficients effects because they suffer from an identification problem (Oaxaca & Ransom, 1999). This is because the contribution of a dummy variable (and of the intercept) to this effect will vary with the choice of the omitted category, while the contribution of continuous variables will vary with affine transformations that involve a location parameter. There are some solutions for the case of dummies in the literature. For example, Yun (2005, 2008) normalized the coefficients for the categorical variables, such that the sum of the coefficients of each set of dummies is 1. The only solution for continuous variables is to rely on specifications that are widely accepted in the literature. However, as pointed out by Fortin et al. (2011a), there is no general solution to this problem and those proposed in the literature are all ad hoc. In our case, we only have one dummy set (degree of urbanization). The rest are continuous variables such as household size and a number of proportions across household members that have a natural normalization. However, these proportions come from dummy variables and we need to exclude some of them to avoid multicolinearity (e.g., the proportion of men in the household when we include the proportion of women), and there is no clear solution for this. For that reason, we are not using any correction here. Note, however, that the main focus of our study is to identify the detailed characteristics effect, which is not affected by this identification problem (neither is the overall coefficients effect).

EMPIRICAL RESULTS: RIF REGRESSIONS

We first discuss the auxiliary RIF regressions used for the decompositions. The dependent variable in the regressions is the RIF($y; G$). The distribution of the average values of this variable by income percentile in Spain and Germany in 2012 is displayed in Fig. 3. A horizontal line indicates the value of the overall average (the Gini index) in each country to identify income percentiles whose RIF lie above or below that average. As expected, RIF values tend to be highest at both ends of the income scale, but the proportion of people with values above the mean is much larger at the bottom (below the 29th percentile in Spain) than at the top (above the 91st

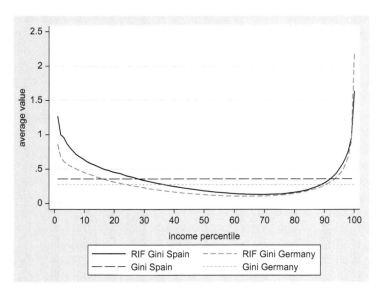

Fig. 3. Average RIF(*y;G*) in Spain and Germany by Income Percentile, 2012. *Notes*: Equivalized household disposable income among active households (OECD-modified scale). Active households (at least one member in the labor force). *Source*: Own construction using EU-SILC 2012 (2011 income).

percentile). Thus, the way characteristics distinctly affect these observations will have a larger impact on inequality. In what follows we discuss the explanatory variables and the estimated coefficients.

Households' Characteristics

Table 3 shows the extent to which Spanish and German active households differ across a number of relevant dimensions. It reports the average and standard deviation of the explanatory variables across individuals in both countries and years, although all the characteristics, like income, are determined at the household level.

In 2012, Spain has a higher proportion of people living in active households residing in densely populated areas (50 vs. 34 percent in Germany). The proportion of married adults and women is pretty similar in both countries, but they have a different demographic profile. On average, Spanish people live in larger active households (3.4 vs. 3 members), with a

Table 3. Mean and Standard Deviation (SD) among Active Households: Explanatory Variables.

	Spain				Germany			
	2008		2012		2008		2012	
	Mean	SD	Mean	SD	Mean	SD	Mean	SD
Densely populated area (omitted)	0.516	0.500	0.504	0.500	0.484	0.500	0.337	0.473
Intermediate area	0.226	0.418	0.237	0.425	0.356	0.479	0.393	0.489
Thinly populated area	0.258	0.437	0.259	0.438	0.159	0.366	0.270	0.444
Household size	3.604	1.359	3.434	1.279	3.022	1.349	2.962	1.370
Age 0–16	0.180	0.211	0.188	0.217	0.191	0.232	0.186	0.233
Age 16–24	0.132	0.198	0.117	0.192	0.142	0.228	0.137	0.225
Age 25–34	0.240	0.335	0.210	0.320	0.191	0.350	0.196	0.355
Age 35–44 (omitted)	0.275	0.365	0.293	0.378	0.313	0.396	0.273	0.388
Age 45–54	0.176	0.267	0.200	0.286	0.214	0.318	0.237	0.333
Age 55–64	0.106	0.225	0.110	0.238	0.114	0.272	0.132	0.291
Age 65 +	0.071	0.173	0.070	0.174	0.027	0.120	0.025	0.116
Married	0.660	0.344	0.659	0.363	0.661	0.401	0.642	0.410
Women	0.499	0.195	0.503	0.205	0.508	0.241	0.512	0.248
Foreign citizens	0.131	0.320	0.131	0.319	0.028	0.136	0.034	0.149
Immigrant (10 or less years)	–	–	0.129	0.314	–	–	0.020	0.120
Immigrant (>10 years)	–	–	0.029	0.132	–	–	0.046	0.175
Health limitations	0.161	0.255	0.139	0.244	0.207	0.317	0.209	0.324
Activity rate	0.730	0.258	0.749	0.259	0.773	0.250	0.795	0.245
Full-time employment rate	0.794	0.294	0.653	0.371	0.679	0.365	0.672	0.361
Part-time employment rate	0.092	0.207	0.098	0.222	0.217	0.307	0.252	0.322
Self-employment rate (with employees)	0.051	0.188	0.048	0.181	0.026	0.136	0.024	0.128
Self-employment rate (without employees)	0.102	0.250	0.090	0.240	0.049	0.189	0.039	0.165
Months as full-time employee (rate)	–	–	0.540	0.393	–	–	0.622	0.380
Months as full-time self-employee (rate)	–	–	0.113	0.269	–	–	0.050	0.186
Months as part-time time employee (rate)	–	–	0.091	0.214	–	–	0.237	0.315
Months as part-time self-employee (rate)	–	–	0.007	0.064	–	–	0.015	0.096
Managers	0.050	0.186	0.047	0.178	0.055	0.195	0.049	0.181
Professionals	0.113	0.272	0.126	0.290	0.185	0.347	0.203	0.353

Table 3.   (*Continued*)

	Spain				Germany			
	2008		2012		2008		2012	
	Mean	SD	Mean	SD	Mean	SD	Mean	SD
Technicians and associate professionals	0.098	0.241	0.098	0.243	0.257	0.369	0.256	0.368
Clerical support workers	0.112	0.250	0.109	0.257	0.120	0.270	0.128	0.279
Services and sales workers	0.160	0.290	0.176	0.309	0.106	0.252	0.120	0.273
Skilled agriculture, forestry, and fishery workers	0.029	0.144	0.034	0.161	0.015	0.104	0.012	0.089
Craft and related trades workers	0.159	0.294	0.157	0.294	0.127	0.275	0.100	0.242
Plant and machine operators and assemblers	0.072	0.207	0.066	0.202	0.054	0.190	0.075	0.223
Elementary occupations (omitted)	0.185	0.323	0.149	0.294	0.060	0.204	0.045	0.177
Agriculture, forestry, and fishing	0.038	0.163	0.036	0.162	0.010	0.088	0.015	0.106
Mining; manufacturing; electricity, gas, and water supply (omitted)	0.143	0.286	0.112	0.262	0.154	0.308	0.209	0.343
Construction	0.105	0.247	0.049	0.175	0.046	0.173	0.039	0.158
Wholesale and retail trade; repair vehicles	0.116	0.261	0.097	0.243	0.109	0.265	0.070	0.212
Transport, storage, and communications	0.038	0.157	0.042	0.166	0.042	0.170	0.037	0.162
Accommodation and food service	0.056	0.190	0.047	0.176	0.017	0.109	0.022	0.123
Information and communication	0.024	0.125	0.019	0.114	0.034	0.160	0.044	0.178
Financial and insurance	0.025	0.126	0.022	0.121	0.044	0.176	0.042	0.173
Real state, professional, scientific, administrative, and support service	0.061	0.193	0.062	0.199	0.076	0.225	0.066	0.211
Public administration and defense; social security	0.069	0.209	0.055	0.191	0.083	0.236	0.099	0.256
Education	0.051	0.184	0.050	0.179	0.068	0.218	0.071	0.219
Human health and social work	0.049	0.177	0.055	0.187	0.104	0.255	0.111	0.266
Other services	0.061	0.188	0.054	0.178	0.083	0.238	0.046	0.175
Unit size: 1–2 workers (omitted)	0.145	0.289	0.132	0.281	0.057	0.202	0.052	0.189
Unit size: 3–5 workers	0.110	0.254	0.094	0.241	0.062	0.200	0.055	0.189
Unit size: 6–10 workers	0.093	0.235	0.071	0.208	0.076	0.220	0.080	0.225
Unit size: 11–49 workers	0.221	0.334	0.193	0.324	0.207	0.344	0.196	0.335
Unit size: 50 + workers	0.236	0.353	0.201	0.337	0.466	0.426	0.483	0.428
Temporary contract	0.298	0.375	0.289	0.374	0.074	0.221	0.145	0.293

Table 3. (*Continued*)

	Spain				Germany			
	2008		2012		2008		2012	
	Mean	SD	Mean	SD	Mean	SD	Mean	SD
Experience <1 year	0.051	0.181	0.037	0.146	0.028	0.135	0.022	0.125
Experience 1–2 years	0.055	0.161	0.044	0.150	0.042	0.148	0.045	0.164
Experience 3–5 years	0.086	0.208	0.064	0.187	0.066	0.199	0.064	0.198
Experience 6–9 years	0.101	0.236	0.097	0.236	0.083	0.239	0.074	0.222
Experience 10 + years	0.707	0.350	0.758	0.338	0.781	0.344	0.794	0.338
Labor unknown	0.026	0.120	0.125	0.265	0.032	0.146	0.071	0.212
Primary education (omitted)	0.196	0.324	0.154	0.296	0.013	0.098	0.012	0.092
Lower secondary education	0.245	0.352	0.267	0.366	0.078	0.215	0.079	0.221
Upper secondary, non-tertiary postsecondary education	0.231	0.335	0.233	0.338	0.496	0.428	0.518	0.424
Tertiary education	0.301	0.391	0.325	0.401	0.412	0.432	0.392	0.427

Source: Own construction using EU-SILC 2008 and 2012 (2007 and 2011 income).
Notes:
– Active households (at least one member in the labor force).
– See "Households' characteristics" section for a description of variables.

higher proportion of adults in their middle-age (25–44 years old) or 65 or older (7 vs. 2.5 percent), a similar proportion of children (up to 16 years old), and fewer adults with health limitations (14 vs. 21 percent). There is also a higher proportion of recent immigrants (less than 10 years of residence, 13 vs. 2 percent) and a smaller proportion of immigrants with longer time of residence (3 vs. 5 percent) in Spanish active households. The main demographic changes observed in Spain between 2008 and 2012 refer to the decline in the average household size, driven by a reduction in the proportion of young adults (16–34 years old).[25] Compared with Germany, Spanish households also exhibit in 2012 a lower proportion of adults who

---

[25]There was a net increase of about 0.25 million of individuals in active households between 2008 and 2012, with a substantial increase of almost 1.3 million people in the range of 35–64 years old and 0.3 of children, but a reduction of near 1.4 million of 16–34-year-old people. Similar changes are observed in the entire population (which increased by about 1 million), probably the result of the inversion of migration flows.

attained upper secondary/postsecondary education (23 vs. 52 percent) and tertiary education (32.5 vs. 39 percent).[26]

The activity rate in 2012 is lower in Spanish households (75 vs. 80 percent of months spent in the labor force) with also lower employment rates as employees either part-time (9 percent of moths in Spain, 24 percent in Germany) or full-time (54 vs. 62 percent). The proportion of months worked as self-employed is, however, higher in Spain (12 vs. 6 percent, including part- and full-time). The average proportion of adults with temporary contracts in Spain doubles that in Germany (29 vs. 14.5 percent), while the average proportion of workers with 6 or more years of experience is larger in Germany. Regarding the structure of the economy, Spanish households have a higher proportion of adults in low-skilled occupations (elementary; craft and related trades; services and sales workers) and a smaller proportion of professionals and technicians. Similarly, a lower proportion of adults work in Spain in manufacturing, and a relatively higher number work in accommodation and food services or wholesale and retail trade. A higher proportion of adults are working in smallest firms (1−2 employees: 13 vs. 5 percent) and a lower share in larger firms (above 50 workers: 20 vs. 48 percent).

The changes observed between 2008 and 2012 in the labor market in Spain are, not surprisingly, important. There is a small increase in the activity rate (2 percentage points, driven by higher women's participation), with a fall in full-time employment rates of 14 percentage points, and an increase in part-time (6 percentage points). Employment losses were not random and also changed the structure of jobs, with a reduction of workers in larger working units and in elementary occupations, especially in the construction and manufacturing sectors. There was only a small 1-percentage-point reduction in the proportion of temporary contracts, while more experienced workers represent a larger share in 2012.[27]

---

[26]The gap in education is smaller for youngest cohorts. Spain exhibits a similar proportion of people with tertiary education (42 percent) among those between 25 and 34 years old, but still a much higher proportion of people who did not reached upper-secondary studies (32 vs. 7 percent).

[27]In the case of Germany there is a reduction in the proportion of middle-aged members (35−44), an increase in part-time and temporary work, also with more workers in the manufacturing sector and less in trade. There was also a reduction in the population living in densely populated areas. This might be associated with the change in the construction of this variable by Eurostat since 2012 (based on *Eurostat Labour Market Working Group* in 2011).

Gini-RIF Coefficients

The coefficients in the RIF regressions indicate the magnitude and direction of the expected change in the Gini index after a small increase in the average value of the corresponding variable, ceteris paribus. Given that RIF(y; G) is a non-monotonic transformation of incomes whose average is the Gini index, a marginal increase in the average value of a characteristic will increase inequality whenever it increases the relative income of the rich or decreases that of the poor. This will be clearly the case of characteristics with an association with conditional income following a U-shaped curve. The reverse will decrease inequality instead (inverted U-shaped curves). Fig. 4 shows the examples of the association between activity/employment rates with unconditional income and RIF in Spain. Household disposable income inequality is the result of the interplay between the earnings generation process, the tax-benefit model, and the formation of households. Thus, the exact mechanisms that produce these coefficients might not always be obvious.

The estimated coefficients of the Gini-RIF regressions are reported in Table 4 for Spain and Germany in 2012. While there are important coincidences, it is clear that the labor market and demographics work differently in both countries in terms of how they shape inequality as we now discuss in more detail. There is a large intercept in both countries. This is the expected Gini for the limit case in which all explanatory variables are set to zero. It reflects the net effect on inequality of unobservables and variables

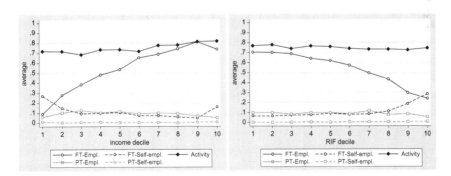

Fig. 4. Employment by Income and Gini-RIF Deciles in Spain, 2012. *Notes*: Equivalized household disposable income (OECD-modified scale) among active households (at least one member in the labor force). See "Households' characteristics" section for a description of variables. *Source*: Own construction using EU-SILC 2012 (2011 income).

Table 4. (Gini) RIF Regressions of Disposable Household Income for
Active Households, 2012.

	Spain		Germany	
	Coeff.	St. E.	Coeff.	St. E.
Intermediate area	−0.023**	0.008	0.009	0.008
Thinly populated area	−0.027***	0.008	0.003	0.007
Household size	−0.016***	0.004	−0.021***	0.005
Age 0−16	0.084**	0.027	0.053*	0.026
Age 16−24	0.069*	0.030	−0.022	0.019
Age 25−34	0.007	0.013	−0.010	0.012
Age 45−54	0.006	0.013	0.015	0.011
Age 55−64	−0.015	0.018	0.037*	0.018
Age 65 +	−0.163***	0.026	0.033	0.064
Married	−0.011	0.010	−0.011	0.009
Women	−0.014	0.016	−0.015	0.012
Immigrant (10 or less years)	0.084***	0.012	0.074	0.048
Immigrant (>10 years)	0.067	0.040	−0.010	0.015
Health limitations	−0.011	0.014	−0.021*	0.009
Activity rate	−0.064***	0.017	−0.046*	0.022
FT-E employment rate	−0.237***	0.018	−0.213***	0.028
FT-SE employment rate	0.096***	0.026	0.062	0.039
PT-E employment rate	−0.179***	0.020	−0.179***	0.028
PT-SE employment rate	−0.039	0.064	−0.043	0.051
Managers	0.089**	0.029	0.182***	0.045
Professionals	0.075***	0.020	0.014	0.016
Technicians and associate professionals	−0.068***	0.015	−0.038**	0.014
Clerical support workers	−0.071***	0.015	−0.032	0.018
Services and sales workers	−0.041**	0.012	−0.011	0.014
Skilled agric., forestry, and fishery workers	−0.006	0.039	−0.058	0.039
Craft and related trades workers	−0.012	0.013	−0.048**	0.015
Plant and machine operators/assemblers	−0.072***	0.014	−0.012	0.015
Agriculture, forestry, and fishing	−0.031	0.033	−0.023	0.036
Construction	−0.035	0.019	−0.020	0.023
Wholesale and retail trade; repair vehicles	−0.002	0.017	−0.041**	0.016
Transport, storage, and communications	−0.009	0.019	0.025	0.024
Accommodation and food service	−0.016	0.019	0.001	0.023

Table 4. (*Continued*)

	Spain		Germany	
	Coeff.	St. E.	Coeff.	St. E.
Information and communication	0.014	0.034	−0.023	0.020
Financial and insurance	0.189***	0.043	0.005	0.023
Real state, professional, etc.	−0.035	0.019	0.005	0.028
Public adm. and defense; soc. sec.	−0.005	0.017	−0.063***	0.013
Education	−0.037	0.023	−0.091***	0.017
Human health and social work	0.030	0.023	−0.032	0.018
Other services	−0.049*	0.021	−0.027	0.024
Unit size: 3−5 workers	−0.014	0.020	0.029	0.034
Unit size: 6−10 workers	−0.020	0.018	0.062	0.037
Unit size: 11−49 workers	−0.024	0.017	0.012	0.029
Unit size: 50 + workers	−0.006	0.016	0.003	0.027
Temporary	0.013	0.011	0.059***	0.015
Experience 1−2 years	−0.032	0.031	−0.021	0.039
Experience 3−5 years	0.022	0.029	−0.073*	0.036
Experience 6−9 years	−0.012	0.026	−0.031	0.036
Experience 10 + years	0.002	0.023	−0.058	0.035
Labor unknown	−0.011	0.015	0.010	0.029
Lower secondary education	−0.035**	0.012	−0.045	0.026
Upper secondary, non-tertiary postsecondary	−0.056***	0.013	−0.057*	0.025
Tertiary education	−0.037**	0.014	−0.042	0.026
Intercept	0.657***	0.033	0.661***	0.046
N	27,751	p-Value	20,893	p-Value
F	27.56	0	32.75	0
R^2	0.214		0.104	

Source: Own construction using EU-SILC 2012 (2011 income).
Notes:
− "Dependent variable is the Gini-RIF of equivalized" household disposable income (OECD-modified scale) among active households (at least one member in the labor force).
− See "Households' characteristics" section for a description of variables.
− *p* < 0.05; **p* < 0.01; ***p* < 0.001.

omitted to prevent multicolinearity (implying no activity/employment, low-est education, etc.). A marginal increase in most characteristics included as explanatory variables, such as education or employment, produce an equal-izing effect, given how the model was specified.

Inequality in both countries decreases, ceteris paribus, with the size of the household (which allows to diversify income sources). We do not find any statistically significant relationship between inequality and gender or civil status (although the effects are also negative), while health limitations significantly decrease inequality only in Germany. Regarding age composi-tion, inequality increases more intensely in Spain with the proportion of children. This might be the result of the failure of family policies to compen-sate the increase in needs. In Spain, unlike in Germany, inequality increases also with the proportion of young adults (16−24 years old). Inequality in Spain, however, is strongly and negatively associated with the proportion of 65-year-old people, a group with higher incidence among intermediate income deciles, consistent with the equalizing effect of old-age and survi-vors' pensions already mentioned. This effect is positive but statistically not significant in Germany (it is, however, positive and significant for the proportion of 55−64 years old). Inequality increases in Spain with a higher presence of recent immigrants, who are over-represented at the bottom of the distribution even after controlling for other characteristics (probably induced by their lower wages, over-education, etc.).[28] Inequality in Spain (but not in Germany) decreases with the proportion of people living in less densely populated areas, what might reflect the fact that the distribution of income in less densely populated areas tends to be more homogenous.[29]

In Spain, there is also a negative relationship between inequality and the proportion of active household members that went beyond primary education − the omitted category. In Germany, the negative educational effect on inequality is only statistically significant in the cases of upper/postsecondary studies.

Regarding labor variables, inequality is reduced in both countries with the proportion of time spent in the labor force. As Fig. 4 shows, the activity rate tends to be increasing with households' income (and decreasing

---

[28]For example, Canal-Domínguez and Rodríguez-Gutiérrez (2008) found a significant unex-plained wage gap between native and immigrants in Spain after controlling for differences in productivity.

[29]In the case of Germany we do find a locational effect in 2008 but not in 2012. This might be associated with the change in the construction of this variable mentioned earlier.

with RIF): in Spain from 68 percent in the third decile to 82 percent in the top one. Inequality is even more intensely reduced with the proportion of months spent as full-time and part-time employees. However, inequality increases in Spain with the proportion of time spent in full-time self-employment.[30] The negative association between employment rates and inequality is higher in the case of full-time employees, although the differential with part-timers is small. To be more precise, an increase in one percentage point in the average full-time (part-time) employment rate, reduces the Gini index in Spain around 0.7 (0.5) percent, while a similar increase in the activity rate produces a smaller decline of 0.2 percent in inequality. The omitted category is the unemployment rate, so what the employment coefficients predict is a decline in inequality, after an increase in employment at the expense of unemployment (while keeping constant the activity rate and the other type of employment among other things) which is a bit larger in the case of a full-time job. While part-time employment has a lower impact on income, it mostly benefits poor and middle incomes (Fig. 4). The effect of an increase in full-time employment on income is much larger, but its impact on inequality is attenuated because it is more likely to benefit relatively higher incomes.

We do not find much evidence of a significant relationship between experience and inequality. The proportion of temporary workers increases inequality in Germany but not in Spain. This lack of association between the share of temporary workers and inequality in Spain might be surprising, as the duality between temporary and permanent contracts has been profusely identified as one of the major weaknesses of the labor market. There is a strong negative correlation between the share of temporary jobs and income and thus a negative correlation with RIF. It is after we control for other characteristics that this effect vanishes. A possible explanation is that temporary jobs are expected to affect inequality mostly through their impact on employment because they imply a rotation of workers between jobs and unemployment during short periods. Thus, this main effect on inequality will be captured by the employment rates, which are controlled for here. Temporary jobs are also highly correlated with

---

[30]Álvarez, Gradín, and Otero (2013) have shown with evidence for 1994–2001 in Spain that self-employment was the only alternative for some people to become employed due to constraints in the labor market. Considering the previous working status, the unemployed were the most likely to become self-employed, while employees were the least likely to do so.

unskilled workers, low-paid occupations, etc., variables also controlled for in the regression.[31]

Inequality is associated with the structure of the economy in Spain more strongly than in Germany. Inequality in Spain increases with the proportion of managers and professionals, or people working in the financial sector, and to decrease with the proportion of technicians and clerks, and people in other services.

Table B2 in the appendix reports the coefficients for the regressions that allow to compare 2008 and 2012 in Spain. They are pretty similar. Among the most salient differences, the positive effect of the proportion of young adults on inequality and the negative effect of tertiary education did not appear in 2008, while the negative association of the proportion of elderly was already present but smaller. In 2008, however, the proportion of women in the household had a positive association with higher inequality that disappeared in 2012. We also observe important changes in the contribution of industries (financial sector and other services) and occupations (technicians and associate professionals, and craft and related trades workers).[32] These trends are likely reflecting the deep changes during the recession such as the larger contribution of elderly's pensions and women's earnings to households' income, the lack of opportunities of the youngest members of the household, or the relative situation of some economic activities.

EMPIRICAL RESULTS: DECOMPOSING THE INTER-COUNTRY INEQUALITY GAP AMONG ACTIVE HOUSEHOLDS

More than three quarters of the Gini differential in income inequality among active households between Spain and Germany in 2012 (0.063 out

---

[31]However, there remains a direct and significant effect on income after controlling for all those other characteristics but not on inequality. In the case of a log-linear regression of household disposable income on the same set of characteristics the coefficient associated with temporary jobs is -0.097 in Spain (-0.126 in Germany) and statistically significant.

[32]In Table A2, we do not distinguish the proportion of months spent as employee or as self-employee because that information is not available in 2008. We use instead the proportion of people in self-employment at the time of the interview. The effect of using this poorer information is that it reduces the absolute magnitude of the coefficients associated with months spent in full- or part-time employment, and increases the contribution of the proportion of temporary contracts, among other effects.

of 0.083) are explained by inter-country differences in average characteristics (Table 5, first two columns). This is the inequality that would be gone if active households in Spain had German average characteristics, while keeping Spanish coefficients, and corresponds with a Gini of 0.295 in Spain. The remaining unexplained effect (that would be gone only after additionally shifting the coefficients) is significant but much smaller: 0.020.

The Detailed Explained or Compositional Effect in 2012

The largest explained effect (0.054, 66 percent of the total Gini gap) is related with differences in the set of labor market variables. The largest contribution (0.055) comes from the low work intensity of Spanish households as the result of the recession (proportion of months spent in activity and employment). More specifically, a small portion of the gap (0.003, 4 percent) is explained by a lower activity rate; the shorter time spent working as employees makes the largest contributions either part-time (0.026, 32 percent) or full-time (0.019, 23 percent). The higher proportion of months spent in full-time self-employment explained another significant 0.006 or 7 percent of the gap. Other job or worker' characteristics, such as type of contract, unit size, experience, or occupation do not help to explain the higher inequality in Spain, however, because these differences valued with Spanish coefficients are small and statistically not significant. We, however, found a negative and significant effect of the industrial mix (e.g., the smaller size of the financial sector) that helps to reduce inequality in Spain as compared with Germany (−0.006, 8 percent).

After the labor market, the lower attained education is the main driving factor of higher inequality in Spain: it explains another 0.012 Gini points differential (14 percent of the gap), while the different degrees of urbanization play only a marginal role (0.004, 5 percent). We will turn back later to the role of education and labor characteristics when we analyze how their impact change across households with different employment rates.

The difference in the demographic composition of households has a net negative contribution of −0.007 (9 percent if the gap). If household size and composition by age in Spain were similar to those in Germany, inequality would increase by about 0.016 Gini points (20 percent of the observed gap). The fact that Spain has larger economically active households and these cohabits with more people above 65 years old, make the largest negative contributions (each factor explaining −0.007, equivalent to 9 percent of the gap). These two demographic effects are, however,

Table 5. RIF Decomposition of the Gini Gap between Spain and
Germany 2012.

		Spain's Counterfactual with German Characteristics (C)		Spain's Counterfactual with German Coefficients (C*)	
Gap		0.083***		0.083***	
		(0.005)		(0.005)	
		Characteristics and Coefficients Effects			
		Characteristics (ES12-C)	Coefficients (C-DE12)	Characteristics (C*-DE12)	Coefficients (ES12-C*)
Total effect		0.063***	0.020**	0.075***	0.007
		(0.006)	(0.007)	(0.010)	(0.012)
Urbanization		0.004**	−0.021**	−0.001	−0.016**
		(0.001)	(0.006)	(0.001)	(0.005)
Demographic		−0.007*	0.029	0.000	0.021
		(0.003)	(0.022)	(0.008)	(0.026)
	Household size	−0.007***	0.015	−0.010***	0.018
		(0.002)	(0.019)	(0.002)	(0.022)
	Age 0−55	−0.001	0.012	−0.001	0.012
		(0.001)	(0.015)	(0.001)	(0.014)
	Aged 65 +	−0.007***	−0.005**	0.002	−0.014**
		(0.001)	(0.002)	(0.003)	(0.005)
	Married	0.000	0.000	0.000	0.000
		(0.000)	(0.009)	(0.000)	(0.009)
	Women	0.000	0.001	0.000	0.001
		(0.000)	(0.010)	(0.000)	(0.010)
	Immigrant	0.008***	0.004	0.008	0.003
		(0.002)	(0.002)	(0.005)	(0.006)
	Health	0.001	0.002	0.001*	0.001
		(0.001)	(0.003)	(0.001)	(0.002)
Labor		0.054***	0.013	0.066***	0.001
		(0.005)	(0.043)	(0.004)	(0.042)
	Employment	0.055***	−0.027	0.050***	−0.023
		(0.004)	(0.037)	(0.006)	(0.033)
	Activity	0.003***	−0.015	0.002*	−0.014
		(0.001)	(0.022)	(0.001)	(0.021)
	FT-E	0.019***	−0.015	0.017***	−0.013
		(0.002)	(0.020)	(0.003)	(0.018)

Table 5.   (*Continued*)

		Characteristics and Coefficients Effects			
		Characteristics (ES12-C)	Coefficients (C-DE12)	Characteristics (C*-DE12)	Coefficients (ES12-C*)
	FT-SE	0.006***	0.002	0.004	0.004
		(0.002)	(0.002)	(0.002)	(0.005)
	PT-E	0.026***	0.000	0.026***	0.000
		(0.003)	(0.008)	(0.004)	(0.003)
	PT-SE	0.000	0.000	0.000	0.000
		(0.001)	(0.001)	(0.000)	(0.001)
	Occupation	0.004	−0.009	0.001	−0.006
		(0.003)	(0.016)	(0.003)	(0.013)
	Industry	−0.006**	0.023*	0.005**	0.011
		(0.002)	(0.011)	(0.002)	(0.010)
	Unit size	0.001	−0.020	0.000	−0.019
		(0.004)	(0.026)	(0.007)	(0.018)
	Contract	0.002	−0.007*	0.008***	−0.013*
		(0.002)	(0.003)	(0.002)	(0.005)
	Experience	0.000	0.055	0.001	0.053
		(0.001)	(0.040)	(0.001)	(0.040)
	Unknown	−0.001	−0.001	0.001	−0.003
		(0.001)	(0.002)	(0.002)	(0.004)
Education		0.012**	0.003	0.011*	0.004
		(0.003)	(0.027)	(0.005)	(0.023)
Intercept			−0.004		−0.004
			(0.057)		(0.057)

Source: Own construction using EU-SILC 2012 (2011 income).

Notes:

− Equivalized household disposable income (OECD-modified scale) among active households (at least one member in the labor force).

− FT = full-time, PT = part-time, E = employee, SE = self-employee.

− Counterfactuals: (C) Spanish coefficients, German characteristics; (C*) Spanish characteristics, German coefficients.

− See "Households' characteristics" section for a description of variables. Average characteristics in Table 2 and regression coefficients in Table 3.

− Standard errors in parentheses; *$p < 0.05$; **$p < 0.01$; ***$p < 0.001$.

partially offset by the positive effect of immigration on the inequality gap, due to a higher proportion of recent immigrants in Spain (0.008; 10 percent of the gap).[33]

On summary, lower working intensity and attained education, and a more recent immigration profile jointly explain almost entirely the observed higher inequality in Spain compared with Germany, although the equalizing role of Spanish extended families makes this gap smaller. One obvious limitation of comparative approaches is to assess how much of this depends on the specific choice of the reference. For that reason, we now extend the analysis to other countries, and we will check as well how much of the nature of inequality in Spain changed during the recession.

Comparison with other Countries

The results when other countries (France, Italy, Sweden, and the United Kingdom) are taken as the reference are reported in Table 6 (mean characteristics and estimated coefficients can be found in Tables B3 and B4). All these countries exhibit lower inequality than Spain, but only Sweden has lower inequality than Germany. The characteristics of households explain to a large extent the higher inequality of Spain, going from only 0.013 Gini points with Italy to 0.047 with Sweden. In relative terms, characteristics account for the entire gap with the United Kingdom, for 71 percent with France, 39 percent with Sweden, and 34 percent with Italy. The results generally point in the same direction to those found when Germany was the reference.

Of these countries, Italy outstands as a particular case. Spain exhibits higher inequality to some extent due to the lower attained education (0.007), a higher recent immigration (0.003), and the occupational mix (0.002), only partially compensated by a higher activity rate (−0.004). Regarding employment rates, there is no overall effect because the positive effect of the shorter time Spanish households spent in full-time employment is compensated by the opposite effect of the lower intensity in full-time self-employment (which increases rather than decreases inequality). Household

---

[33]Lacuesta and Izquierdo (2012), for example, found that increasing immigration between 1995 and 2002 contributed to increase heterogeneity in earnings among men in Spain, consistently with previous results for the United States and Germany.

Table 6. RIF Decomposition of the Gini Gap between Spain and Selected Countries, 2012.

	France		Italy		Sweden		UK	
Gap	0.058***		0.038***		0.122***		0.030***	
	(0.007)		(0.005)		(0.005)		(0.008)	
	Characteristics (ES-C)	Coefficients (C-FR)	Characteristics (ES-C)	Coefficients (C-IT)	Characteristics (ES-C)	Coefficients (C-SE)	Characteristics (ES-C)	Coefficients (C-UK)
Characteristics and Coefficients Effects								
Total effect	0.041***	0.017*	0.013**	0.025***	0.047***	0.074***	0.033***	–003
	(0.005)	(0.008)	(0.005)	(0.006)	(0.008)	(0.009)	(0.006)	(0.009)
Urbanization	0.001*	0.014	0.001	0.006	0.008**	0.004	–0.002*	–0.010
	(0.001)	(0.007)	(0.001)	(0.005)	(0.003)	(0.010)	(0.001)	(0.006)
Demographic	–0.010**	–0.055	0.003	–0.024	–0.020***	–0.011	–0.007*	0.019
	(0.003)	(0.030)	(0.002)	(0.022)	(0.004)	(0.030)	(0.003)	(0.033)
Household size	–0.002**	–0.007	–0.001	0.045*	–0.004***	0.032	–0.003**	0.004
	(0.001)	(0.023)	(0.000)	(0.021)	(0.001)	(0.020)	(0.001)	(0.025)
Age 0–55	–0.007**	0.005	0.000	–0.044**	–0.007**	–0.038	–0.004*	0.021
	(0.002)	(0.024)	(0.001)	(0.015)	(0.003)	(0.022)	(0.002)	(0.023)
Age 65 +	–0.008***	–0.008	0.000	–0.012***	–0.007***	–0.007**	–0.001	–0.009**
	(0.001)	(0.005)	(0.000)	(0.003)	(0.001)	(0.002)	(0.001)	(0.003)
Married	0.000	–0.032*	0.000	–0.014	0.000	0.003	0.000	–0.006
	(0.000)	(0.013)	(0.000)	(0.009)	(0.000)	(0.011)	(0.000)	(0.012)
Women	0.000	–0.014	0.000	–0.011	0.000	–0.002	0.000	0.000
	(0.000)	(0.014)	(0.000)	(0.010)	(0.000)	(0.011)	(0.000)	(0.017)
Immigrant	0.006**	0.000	0.003**	0.007**	–0.001	0.002	0.001	0.006
	(0.002)	(0.004)	(0.001)	(0.002)	(0.002)	(0.004)	(0.002)	(0.005)

Table 6. (*Continued*)

	Characteristics (ES-C)	Coefficients (C-FR)	Characteristics (ES-C)	Coefficients (C-IT)	Characteristics (ES-C)	Coefficients (C-SE)	Characteristics (ES-C)	Coefficients (C-UK)
			Characteristics and Coefficients Effects					
Health	0.000	0.001	0.000	0.006	−0.001	−0.001	0.000	0.002
	(0.000)	(0.004)	(0.001)	(0.003)	(0.001)	(0.001)	(0.000)	(0.003)
Labor	0.041***	−0.093**	0.003	0.074*	0.048***	−0.055	0.036***	−0.015
	(0.004)	(0.034)	(0.003)	(0.036)	(0.007)	(0.036)	(0.005)	(0.041)
Employment	0.040***	−0.089**	−0.003	0.050	0.061***	−0.054	0.044***	−0.054
	(0.003)	(0.033)	(0.003)	(0.027)	(0.004)	(0.034)	(0.004)	(0.043)
Activity	0.003***	0.008	−0.004***	0.016	0.006***	0.015	0.003**	−0.011
	(0.001)	(0.022)	(0.001)	(0.016)	(0.002)	(0.026)	(0.001)	(0.025)
FT-E	0.023***	−0.069***	0.006**	−0.009	0.031***	−0.066***	0.018***	−0.040
	(0.002)	(0.017)	(0.002)	(0.015)	(0.003)	(0.019)	(0.002)	(0.022)
FT-SE	0.002**	−0.010	−0.006***	0.040***	0.005***	0.010***	0.003**	0.013*
	(0.001)	(0.005)	(0.002)	(0.006)	(0.001)	(0.003)	(0.001)	(0.006)
PT-E	0.011***	−0.017**	0.001	0.003	0.018***	−0.012*	0.020***	−0.017*
	(0.002)	(0.006)	(0.001)	(0.003)	(0.002)	(0.006)	(0.002)	(0.008)
PT-SE	0.000	−0.001	0.001	0.000	0.000	−0.001	0.001	0.001
	(0.000)	(0.001)	(0.001)	(0.002)	(0.000)	(0.002)	(0.002)	(0.003)
Occupation	0.000	0.006	0.002*	0.010	−0.010***	0.023	−0.011***	−0.004
	(0.002)	(0.016)	(0.001)	(0.013)	(0.003)	(0.016)	(0.003)	(0.015)
Industry	0.000	0.040	0.000	−0.007	−0.002	−0.005	−0.002	−0.020
	(0.002)	(0.024)	(0.001)	(0.010)	(0.003)	(0.010)	(0.003)	(0.020)
Unit size	0.000	−0.048**	0.002	−0.007	−0.003	−0.010	0.001	0.034
	(0.002)	(0.018)	(0.002)	(0.014)	(0.002)	(0.012)	(0.003)	(0.022)

Contract	0.002	−0.003	0.002	−0.004	0.003	−0.005**	0.003	−0.001
	(0.002)	(0.003)	(0.002)	(0.002)	(0.002)	(0.002)	(0.003)	(0.002)
Experience	–	–	0.000	0.034	–	–	0.000	0.035
	–	–	(0.000)	(0.035)	–	–	(0.000)	(0.036)
Unknown	−0.001	0.001	−0.001	−0.002	0.000	−0.004	−0.001	−0.006**
	(0.001)	(0.002)	(0.001)	(0.002)	(0.000)	(0.003)	(0.001)	(0.002)
Education	0.009**	−0.116***	0.007**	−0.038*	0.011**	−0.046	0.007**	−0.051*
	(0.003)	(0.032)	(0.002)	(0.017)	(0.003)	(0.032)	(0.002)	(0.021)
Intercept		0.267***		0.006		0.182**		0.054
		(0.063)		(0.049)		(0.053)		(0.063)

Source: Own construction using EU-SILC 2012 (2011 income).

Notes:

– Equivalized household disposable income (OECD-modified scale) among active households (at least one member in the labor force).

– FT = full-time, PT = part-time, E = employee, SE = self-employee.

– Counterfactual (C): Spanish coefficients, other country characteristics. See "Households' characteristics" section for a description of variables. Average characteristics in Table 3 and regression coefficients in Table 4.

– Standard errors in parentheses; *$p < 0.05$; **$p < 0.01$; ***$p < 0.001$.

size and composition by age are pretty similar in both Mediterranean countries and play no role in explaining differences in inequality.

The results in the other cases are more similar to those found in the case
of Germany. Lower activity and employment rates in Spain explain the gap
to a large extent, while the size and composition of Spanish households
tend to attenuate that differential. The main difference among these countries is the role of part- and full-time jobs. The effect of time spent in part-
time jobs is largest in the comparison with the United Kingdom (0.020)
and smallest with France (0.011), while the effect of full-time jobs is largest
with Sweden (0.031) and smallest with the United Kingdom (0.018). The
higher recent immigration is only relevant in the comparison with France
(0.006). Among the other labor variables, the only relevant effect is that the
occupational mix tends to reduce inequality in Spain as compared with the
United Kingdom and Sweden.

The contribution of lower attained education in Spain on inequality is
always large, varying between 0.007 (the United Kingdom) and 0.011
(Sweden). On the other hand, the overall effect of the size and age composition of households when the reference is France (−0.017) or Sweden
(−0.019) is similar to the case of Germany (−0.016), but it is substantially
smaller for the United Kingdom (−0.008). However, the role of each factor
varies. While the effect of the differential in households' size is smaller in
these countries than in the comparison with Germany, the importance of
the proportion of children is much larger in the comparison with France
(−0.004) and with Sweden (−0.006), because these countries have higher
fertility rates.

The Recession and the Explained Effect

Our next step is to ask how much of the nature of inequality in Spain changed between 2008 and 2012. This allows to separate more permanent factors from those strongly associated with the recession. For that, we first
obtain the decomposition for the inter-country gap between Spain and
Germany in 2008 in Table 7 (first two columns). The gap was much smaller
(0.014) and entirely associated with the lower activity and part-time
employment rates in Spain, and the higher level of self-employment. These
effects were only partially compensated by the higher full-time employment
rates. The occupational distribution and the size of working units contributed to reduce the gap in 2008, effects that vanished during the recession
after the asymmetric destruction of jobs. On the other hand, the role of

Table 7. RIF Decomposition of the Gini Gap between Spain and Germany 2008 and Over Time.

	Spain-Germany 2008			Spain 2012–2008			
	Spain's Counterfactual with German Characteristics (C)			2012 Counterfactual with 2008 Characteristics (C⁺)		2012 Counterfactual with 2008 Coefficients (C')	
Gap	0.014* (0.006)			0.043*** (0.005)		0.043*** (0.005)	
	Characteristics and Coefficients Effects						
	Characteristics (ES08-C)	Coefficients (C-DE08)	Characteristics (ES12-C⁺)	Coefficients (C⁺-ES08)	Characteristics (C*-ES08)	Coefficients (ES12-C*)
Total effect	0.013*	0.002	0.022***	0.021***	0.037***	0.006
	(0.006)	(0.008)	(0.004)	(0.006)	(0.006)	(0.008)
Urbanization	0.001	-0.002	0.000	-0.001	0.000	-0.001
	(0.001)	(0.006)	(0.000)	(0.005)	(0.000)	(0.005)
Demographic	-0.008**	0.075**	0.003	-0.041	0.003**	-0.042
	(0.003)	(0.027)	(0.002)	(0.026)	(0.001)	(0.025)
Household size	-0.007**	0.056**	0.003**	-0.012	0.002**	-0.012
	(0.002)	(0.019)	(0.001)	(0.020)	(0.001)	(0.019)
Age 0–55	-0.002	0.008	0.000	0.007	0.001	0.006
	(0.001)	(0.019)	(0.001)	(0.017)	(0.001)	(0.017)
Aged 65+	-0.005***	-0.006**	0.000	-0.003	0.000	-0.003
	(0.001)	(0.002)	(0.000)	(0.003)	(0.000)	(0.003)
Married	0.000	-0.006	0.000	-0.016	0.000	-0.016
	(0.000)	(0.011)	(0.000)	(0.010)	(0.000)	(0.010)
Women	0.000	0.021	0.000	-0.023*	0.000	-0.023*
	(0.000)	(0.012)	(0.000)	(0.011)	(0.000)	(0.011)

Table 7. (Continued)

	Characteristics (ES08-C)	Coefficients (C-DE08)	Characteristics (ES12-C⁺)	Coefficients (C⁺-ES08)	Characteristics (C*-ES08)	Coefficients (ES12-C*)
Immigrant	0.005***	−0.001	0.000	0.006*	0.000	0.006*
	(0.001)	(0.001)	(0.001)	(0.003)	(0.000)	(0.003)
Health	0.001	0.002	0.000	0.000	0.000	0.000
	(0.001)	(0.004)	(0.000)	(0.003)	(0.000)	(0.003)
Labor	0.012*	−0.072	0.022***	0.062	0.034***	0.049
	(0.006)	(0.042)	(0.004)	(0.037)	(0.005)	(0.037)
Employment	0.022***	−0.133***	0.019***	0.094**	0.027***	0.086**
	(0.003)	(0.034)	(0.003)	(0.031)	(0.003)	(0.028)
Activity	0.004***	−0.064**	−0.001**	0.023	−0.002**	0.023
	(0.001)	(0.024)	(0.000)	(0.017)	(0.001)	(0.018)
Full-time	−0.027***	−0.034*	0.025***	0.047*	0.034***	0.038*
	(0.003)	(0.019)	(0.003)	(0.023)	(0.003)	(0.019)
Part-time	0.032***	−0.020**	−0.001	0.010**	−0.002	0.011**
	(0.003)	(0.007)	(0.001)	(0.003)	(0.001)	(0.003)
Self-empl.	0.013***	−0.015**	−0.004**	0.015**	−0.003**	0.014**
	(0.002)	(0.005)	(0.002)	(0.005)	(0.001)	(0.004)
Occupation	−0.007*	0.021	0.001	0.000	0.000	0.001
	(0.004)	(0.018)	(0.001)	(0.011)	(0.001)	(0.012)
Industry	0.000	0.026	0.002	−0.011	−0.001	−0.009
	(0.002)	(0.016)	(0.002)	(0.011)	(0.001)	(0.010)
Unit size	−0.007*	0.016	0.004*	−0.034*	−0.001	−0.029*
	(0.003)	(0.024)	(0.002)	(0.014)	(0.001)	(0.012)

Contract	0.005*	0.000	0.000	0.003	0.000	0.003
	(0.002)	(0.001)	(0.000)	(0.004)	(0.000)	(0.004)
Experience	0.001	−0.005	0.000	0.013	0.000	0.013
	(0.001)	(0.034)	(0.001)	(0.030)	(0.001)	(0.030)
Unknown	−0.001	0.001	−0.003	−0.003*	0.009*	−0.015*
	(0.000)	(0.002)	(0.002)	(0.001)	(0.004)	(0.006)
Education	0.008*	0.020	−0.002**	−0.019	−0.001	−0.020
	(0.004)	(0.042)	(0.001)	(0.012)	(0.001)	(0.013)
Intercept	−0.019			0.020		0.020
	(0.064)			(0.050)		(0.050)

Source: Own construction using EU-SILC 2012 (2011 income).

Notes:

– Equivalized household disposable income (OECD-modified scale) among active households (at least one member in the labor force).

– Counterfactuals: (C) Spanish coefficients, German characteristics; (C^{+}) Spanish 2012 coefficients, Spanish 2008 characteristics.

– See "Households' characteristics" section for a description of variables. Average characteristics in Table 2 and regression coefficients in Table 3.

– Standard errors in parentheses; $^{*}p < 0.05$; $^{**}p < 0.01$; $^{***}p < 0.001$.

education increased between 2008 and 2012, while the effect of the demographic factors remained at a similar level.

Table 7 (two columns in the middle) also reports the results when we compare inequality in Spain in 2008 and in 2012 (the counterfactual has 2008 characteristics and 2012 coefficients). Our results identify the fall in employment as the main responsible factor for the rise in inequality over time. Of the total increase in inequality between 2008 and 2012, near 60 percent (0.025) is associated with the reduction in the time households spent in full-time jobs, with an additional effect (0.004) associated with the larger loss of jobs in bigger working units. These effects were only partially offset by the opposite effect of the increases in the activity rate and time spent in part-time jobs, as well as the decrease in the importance of self-employment (summing up −0.006). The reduction in the average size of households (likely following a long-term demographic trend) accounted for a small 6 percent (0.012) of increase in inequality. We do not find evidence of the change in the composition of jobs by sector or occupation to have affected inequality of households' disposable income in Spain during the recession, contrary to what was found in the (individual) earnings inequality literature using other data sources for earlier years.[34]

The Detailed Unexplained Effects

An inspection of the coefficients effects in Table 5 (second column) highlights the fact that the different impact of household characteristics on inequality in Spain and Germany in 2012 (valued at the average characteristics in Germany) is also playing a role, but with some counterbalancing effects. We need to take these effects with caution given that they suffer from well-known identification problems. By main dimensions, the only significant effect is that of location, −0.021, because the less densely populated areas contribute to reduce inequality in Spain, but not in Germany as was previously discussed. The overall effects of labor and education are

---

[34]If with our EU-SILC data, we undertake the decomposition analysis for the 2008−2012 increase (0.015) in the Gini of individual gross earnings (conditional on individual characteristics) for people employed all 12 months during the reference period, we only find evidence of a small reduction in inequality associated with the smaller proportion of temporary workers (−0.002), and an increase in inequality (0.005) due to the higher proportion of part-timers. We still do not find any effect of the change in occupation or industry unlike other studies using alternative datasets.

positive and large but statistically not significant, indicating a high degree of heterogeneity.

At the more detailed level of disaggregation, we observe some statistically significant effects. In the labor market, the more disequalizing effect of temporary workers in Germany, would produce, if brought to Spain, an increase in inequality (the contribution has a negative sign) of 0.007 (about 8 percent of the gap). On the other hand, the effects associated with industry composition of the labor force helps to explain a substantial gap of 0.023. Among the demographic factors, we also find that, as expected, the gap in inequality would be a 6 percent larger (0.005) if we import the effect of the share of elderly people in active households (which attenuates inequality in Spain but not in Germany), a similar effect is found in 2008.

Comparing the situation in Spain in 2008 and 2012, we find that most aggregate coefficient effects are poorly significant. Only at the most detailed level we find statistically significant negative changes, characteristics associated with a more (less) equalizing (disequalizing) effect in 2012, for tertiary education, large working units, or the percentage of women. The opposite is found for employment, which was less effective in 2012 to lower inequality, and immigration, which increased its disequalizing effect.

Regarding the comparison with other countries, the overall coefficients effects were also found to be positive and statistically significant in the cases of France (0.017), Italy (0.025), and, especially, Sweden (0.074), but barely zero in the case of the United Kingdom, indicating that the distribution of the relevant characteristics and local institutions also matter for explaining the higher level of inequality in Spain. However, the presence of large fixed effects of the intercept in the cases of France and Sweden makes it difficult to identify what factors might be behind this. The large and positive effects of (full-time) self-employment (except with France) indicate that these type of jobs are strongly associated with higher inequality in Spain but not in these countries. The negative effects of part-time jobs (except for Italy) indicate that they reduced inequality more intensely in Spain. In all cases (except with France), we find a negative and significant coefficients effect associated with the proportion of elderly in the household, which reinforces the strong equalizing effect of pensioners cohabiting in active households in Spain.

Households Heterogeneity in Employment Rates

Working intensity of active households is quite heterogeneous, going from households fully employed during the reference year (making up 56 and 87 percent of the target population in Spain and Germany), to households fully deprived from employment (9 and 5 percent, respectively).[35] In order to better assess the importance of the factors determining inequality we now evaluate how much the relevance of each factor changes in explaining inequality within economically active households when starting with the subsample of those in households with the maximum employment rate equal to 1 (implying 12 months worked in any type of job) we sequentially lower this limit to > 0.75, > 0.5, > 0.25, > 0, and ≥ 0 (the case previously analyzed). Results are reported in Table 8.

The results show the increasing importance of the full-time employment effects that raise the inter-country inequality gap as we sequentially include households with lower employment rates. They also show that the lower proportion of time spent in part-time jobs in Spain (compared with Germany) reduces inequality among highly employed households (because the alternative of full-time jobs is more effective in reducing inequality). However, it contributes to explain higher inequality in Spain as we include households with low employment rates (as part-time jobs reduce inequality when the alternative is unemployment). At the same time, the importance of self-employment (and to a much lower extent the size of working units) in explaining higher inequality in Spain decreases as we include households with lower employment rates.

Particularly interesting is to note that education and industry increase their relevance (with a positive and negative effect, respectively) as we reduce the working intensity threshold. We do not find a significant effect of education to explain higher inequality among yearly employed households in Spain. This is in line with previous results in the earnings inequality literature that have shown that the educational premium declined in Spain before the recession, unlike in other countries. Felgueroso, Hidalgo-Pérez, and Jiménez-Martín (2016) associated this trend with a large level of over-education and to the extraordinary share of tourism and the construction sector in the Spanish economy. However, we find that the effect of education becomes more important to explain the inter-country inequality gap as we include people in households with lower or none employment. The same trend (but with the opposite sign) can be found with the industrial composition that prevents the gap in inequality to be even higher in Spain, mostly due to the lower proportion of workers in the financial

---

[35]Gradín et al. (2015a) provide an extensive analysis of patterns of employment deprivation of households across the EU at the beginning of the recession.

Table 8. Characteristics Effects in the Gini Gap between Spain and Germany for Different Employment Rates, 2012.

	Household Employment Rate					
	= 1	> 0.75	> 0.50	> 0.25	> 0	≥ 0 (All)
Gap	0.053***	0.056***	0.056***	0.069***	0.075***	0.083***
Total explained effect	0.041***	0.038***	0.038***	0.048***	0.054***	0.063***
Urbanization	0.005**	0.006***	0.005**	0.004**	0.005***	0.004**
Demographic	−0.009*	−0.008*	−0.008*	−0.005	−0.006	−0.007*
Household size	−0.008***	−0.006**	−0.007***	−0.008***	−0.008***	−0.007***
Age 0–55	−0.002	−0.003	−0.002	−0.002	−0.002	−0.001
Age 65 +	−0.007***	−0.006***	−0.005***	−0.005***	−0.005***	−0.007***
Married	0.000	0.000	0.000	0.000	0.000	0.000
Women	0.000	0.000	0.000	0.000	0.000	0.000
Immigrant	0.008***	0.007***	0.007***	0.008***	0.008***	0.008***
Health	0.000	0.000	0.000	0.001	0.001	0.001
Labor	0.042***	0.037***	0.036***	0.041***	0.047***	0.054***
Employment	0.030***	0.027***	0.028***	0.037***	0.045***	0.055***
Activity	0.008***	0.007***	0.005***	0.003***	0.003***	0.003***
FT-E	(omitted)	0.001	−0.001	0.008***	0.012***	0.019***
FT-SE	0.033***	0.034**	0.019***	0.012***	0.009***	0.006***
PT-E	−0.010***	−0.013	0.006	0.015***	0.021***	0.026***
PT-SE	−0.001*	−0.002	−0.001	0.000	0.000	0.000

Table 8. (*Continued*)

			Household Employment Rate			
	= 1	>0.75	>0.50	>0.25	>0	≥0 (All)
Occupation	0.005	0.004	0.004	0.002	0.003	0.004
Industry	0.001	-0.001	-0.001	0.004	-0.005*	-0.006**
Unit size	0.004	0.004	0.002	0.003	0.001	0.001
Contract	0.001	0.001	0.002	0.002	0.002	0.002
Experience	0.000	0.000	0.000	0.000	0.000	0.000
Unknown	0.000	0.000	0.001	0.000	0.001	-0.001
Education	0.004	0.003	0.005	0.009*	0.009**	0.012**

Source: Own construction using EU-SILC 2012 (2011 income).

Notes:

– Household employment rate is the proportion of months worked by active household members during the reference year (out of their potential).

– Equivalized household disposable income (OECD-modified scale) among active households (at least one member in the labor force).

– FT = full-time, PT = part-time, E = employee, SE = self-employee.

– Counterfactual (C): Spanish coefficients, other country characteristics. See "Households' characteristics" section for a description of variables. Average characteristics in Table 3 and regression coefficients in Table 4.

– Significance: *$p < 0.05$; **$p < 0.01$; ***$p < 0.001$.

sector. The change in the importance of these two variables is reflecting that they probably affect between-group inequality for households with very low employment rates and the rest, rather than within-group inequality among those actually employed.[36] The importance of other labor variables such as experience, unit size, or contract type remains very low at all employment rates. The impact of occupation is a bit larger at the extremes but poorly significant.[37]

Using an Alternative Counterfactual

Finally, we address the question of robustness with the choice of the counterfactual in the comparison with Germany. Would these results be different if we had chosen instead a counterfactual in which Spanish households in 2012 were given German coefficients while keeping their own average characteristics? The corresponding coefficients effect (comparing the original Spanish distribution and the counterfactual) is even smaller (0.007) and statistically not significant (Table 5, last two columns). Thus, bringing to Spain the German association between characteristics and inequality, but maintaining the distribution of characteristics would not reduce any inequality at all. All the reduction in inequality would be produced going from this counterfactual to the German distribution of income (0.075, 91 percent of the gap), confirming the importance of the characteristics effect regardless of whether this is valued with Spanish or with German coefficients.

The detailed characteristics effects show that the main contribution is, again, associated with the shortage in employment, especially part-time, and to a much lower extent the industrial structure (0.005). An important novelty of using German coefficients is the significant contribution of the higher proportion of temporary workers in Spain. In the case of

---

[36]They could also affect the degree of overlapping of both groups over incomes. When population groups overlap over the space of incomes, the overall Gini index can be written as the sum of the between-group Gini and the weighted sum of the product of each within-group Gini and an index of overlapping with the other groups (Gradín, 2000).

[37]Similarly, if we decompose the increase in inequality between 2008 and 2012 in Spain for households employed all the year around, we only find a small increase in inequality (0.010), and the only significant explained effects are those associated with the decline in households' size (increasing inequality by 0.004) and the smaller proportion of temporary workers (reducing inequality by 0.002). These results are consistent with the earnings inequality decomposition explained earlier in footnote 34.

demographic variables, the contribution is larger for household size (−0.010) but smaller and not significant for age composition and immigration. This is because German coefficients show a smaller equalizing effect of the share of elderly people, a larger equalizing effect of household size, and less disequalizing effect of recent immigration. The contribution of education would be still positive and significant (0.011). Regarding the coefficients effect (now valued using Spanish characteristics) we would still find negative and significant values for degree of urbanization, elderly population, and temporary contract.

Similarly, if we compare Spain in 2012 and 2008, but using as the counterfactual the distribution that keeps the 2008 coefficients and 2012 characteristics (Table 7, last two columns), the characteristics effect is larger, 0.037 (86 percent of the increase in inequality over time), with most accounted by the fall in full-time employment (0.034), again only partially compensated by the increases in activity, part-time and the fall in self-employment like in our previous results.

CONCLUDING REMARKS

In this paper, we have investigated the reasons explaining why inequality in Spain is higher than in other EU countries, and why it has sharply increased in recent years. Using a comparative approach, we have analyzed the role of earnings and the tax-benefit model, as well as that of the composition of households by characteristics. We show that the high level of inequality in Spain in 2012 was the result of a combination of circumstantial factors, especially the low level of employment after the recession, and factors already present before the recession, such as the low level of education, the recent immigration profile, or the weakness of the redistributive effect of taxes and family or housing benefits. We have also shown that other factors help to lower the level of inequality. That is the case of the higher prevalence of extended households, or the increase in unemployment benefits during the recession. The structure of employment by occupation or industry (with an underrepresentation of high-skilled jobs, or jobs in the financial sector) seems also to help to reduce rather than increase income inequality.

An important lesson from all these results is that there are three main sources through which inequality could be reduced in Spain. The main way is by increasing the level of employment. Our results suggest that increasing part-time employment may have a significant impact on reducing inequality, provided it is the alternative to unemployment or inactivity, and provided it keeps its current distributional pattern. Increasing full-time employment, especially at the bottom of the distribution where it is currently scarce, is likely to have a much larger effect, however.

A second way to push inequality down is by increasing the level of education. This necessarily calls for a reduction of the large drop-out rates in secondary education and the recycling of those who abandoned the educational system to work during the housing bubble. The huge youth unemployment rates imply that a large part of the Spanish labor force is neither in education nor accumulating experience, while students in tertiary education face increasing costs with fewer scholarships. After a long debate about the convenience of the intense immigration flows, the country has witnessed a sudden flow of outmigration with especial incidence among young people with higher education.

Finally, inequality can be reduced through a more redistributive tax-benefit system. Most social benefits are devoted to unemployment and very few to child or housing support in comparison to Germany and other EU countries. The current equalizing effect of social benefits in Spain is strongly linked to the low employment levels and the extension of unemployment benefits. A reduction in unemployment if the economy returns to a normal situation would then be accompanied by a reduction in social protection and its equalizing effect. Direct taxes, although nominally very progressive, are full of loopholes and face large evasion levels, reducing its effectiveness in reducing inequality.

ACKNOWLEDGMENTS

I would like to thank two anonymous reviewers for their helpful comments and to acknowledge the financial support from the Spanish *Ministerio de Economía y Competitividad* (ECO2013-46516-C4-2-R) and *Xunta de Galicia* (GRC2015/014 and AGRUP2015/08).

REFERENCES

Addabbo, T., Rodríguez-Modroño, P., & Gálvez-Muñoz, L. (2013). *Gender and the great recession: Changes in labour supply in Spain*. DEMB Working Paper Series 10. Dipartimento di Economia Marco Biagi, University of Modena.

Álvarez, G., Gradín, C., & Otero, M. S. (2013). Self-employment in Spain: Transition and earnings differential. *Revista de Economía Aplicada, 62*(21), 61−69.

Arranz, J. M., & García-Serrano, C. (2012). Diferencias salariales, característicasdel puesto de trabajo y cualificación: un análisis para el periodo 2005-2010. *Presupuesto y Gasto Público, 67*(2), 195−212.

Arranz, J. M., & García-Serrano, C. (2014). How green was my valley. *International Journal of Manpower*, *35*(7), 1059–1087.

Ayala, L. (2014). *Desigualdad y pobreza en España en el largo plazo, la continuidad de un modelo*. Documento de Trabajo 2.1, VII Informe sobre Exclusión y Desarrollo en España 2014, Fundación FOESSA, Madrid.

Ayala, L., Martínez, R., & Ruiz-Huerta, J. (2013). *Desigualdad y redistribución en los países de la OCDE*. 1er Informe sobe la Desigualdad en España, Fundación Alternativas, Madrid, pp. 25–74.

Becchetti, L., Massari, R., & Naticchioni, P. (2014). The drivers of happiness inequality. Suggestions for promoting social cohesion. *Oxford Economic Papers*, *66*, 419–442.

Blinder, A. S. (1973). Wage discrimination: Reduced form and structural estimates. *Journal of Human Resources*, *8*(4), 436–455.

Bonhomme, S., & Hospido, L. (2013a). The cycle of earnings inequality: Evidence from Spanish social security data. Paper presented at 13th IZA/SOLE Transatlantic Meeting of Labor Economists, Inning/Buch, Germany.

Bonhomme, S., & Hospido, L. (2013b). Earnings inequality in Spain: New evidence using tax data. *Applied Economics*, *45*(30), 4212–4225.

Bredtmann, J., Otten, S., & Rulff, C. (2014). *Husband's unemployment and wife's labor supply – The added worker effect across Europe*. Economics Working Papers 13. Department of Economics and Business, Aarhus University.

Brenke, K., Rinne, U., & Zimmermann, K. (2013). Short-time work: The German answer to the great recession. *International Labour Review*, *152*(2), 287–305.

Canal-Domínguez, J. F., & Rodríguez-Gutiérrez, C. (2008). Analysis of wage differences between native and immigrant workers in Spain. *Spanish Economic Review*, *10*, 109–134.

Cantó, O. (2014). *La contribución de las prestaciones sociales a la redistribución*. Documento de Trabajo 2.7, VII Informe sobre Exclusión y Desarrollo en España 2014. Fundación FOESSA, Madrid.

Cantó, O., Gradín, C., & Del Río, C. (2000). *La situación de los estudios sobre pobreza y desigualdad en España*. Cuadernos de Gobierno y Administración, 2, Pobreza y Desigualdad en España: Enfoques, fuentes y acción pública, pp. 25–94.

Casado, J. M., & Simón, H. (2013). La evolución de la estructura salarial en España (2002-2010). Paper presented at Jornadas de Economía Laboral, Universidad Autónoma de Madrid, Madrid.

Chen, C.-N., Tsaur, T. W., & Rhai, T. S. (1982). The Gini coefficient and negative income. *Oxford Economic Papers*, *34*(3), 473–478.

Cowell, F. A., & Flachaire, E. (2007). Income distribution and inequality measurement: The problem of extreme values. *Journal of Econometrics*, *141*, 1044–1072.

Cowell, F. A., & Victoria-Feser, M. P. (1996). Robustness properties of inequality measures: The influence function and the principle of transfers. *Economica*, *64*, 77–101.

Davia, M. A. (2013). *Mercado de trabajo y desigualdad*. 1er Informe sobe la desigualdad en España, Fundación Alternativas, Madrid, pp. 75–133.

Dolado, J. J., García-Serrano, C., & Jimeno, J. F. (2002). Drawing lessons from the boom of temporary jobs in Spain. *The Economic Journal*, *112*(480), F270–F295.

Dustmann, C., Fitzenberger, B., Schönberg, U., & Spitz-Oener, A. (2014). From sick man of Europe to economic superstar: Germany's resurgent economy. *Journal of Economic Perspectives*, *28*(1), 7–188.

Essama-Nssah, B., & Lambert, P. J. (2012). Influence functions for policy impact analysis. In J. A. Bishop & R. Salas (Eds.), *Inequality, mobility and segregation: Essays in honor of Jacques Silber* (Vol. 20, pp. 135–159). Research on Economic Inequality. Bingley, UK: Emerald Group Publishing Limited.

European Commission. (2010). *Employment in Europe.* Employment, Social Affairs and Inclusion, Report, 2010.

Felgueroso, F., Hidalgo-Pérez, M., & Jiménez-Martín, S. (2016). The puzzling fall of the wage skill premium in Spain. *The Manchester School, 84*(3), 390–435.

Ferreira, F. H. G., Firpo, S. P., & Messina, J. (2014). *A more level playing field? Explaining the decline in earnings inequality in Brazil, 1995–2012.* IRIBA Working Paper 12.

Ferrer-i-Carbonell, A., Ramos, X., & Oviedo, M. (2014). Spain: What can we learn from past decreasing inequalities? In B. Nolan, W. Salverda, D. Checchi, I. Marx, A. McKnight, I. György Tóth, & H. G. van de Werfhorst (Eds.), *Changing inequalities and societal impacts in thirty rich countries* (Vol. 2, pp. 616–640). Oxford: Oxford University Press.

Fields, G. S. (2003). Accounting for income inequality and its change: A new method with application to U.S. earnings inequality. In S. W. Polacheck (Ed.), *Research in labor economics, 22: Worker well-being and public policy* (pp. 1–38). Oxford: JAI.

Firpo, S., Fortin, N. M., & Lemieux, T. (2007). *Decomposing Wage Distributions Using Recentered Influence Function Regressions.* Unpublished Manuscript, University of British Columbia.

Firpo, S., Fortin, N. M., & Lemieux, T. (2009). Unconditional quantile regressions. *Econometrica, 77,* 953–973.

Fortin, N. M., Lemieux, T., & Firpo, S. (2011a). Decomposition methods in economics. In O. Ashenfelter & D. Card (Eds.), *Handbook of labor economics* (Vol. 4, pp. 1–102). North Holland, Amsterdam: Elsevier.

Fortin, N. M., Lemieux, T., & Firpo, S. (2011b). *Occupational tasks and changes in the wage structure.* IZA discussion paper 5542. IZA, Bonn.

Frick, J. R., & Krell, K. (2010). *Measuring income in household panel surveys for Germany: A comparison of EU-SILC and SOEP.* SOEP papers on Multidisciplinary Panel Data Research, 265. The German Socio-Economic Panel Study at DIW Berlin.

García-Serrano, C., & Arranz, J. M. (2013). Crisis económica y desigualdad salarial. *Papeles de economía española, 135,* 68–82.

García-Serrano, C., & Arranz, J. M. (2014). *Evolución de la desigualdad salarial en los paisesdesarrollados y en España en los últimos treintaaños,* Documento de Trabajo 2.5, VII Informe sobre Exclusión y Desarrollo en España2014, Fundación FOESSA, Madrid.

Gâteaux, R. (1913). Sur les fonctionnelles continues et les fonctionnelles analytiques. *CRAS, 157,* 325–327.

Gradín, C. (2000). Polarization by sub-populations in Spain, 1973–91. *Review of Income and Wealth, 46*(4), 457–474.

Gradín, C., Cantó, O., & Del Río, C. (2015a). Measuring employment deprivation in the EU using a household-level index. *Review of Economics of the Household,* forthcoming. Accessed online from May 3, 2014. doi:10.1007/s11150-014-9248-7

Gradín, C., Cantó, O., & Del Río, C. (2015b). Unemployment and spell duration during the great recession in the EU. *International Journal of Manpower, 36*(2), 216–235.

Gradín, C., & Del Río, C. (2013). *El desempleo de inmigrantes, mujeres y jóvenes.* 1er Informe sobe la Desigualdad en España, Fundación Alternativas, Madrid, pp. 135–191.

Groisman, F. (2014). Empleo, salarios y desigualdad en Argentina: Análisis de los determinantes distributivos. *Revista Problemas del Desarrollo, 177*(45), 59–86.

Hampel, F. R. (1974). The influence curve and its role in robust estimation. *Journal of the American Statistical Association, 60*, 383–393.

ILO. (2015). *ILO global wage report 2014/15, wages and income inequality.* Geneva: International Labor Organization.

Juhn, C., Murphy, K. M., & Pierce, B. (1993). Wage inequality and the rise in returns to skill. *Journal of Political Economy, 101*(3), 410–442.

Lacuesta, A., & Izquierdo, M. (2012). The contribution of changes in employment composition and relative returns to the evolution of wage inequality: The case of Spain. *Journal of Population Economics, 25*(2), 511–543.

Monti, A. C. (1991). The study of the Gini concentration ratio by means of the influence function. *Statistica, 51*(4), 561–577.

Morduch, J., & Sicular, T. (2002). Rethinking inequality decomposition, with evidence from rural China. *The Economic Journal, 112*, 93–106.

Oaxaca, R. L. (1973). Male-female wage differentials in urban labor markets. *International Economic Review, 14*(3), 693–709.

Oaxaca, R. L., & Ransom, M. R. (1999). Identification in detailed wage decompositions. *Review of Economics and Statistics, 81*, 154–157.

OECD. (2008). *Growing unequal? Income distribution and poverty in OECD countries.* Paris: OECD.

OECD. (2010). *Employment outlook 2010: Moving beyond the jobs crisis.* Paris: OECD.

OECD. (2011). *Divided we stand, why inequality keeps rising?* Paris: OECD.

Rehm, M., Schmid, K. D., & Wang, D. (2014). *Why has inequality in Germany not risen further after 2005?* SOEP papers on Multidisciplinary Panel Data Research, 690. The German Socio-Economic Panel Study at DIW Berlin.

Ruiz-Huerta, J. (2014). ¿*Afectan los impuestos a la distribución de la renta?* Documento de Trabajo 2.6, VII Informe sobre Exclusión y Desarrollo en España 2014. Fundación FOESSA, Madrid.

Shorrocks, A. F. (1982). Inequality decomposition by factor components. *Econometrica, 50*(1), 193–211.

Shorrocks, A. (2007). Decomposition procedures for distributional analysis: A unified framework based on the Shapley value. *The Journal of Economic Inequality, 11*(1), 99–126.

Starr, M. A. (2014). Gender, added-worker effects, and the 2007–2009 recession: Looking within the household. *Review of Economics of the Household, 12*, 209–235.

Torregrosa-Hetland, S. (2016). Sticky income inequality in the Spanish transition (1973–1990). *Revista de Historia Económica. [Journal of Iberian and Latin American Economic History], 34*(1), 39–80. doi:10.1017/S0212610915000208

Wan, G. (2002). *Regression-based inequality decomposition: Pitfalls and a solution procedure.* World Institute for Development Economics Research Discussion Paper No. 2002/101, Helsinki.

Yun, M. S. (2005). A simple solution to the identification problem in detailed wage decompositions. *Economic Inquiry, 43*, 766–772.

Yun, M. S. (2006). Earnings inequality in USA, 1969–99: Comparing inequality using earnings equations. *Review of Income and Wealth, 52*(1), 127–144.

Yun, M. S. (2008). Identification problem and detailed Oaxaca decomposition: A general solution and inference. *Journal of Economic and Social Measurement, 33*(1), 27–38.

APPENDIX A: THE (RECENTERED) INFLUENCE
FUNCTION OF GINI

Let F be the cumulative distribution of income y, with mean μ and Gini index $G(F)$. For $0 < \varepsilon < 1$, $T = (1 - \varepsilon)F + \varepsilon\delta_y$ is the mixture distribution[38] obtained by the contamination of F in y, where δ_y is the cumulative distribution function for a probability measure which gives mass 1 to income y. Then, the influence function of the Gini index, IF(y; G), first obtained by Monti (1991), is the directional derivative of $G(T)$ with respect to ε at $\varepsilon = 0$, has zero expectation, and can be represented as follows (Essama-Nssah & Lambert, 2012):

$$\text{IF}(y, G) = \frac{d}{\varepsilon} G(T)\Big|_{\varepsilon=0} = \lim_{\varepsilon \to 0} \frac{G(T) - G(F)}{\varepsilon} = 1 - \frac{\mu + y}{\mu}G - \frac{y}{\mu} + \frac{2}{\mu}\int_0^y F(x)\,dx$$

(A.1)

Integrating by parts, $\frac{1}{\mu}\int_0^y F(x)dx = \frac{y}{\mu}F(y) - L_{F(y)}$, where $L_{F(y)}$ is the Lorenz curve at $F(y)$:

$$\text{IF}(y, G) = 2\frac{y}{\mu}\left[F(y) - \frac{1+G}{2}\right] + 2\left[\frac{1-G}{2} - L_{F(y)}\right]$$

(A.2)

As Monti (1991) mentioned, the variability in IF(y, G) increases with the distance between the abscissa (F) and ordinate (L) of the Lorenz curve from their corresponding weighted averages, that is, the areas above and below the Lorenz curve: $1 + G/2$ and $1 - G/2$. The first term is unbounded because it is increased by the factor y/μ, while the second one is bounded between $G - 1$ and $1 + G$. These two terms cancel out each other in the case of perfect equality.

The recentered influence function, RIF(y; G), is just obtained by adding G to IF(y; G), so that its expected value $E(\text{RIF}(y, G)) = G$:

---

[38]The mixture distribution attaches a probability $1 - \varepsilon$ of y being generated by the distribution F and ε of being generated instead by δ_y.

$$\text{RIF}(y, G) = \text{IF}(y, G) + G = 1 - \frac{y}{\mu}G - \frac{y}{\mu} + \frac{2}{\mu}\int_0^y F(x)dx \qquad \text{(A.3)}$$

The IF(y, G) (and RIF) of a continuous function is continuous and convex in y, reaching its minimum when $F(y) = 1 + G/2$.[39] Given the usual ranges in developed countries for the Gini index of disposable income (around 0.3) and the rank of the average income (around the 60–70 percentiles), this minimum will typically happen near the mean. The function is unbounded from above.[40] As a result, extremely high incomes (and to a lower extent also low incomes) will have a disproportionally large influence in the Gini coefficient, like in other inequality measures.[41] However, our empirical analysis shows that given that low incomes with a disproportionally influence on Gini are more common than extremely high incomes, the former as a whole will more strongly influence the Gini index, and so their characteristics will be determinant.

---

[39]Note that the first and second derivatives of the IF are $2/\mu(F(y) - 1 + G/2)$, and $(2/\mu)\ dF/dy \geq 0$.

[40]This property was used by Cowell and Victoria-Feser (1996) to show that the Gini index, like other inequality measures, is not robust to data contamination in high incomes. Cowell and Flachaire (2007) compared the rate of increase to infinity of the influence function of different inequality indices when y goes to infinity, which is equal to y in the cases of Gini, Atkinson, and Generalized Entropy ($\alpha \leq 1$). Note that the IF is usually defined for non-negative incomes. In our case, we have to take into account that the income distributions of Germany and Spain have a limited number of negative incomes that are going to be used in the analysis. In this context, the influence function is also unbounded from below.

[41]As Cowell and Victoria-Feser (1996) pointed out, this has not to be confused with the fact that the impact of a progressive transfer produces the largest increase in the Gini index when it takes place around the mode of the distribution.

APPENDIX B

Table B1. Average Income, Current Amounts in €.

Equivalized Household Income		2008			2012		
		Spain (ES)	Germany (DE)	Ratio ES/DE (× 100)	Spain (ES)	Germany (DE)	Ratio ES/DE (× 100)
All households	Disposable income	14,214 (114)	21,086 (149)	67.4	13,885 (114)	22,022 (147)	63.1
	Gross income	16,745 (144)	28,503 (216)	58.7	16,151 (140)	29,998 (223)	53.8
	Market income + pensions	16,040 (148)	26,432 (223)	60.7	14,989 (143)	27,832 (230)	53.9
	Market income	13,681 (150)	21,901 (232)	62.5	12,089 (146)	22,915 (237)	52.8
Inactive households	Disposable income	10,665 (143)	16,926 (161)	63.0	12,208 (173)	18,632 (232)	65.5
Active households	Disposable income	14,777 (129)	22,405 (189)	66.0	14,181 (130)	23,094 (174)	61.4
	Gross income	17,604 (164)	31,346 (276)	56.2	16,711 (161)	32,605 (268)	51.3
	Market income + pensions	16,870 (167)	28,908 (285)	58.4	15,484 (165)	30,138 (279)	51.4
	Market income	15,645 (166)	27,958 (283)	56.0	14,022 (164)	29,209 (278)	48.0
	Labor income	15,231 (162)	26,848 (272)	56.7	13,654 (162)	28,266 (267)	48.3
Individual income							
Labor force	Labor income (annual)	16,281 (161)	28,243 (275)	57.6	14,681 (167)	28,988 (254)	50.6
Employed workers	Labor income (annual)	18,007 (160)	31,147 (282)	57.8	18,007 (179)	31,147 (259)	57.8

Source: Own construction using EU-SILC 2008, 2012 (2007, 2011 income).
Notes:
− Bootstraps standard errors (1,000 replications) in parentheses (individuals clustered within households).
− A household is active (inactive) if any (none) member was in the labor force in the income reference year.
− Household income has been divided by the number of equivalent adults (OECD-modified scale).
− Income aggregates as defined in "Data" section.
− Employed individuals are those who ever worked during 2011. Individuals in the labor force, also include those that were ever unemployed in 2011.

Table B2. Gini-RIF Regressions of Disposable Household Income for Active Households, 2008−2012.

	Germany		Spain			
	2008		2008		2012*	
	Coeff.	St. E.	Coeff.	St. E.	Coeff.	St. E.
Intermediate area	−0.016	0.010	−0.022*	0.009	−0.022**	0.008
Thinly populated area	−0.023*	0.009	−0.023**	0.008	−0.027***	0.008
Household size	−0.030***	0.005	−0.011**	0.004	−0.015***	0.004
Age 0−16	0.048	0.030	0.112***	0.028	0.080**	0.029
Age 16−24	−0.001	0.026	0.007	0.026	0.055	0.033
Age 25−34	−0.017	0.016	−0.014	0.015	0.005	0.014
Age 45−54	0.008	0.017	−0.004	0.015	0.011	0.013
Age 55−64	0.017	0.022	−0.008	0.021	−0.013	0.019
Age 65 +	0.103	0.077	−0.124***	0.029	−0.167***	0.027
Married	0.020	0.013	0.011	0.011	−0.014	0.010
Women	−0.004	0.017	0.037*	0.016	−0.009	0.016
Foreign citizens	0.089	0.046	0.053***	0.013	0.102***	0.016
Health limitations	−0.023*	0.012	−0.013	0.013	−0.011	0.014
Activity rate	−0.017	0.026	−0.101***	0.016	−0.070***	0.018
FT-E employment rate	−0.188***	0.019	−0.238***	0.020	−0.180***	0.021
FT-SE employment rate	−0.165***	0.021	−0.257***	0.022	−0.148***	0.023
PT-E employment rate	0.768***	0.134	0.166***	0.028	0.278***	0.042
PT-SE employment rate	0.136***	0.038	0.162***	0.020	0.254***	0.023
Managers	0.081*	0.035	0.127***	0.035	0.118***	0.030
Professionals	0.009	0.023	0.074**	0.024	0.086***	0.020
Technicians and associate professionals	−0.058***	0.017	−0.019	0.018	−0.060***	0.015
Clerical support workers	−0.045*	0.022	−0.054***	0.016	−0.064***	0.015
Services and sales workers	−0.028	0.019	−0.053***	0.013	−0.038**	0.012
Skilled agric., forestry, and fishery workers	−0.024	0.066	0.016	0.027	−0.006	0.042
Craft and related trades workers	−0.050**	0.019	−0.039**	0.013	−0.010	0.014
Plant and machine operators/assemblers	−0.017	0.026	−0.043**	0.015	−0.067***	0.015
Agriculture, forestry, and fishing	0.020	0.104	0.027	0.027	−0.029	0.036
Construction	0.012	0.030	0.014	0.017	−0.025	0.020

| | Germany | | Spain | | | |
| | 2008 | | 2008 | | 2012* | |
	Coeff.	St. E.	Coeff.	St. E.	Coeff.	St. E.
Wholesale and retail trade; repair vehicles	−0.039	0.022	−0.003	0.016	0.003	0.017
Transport, storage, and communications	−0.036	0.024	−0.029	0.017	−0.006	0.019
Accommodation and food service	−0.050	0.036	0.018	0.021	−0.011	0.019
Information and communication	−0.022	0.029	0.019	0.037	0.014	0.034
Financial and insurance	0.041	0.035	0.096*	0.038	0.182***	0.042
Real state, professional, etc.	0.003	0.037	0.048	0.027	−0.034	0.019
Public adm. and defense; soc. sec.	−0.081***	0.023	−0.027	0.016	−0.006	0.017
Education	−0.084**	0.026	−0.033	0.026	−0.043	0.023
Human health and social work	−0.013	0.033	0.019	0.024	0.026	0.023
Other services	−0.032	0.021	−0.003	0.018	−0.058**	0.020
Unit size: 3−5 workers	−0.060	0.034	0.014	0.016	−0.036	0.024
Unit size: 6−10 workers	0.022	0.041	−0.002	0.016	−0.037	0.020
Unit size: 11−49 workers	−0.009	0.028	−0.003	0.013	−0.052**	0.019
Unit size: 50+ workers	0.005	0.029	0.032*	0.013	−0.030	0.018
Temporary	0.023	0.014	0.022*	0.009	0.031**	0.012
Experience 1−2 years	0.005	0.032	−0.011	0.029	−0.052	0.034
Experience 3−5 years	−0.030	0.031	−0.042	0.027	0.001	0.029
Experience 6−9 years	−0.010	0.034	−0.052*	0.026	−0.034	0.026
Experience 10+ years	−0.034	0.028	−0.034	0.022	−0.020	0.023
Labor unknown	0.065	0.045	0.092*	0.045	−0.030	0.016
Lower secondary	0.003	0.044	−0.028**	0.011	−0.032**	0.012
Upper secondary, non-tertiary postsecondary	−0.053	0.042	−0.051***	0.012	−0.062***	0.013
Tertiary	−0.045	0.042	0.007	0.016	−0.045**	0.014
Intercept	0.648***	0.053	0.629***	0.036	0.649***	0.034
N	21,549	p-Value	30,339	p-Value	27,751	p-Value
F	22.1	0	16.6	0	24.2	0
R^2	0.105		0.132		0.206	

Source: Own construction using EU-SILC 2008 and 2012 (2007 and 2011 income).
Notes:
− "Dependent variable is Gini-RIF of equivalized" household disposable income (OECD-modified scale) among active households (at least one member in the labor force).
− See "Households' characteristics" section for a description of variables.
− 2012 Regression used for the comparison over time.
− Standard errors in parentheses; *$p < 0.05$; **$p < 0.01$; ***$p < 0.001$.

Table B3.   Mean and Standard Deviation (SD) Among Active
Households: Explanatory Variables.

	FR		IT		SE		UK	
	Mean	SD	Mean	SD	Mean	SD	Mean	SD
Densely populated area (omitted)	0.464	0.499	0.435	0.496	0.218	0.413	0.571	0.495
Intermediate area	0.191	0.393	0.418	0.493	0.161	0.367	0.296	0.456
Thinly populated area	0.345	0.475	0.146	0.353	0.621	0.485	0.134	0.340
Household size	3.290	1.402	3.387	1.233	3.156	1.392	3.222	1.321
Age 0–16	0.239	0.242	0.189	0.218	0.252	0.248	0.201	0.235
Age 16–24	0.151	0.244	0.121	0.193	0.148	0.259	0.160	0.248
Age 25–34	0.224	0.369	0.186	0.298	0.215	0.373	0.210	0.352
Age 35–44 (omitted)	0.286	0.383	0.291	0.371	0.290	0.392	0.244	0.361
Age 45–54	0.195	0.304	0.216	0.292	0.193	0.313	0.198	0.302
Age 55–64	0.120	0.276	0.116	0.232	0.129	0.296	0.122	0.270
Age 65 +	0.023	0.112	0.071	0.181	0.025	0.129	0.066	0.216
Married	0.699	0.388	0.654	0.358	0.683	0.414	0.672	0.394
Women	0.511	0.226	0.500	0.212	0.503	0.240	0.508	0.220
Immigrant (10 or less years)	0.034	0.151	0.080	0.246	0.090	0.283	0.090	0.263
Immigrant (>10 years)	0.064	0.195	0.045	0.161	0.088	0.280	0.064	0.194
Health limitations	0.158	0.279	0.181	0.288	0.060	0.193	0.135	0.264
Activity rate	0.793	0.252	0.693	0.266	0.847	0.244	0.796	0.250
Months as full-time employee (rate)	0.638	0.385	0.564	0.415	0.674	0.436	0.614	0.394
Months as full-time self-employee (rate)	0.090	0.240	0.178	0.334	0.063	0.232	0.083	0.229
Months as part-time time employee (rate)	0.156	0.275	0.096	0.228	0.195	0.368	0.203	0.316
Months as part-time self-employee (rate)	0.013	0.094	0.021	0.117	0.011	0.096	0.033	0.146
Managers	0.076	0.222	0.046	0.183	0.054	0.175	0.088	0.232
Professionals	0.137	0.296	0.127	0.294	0.246	0.359	0.221	0.352
Technicians and associate professionals	0.184	0.317	0.139	0.296	0.151	0.286	0.133	0.276
Clerical support workers	0.096	0.239	0.117	0.271	0.050	0.170	0.084	0.222
Services and sales workers	0.154	0.292	0.148	0.300	0.186	0.314	0.187	0.311
Skilled agriculture, forestry, and fishery workers	0.027	0.143	0.025	0.136	0.015	0.104	0.011	0.082
Craft and related trades workers	0.093	0.235	0.173	0.328	0.089	0.223	0.087	0.226

Table B3. (*Continued*)

	FR		IT		SE		UK	
	Mean	SD	Mean	SD	Mean	SD	Mean	SD
Plant and machine operators and assemblers	0.063	0.198	0.066	0.211	0.070	0.210	0.061	0.200
Elementary occupations (omitted)	0.121	0.281	0.105	0.267	0.044	0.174	0.101	0.255
Agriculture, forestry, and fishing	0.029	0.147	0.029	0.150	0.017	0.103	0.009	0.079
Mining; manufacturing; electricity, gas, and water supply (omitted)	0.132	0.279	0.179	0.332	0.068	0.205	0.114	0.260
Construction	0.096	0.243	0.063	0.212	0.030	0.145	0.065	0.200
Wholesale and retail trade; repair vehicles	0.080	0.224	0.127	0.287	0.050	0.175	0.118	0.265
Transport, storage, and communications	0.045	0.171	0.038	0.165	0.023	0.130	0.044	0.172
Accommodation and food service	0.031	0.151	0.043	0.173	0.011	0.088	0.047	0.178
Information and communication	0.039	0.162	0.018	0.116	0.021	0.121	0.027	0.135
Financial and insurance	0.026	0.134	0.026	0.134	0.009	0.079	0.034	0.146
Real state, professional, scientific, administrative, and support service	0.084	0.231	0.082	0.236	0.066	0.203	0.114	0.262
Public administration and defense; social security	0.063	0.201	0.055	0.198	0.021	0.119	0.057	0.191
Education	0.086	0.237	0.054	0.193	0.050	0.177	0.090	0.232
Human health and social work	0.102	0.245	0.062	0.205	0.093	0.232	0.122	0.269
Other services	0.037	0.153	0.048	0.184	0.021	0.119	0.045	0.167
Unit size: 1–2 workers (omitted)	0.112	0.266	0.156	0.317	0.014	0.099	0.135	0.287
Unit size: 3–5 workers	0.066	0.209	0.105	0.264	0.036	0.154	0.049	0.180
Unit size: 6–10 workers	0.070	0.207	0.091	0.245	0.047	0.175	0.069	0.204
Unit size: 11–49 workers	0.188	0.325	0.238	0.367	0.140	0.275	0.230	0.343
Unit size: 50+ workers	0.353	0.404	0.233	0.369	0.213	0.318	0.381	0.407
Temporary contract	0.131	0.281	0.124	0.277	0.082	0.237	0.033	0.149
Experience <1 year	–	–	0.036	0.147	–	–	0.047	0.171
Experience 1–2 years	–	–	0.040	0.147	–	–	0.046	0.162
Experience 3–5 years	–	–	0.066	0.201	–	–	0.066	0.202
Experience 6–9 years	–	–	0.100	0.252	–	–	0.099	0.248
Experience 10+ years	–	–	0.758	0.350	–	–	0.742	0.368
Labor unknown	0.080	0.227	0.068	0.213	0.128	0.267	0.044	0.176
Primary education (omitted)	0.065	0.205	0.073	0.204	0.020	0.114	0.000	0.000

Table B3. *(Continued)*

	FR		IT		SE		UK	
	Mean	SD	Mean	SD	Mean	SD	Mean	SD
Lower secondary education	0.096	0.236	0.312	0.388	0.085	0.219	0.101	0.262
Upper secondary, non-tertiary postsecondary education	0.493	0.415	0.434	0.409	0.514	0.414	0.425	0.416
Tertiary education	0.337	0.416	0.159	0.319	0.375	0.414	0.370	0.424

Source: Own construction using EU-SILC 2012.
Notes:
− Active households (at least one member in the labor force).
− See "Households' characteristics" section for a description of variables.

Table B4. Gini-RIF Regressions of Disposable Household Income for Active Households, 2012.

	France		Italy		Sweden		UK	
	Coeff.	St. E.	Coeff.	St. E.	Coeff.	St. E.	Coeff.	St. E.
Intermediate area	−0.039**	0.014	−0.035***	0.007	−0.034**	0.013	−0.023*	0.012
Thinly populated area	−0.059***	0.013	−0.035***	0.008	−0.031**	0.011	0.049	0.026
Household size	−0.014*	0.005	−0.029***	0.004	−0.026***	0.005	−0.017**	0.006
Age 0–16	0.051	0.047	0.191***	0.024	0.162***	0.031	0.022	0.041
Age 16–24	0.016	0.033	0.130***	0.024	0.102***	0.020	0.020	0.030
Age 25–34	−0.033	0.018	0.018	0.013	0.005	0.016	−0.015	0.023
Age 45–54	0.050*	0.025	0.011	0.011	0.023	0.019	0.009	0.027
Age 55–64	0.081**	0.028	0.105***	0.020	0.069**	0.021	0.009	0.040
Age 65+	0.188	0.211	0.002	0.032	0.112	0.085	−0.031	0.041
Married	0.035*	0.015	0.010	0.010	−0.015	0.013	−0.002	0.015
Women	0.016	0.022	0.009	0.012	−0.008	0.016	−0.013	0.029
Immigrant (10 or less years)	0.085*	0.039	0.019	0.012	0.102***	0.021	0.060	0.050
Immigrant (>10 years)	0.063	0.037	0.023	0.016	0.024*	0.012	0.011	0.028
Health limitations	−0.020	0.020	−0.042***	0.011	0.005	0.020	−0.026	0.018
Activity rate	−0.074***	0.022	−0.088***	0.016	−0.082**	0.026	−0.050	0.027
FT-E employment rate	−0.126***	0.020	−0.221***	0.019	−0.136***	0.021	−0.171***	0.032
FT-SE employment rate	0.207***	0.052	−0.126***	0.019	−0.068*	0.033	−0.057	0.070
PT-E employment rate	−0.071*	0.030	−0.208***	0.022	−0.117***	0.022	−0.097**	0.035
PT-SE employment rate	0.047	0.063	−0.055	0.044	0.092	0.144	−0.073	0.065
Managers	0.189*	0.086	0.088**	0.030	0.051	0.031	0.111**	0.039
Professionals	0.048	0.031	0.008	0.019	−0.022	0.022	0.066	0.034

Table B4. (Continued)

	France		Italy		Sweden		UK	
	Coeff.	St. E.	Coeff.	St. E.	Coeff.	St. E.	Coeff.	St. E.
Technicians and associate professionals	−0.089***	0.017	−0.035*	0.018	−0.059**	0.018	−0.038	0.019
Clerical support workers	−0.087***	0.023	−0.067***	0.014	−0.042	0.026	−0.087***	0.019
Services and sales workers	−0.047**	0.015	−0.052***	0.012	−0.035*	0.015	−0.045**	0.016
Skilled agric., forestry, and fishery workers	0.029	0.041	0.007	0.024	0.055	0.094	−0.090*	0.044
Craft and related trades workers	−0.073***	0.021	−0.039**	0.013	−0.047*	0.019	−0.033	0.022
Plant and machine operators/assemblers	−0.060***	0.018	−0.077***	0.014	−0.067***	0.017	0.002	0.021
Agriculture, forestry, and fishing	−0.111*	0.048	0.005	0.021	0.127	0.086	−0.068	0.047
Construction	−0.028	0.035	0.025	0.019	−0.026	0.029	−0.004	0.038
Wholesale and retail trade; repair vehicles	−0.061	0.037	0.003	0.012	−0.013	0.024	0.027	0.025
Transport, storage, and communications	−0.061*	0.030	−0.023	0.015	−0.035	0.024	0.018	0.028
Accommodation and food service	−0.088	0.054	−0.003	0.019	0.070	0.083	−0.001	0.031
Information and communication	−0.020	0.064	0.010	0.026	−0.018	0.033	0.116	0.075
Financial and insurance	0.124	0.162	0.051	0.028	0.178*	0.076	0.086*	0.041
Real state, professional, etc.	−0.013	0.040	0.069**	0.024	0.044	0.025	0.065	0.041
Public adm. and defense; soc. sec.	−0.086*	0.042	−0.046**	0.015	−0.041	0.028	0.077	0.041
Education	−0.183***	0.034	−0.087***	0.020	−0.040	0.022	−0.047	0.035
Human health and social work	−0.050	0.030	−0.015	0.017	−0.017	0.021	0.003	0.035
Other services	−0.103**	0.039	0.030	0.029	0.112	0.106	−0.016	0.038
Unit size: 3–5 workers	0.036	0.028	−0.001	0.015	0.057	0.062	−0.037	0.032
Unit size: 6–10 workers	0.106**	0.035	0.001	0.020	−0.050*	0.023	−0.052	0.029
Unit size: 11–49 workers	0.089*	0.035	−0.011	0.018	0.019	0.023	−0.062*	0.028

		p-Value		p-Value		p-Value		p-Value
Unit size: 50+ workers	0.033	0.020	-0.002	0.017	0.006	0.020	-0.063*	0.029
Temporary	0.038	0.023	0.044**	0.014	0.072***	0.018	0.029	0.045
Experience 1–2 years	—	—	-0.086*	0.038	—	—	-0.059	0.039
Experience 3–5 years	—	—	-0.054	0.030	—	—	-0.066*	0.031
Experience 6–9 years	—	—	-0.050	0.032	—	—	-0.033	0.032
Experience 10+ years	—	—	-0.028	0.030	—	—	-0.033	0.031
Labor unknown	-0.026	0.022	0.014	0.017	0.015	0.020	0.132**	0.042
Lower secondary	0.091*	0.037	0.003	0.016	0.004	0.033	0.005	0.025
Upper secondary, non-tertiary postsecondary	0.065*	0.029	-0.033*	0.016	-0.009	0.031	-0.007	0.022
Tertiary	0.094*	0.041	0.061**	0.022	0.012	0.035	0.033	0.022
Intercept	0.391***	0.057	0.650***	0.036	0.475***	0.046	0.602***	0.054
N	22,387	p-Value	37,449	p-Value	13,002	p-Value	18,162	p-Value
F	12.96	0	20.87	0	13.51	0	7.73	0
R^2	0.043		0.078		0.098		0.048	

Source: Own construction using EU-SILC 2012 (2011 income).

Notes:

– "Dependent variable is Gini-RIF of equivalized" household disposable income (OECD-modified scale) among active households (at least one member in the labor force).

– See "Households' characteristics" section for a description of variables.

– Standard errors in parentheses; $*p < 0.05$; $**p < 0.01$; $***p < 0.001$.

THE EFFECTS OF THE MINIMUM WAGE ON EARNINGS INEQUALITY: EVIDENCE FROM CHINA

Carl Lin[a] and Myeong-Su Yun[b]

[a]Bucknell University
[b]Inha University

ABSTRACT

The minimum wage has been regarded as an important element of public policy for reducing poverty and inequality. Increasing the minimum wage is supposed to raise earnings for millions of low-wage workers and therefore lower earnings inequality. However, there is no consensus in the existing literature from industrialized countries regarding whether increasing the minimum wage has helped lower earnings inequality. China has recently exhibited rapid economic growth and widening earnings inequality. Since China promulgated new minimum wage regulations in 2004, the magnitude and frequency of changes in the minimum wage have been substantial, both over time and across jurisdictions. The growing importance of research on the relationship between the minimum wage and earnings inequality and its controversial nature have sparked heated debate in China, highlighting the importance of rigorous research to inform evidence-based policy making. We investigate the contribution

Income Inequality Around the World
Research in Labor Economics, Volume 44, 179−212
Copyright © 2016 by Emerald Group Publishing Limited
All rights of reproduction in any form reserved
ISSN: 0147-9121/doi:10.1108/S0147-912120160000044012

of the minimum wage to the well-documented rise in earnings inequality in China from 2004 to 2009 by using city-level minimum wage panel data and a representative Chinese household survey, and we find that increasing the minimum wage reduces inequality − by decreasing the earnings gap between the median and the bottom decile − over the analysis period.

Keywords: Minimum wage; China; earnings; inequality

JEL Classifications: J31; J38; O15; R23

INTRODUCTION

Since the reform and opening-up policy in 1978, China's economy has been growing remarkably at a rate of at least 9.5% per year. As the economy has grown, Chinese workers' earnings have also increased rapidly over the same period. According to the latest figures from the National Bureau of Statistics of China (NBS), disposable earnings per capita have risen substantially − more than 70-fold − over the past few decades in urban China, rising from 343 RMB in 1978 to 24,565 RMB in 2012, while net earnings per capita in rural China have grown 60-fold, increasing from 134 RMB in 1978 to 7,917 RMB in 2012 (National Bureau of Statistics of China, 2013).

As the Chinese economy has rapidly grown, the earnings distribution has deteriorated. For example, the urban-to-rural earnings per capita ratio increased from 2.57 in 1978 to 2.90 in 2001 and further to 3.10 in 2012. The Gini coefficient, a commonly used measure of inequality, was at a very low level in 1978, at .16 and .22 for urban and rural areas, respectively (Li & Zhao, 1999). However, as shown in Fig. 1, China's overall Gini coefficient began to rise from .376 in 1988 to .439 in 1995 (Wang, 2007) and increased further to .454 and .490 in 2002 and 2007, respectively (Li & Luo, 2011).[1] In contrast, high inequality countries such as Brazil and Mexico had shown declined Gini coefficients over a similar time period, whereas for the United States it was relatively stable.[2]

---

[1] These numbers are consistent with the official statistics published by the NBS in 2013, which also reports high inequality (e.g., .484 in 2007 and .474 in 2012). The publication of these official statistics marks the first time that the Chinese government released information on the Gini coefficient.
[2] According to the 2015 World Development Indicators, the Gini coefficients of Brazil were .614 in 1988, .596 in 1995, .586 in 2002, then decreased to .552 and .527 in 2007 and 2012, respectively. For Mexico, the numbers decreased from .519 in 2000 to .481 in 2012. The Gini coefficient of the United States was .402 in 2000, increased to .416 in 2007, and slightly decreased to .411 in 2010.

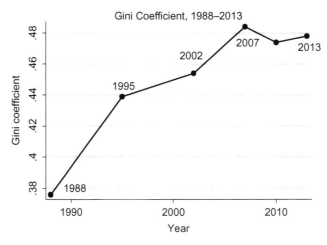

Fig. 1.   Growing Inequality in China. *Notes*: The NBS of China publishes the official Gini coefficients in 2013 for the first time. The numbers of 2007, 2010 and 2013 are from the NBS website; whereas those of 1988 and 1995 are from Wang (2007), and the number of 2002 is from Li and Luo (2011).

The deterioration of the earnings distribution and growing gap between the rich and the poor has engendered challenges to economic development and social stability in China. As shown by the experience of developed countries, public polices, such as tax reforms, can play an essential role in countering rising inequality. Since the early 2000s, the Chinese government has intensively promulgated a series of policies, such as aid to the poor, rural minimal social security, and the minimum wage policy. Among these policy initiatives, the minimum wage policy is the most controversial.[3]

---

[3]Supporters of the minimum wage in China argue that the minimum wage assists individuals or families in achieving self-sufficiency and protects workers in low-paid occupations. The minimum wage can help reduce inequality and serve as an important safety net by providing a wage floor. In addition, rising labor costs due to the minimum wage increases may promote managerial efficiency and labor productivity, inducing employers to invest in productivity-improving technology (Cooke, 2005). Along these lines, many Chinese scholars have argued in favor of a more proactive increase in the minimum wage. In contrast, opponents argue that raising the minimum wage can decrease the employment opportunities of low-wage workers and lead to a reduction in other components of workers' compensation packages. Such regulations can further undermine enterprises' dividend policies to shareholders and reduce China's comparative advantage given the abundance of low-wage labor (Cheung, 2004, 2010). Moreover, rural-urban migrant workers tend to have very low pay, and they may accept jobs that pay less than the current minimum wage; thus, the minimum wage may exist in name only (Chan, 2001).

The contentiousness of the debate on the minimum wage policy in China arises from the difficulty of measuring its effects on employment, wages, and the earnings distribution, among others. However, the initial evidence suggests that the magnitude and frequency of changes to the minimum wage have been substantial both over time and across different jurisdictions, particularly since 2004. These large variations both across jurisdictions and over time facilitate our estimation of minimum wage effects on inequality in China. For example, in January 2004, China promulgated new minimum wage regulations that required local governments to introduce a minimum wage increase at least once every two years, that extended coverage to self-employed and part-time workers, and that quintupled the penalties for violations or noncompliance. The new regulations entered into force in March 2004, engendering frequent and substantial increases in the minimum wage in the years that followed.[4]

Fig. 2 shows the nominal and real minimum wage (monthly average) in China from 1995 to 2012, as well as those of the corresponding provinces that raised the minimum wage standards for each year and the moving average over the same period.[5] Between 1995 and 2003, the average nominal minimum wage increased steadily from 169 to 301 RMB, amounting to 78% growth over 9 years. However, since China promulgated the new minimum wage regulations in 2004, the nominal minimum wage has increased rapidly by more than 200%, reaching 944 RMB in 2012.[6] The real minimum wage grew at a slower pace before 2004 and began to rise thereafter. Furthermore, as shown by the moving average curve in Fig. 2, there is an apparent rise in the number of provinces that raised the minimum wage standards in 2004, indicating that minimum wage adjustments have become more frequent since 2004.

Although the literature widely documents numerous aspects of the minimum wage and its role in the labor market, there is no consensus regarding whether the minimum wage can reduce inequality (Neumark & Wascher, 2008). Moreover, research on the effect of the minimum wage on inequality in developing countries is scant. This study contributes to the literature by

---

[4]According to our calculation, the average growth rate of the minimum wage is 10−20% per year throughout the country since 2004.

[5]There is no national minimum wage in China; the minimum wage standards are determined at the provincial level. We discuss how we calculate the mean nominal and real minimum wage for each year in the section "Data."

[6]The growth rates of the average nominal wage are 155% and 194% for the periods 1995−2003 and 2004−2012, respectively (National Bureau of Statistics of China, 2013).

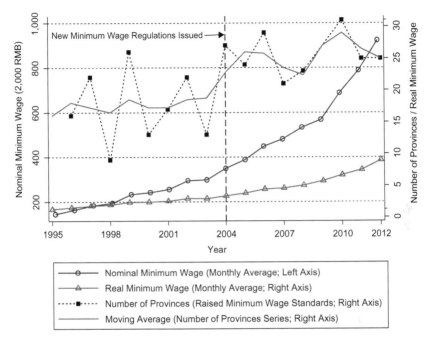

Fig. 2. Minimum Wages in China, 1995 – 2012. *Notes*: Nominal and real minimum wages are adjusted for inflation and expressed in 2,000 RMB.

examining the effect of the minimum wage on inequality in China. China provides a particularly interesting context for such a study since it has experienced both rising inequality and a rising minimum wage (nominal and real), whereas countries such as the United States (Lee, 1999) and Mexico (Bosch & Manacorda, 2010) have experienced rising wage inequality with a declining minimum wage (real).

Using OLS and IV panel regressions at the aggregated city level, we first examine the effect of minimum wage changes on the earnings gaps at the bottom and upper end of the earnings distribution as well as the extent of such an effect. Our analysis shows that minimum wage increases significantly help reduce earnings gaps, particularly at the bottom end of the distribution. Next, to measure the contribution of minimum wage changes to the change in earnings inequality, we construct a counterfactual scenario to capture how China's earnings distribution would have evolved without the rise in the minimum wage. The difference between the observed and the counterfactual scenario is the real effect of the minimum wage. Indeed, we find that the contribution of minimum wage changes in reducing inequality is substantial, particularly at the bottom end of the earnings distribution. That is, had it not been for the increase in the minimum wage, the earnings gap at the bottom end of the earnings distribution would have been larger.[7]

The remainder of this study is organized as follows. We briefly review the literature in the section "Literature on the Distributional Effect of the Minimum Wage" and provide a review of the development of the minimum wage in China in the section "The Minimum Wage Policy in China." The section "Data and Research Design" provides details regarding the data and research design. In the section "Empirical Results and Discussion," we present and discuss the empirical results. The final section presents the conclusions.

LITERATURE ON THE DISTRIBUTIONAL EFFECT OF THE MINIMUM WAGE

Most evidence on the distributional effect of the minimum wage comes from the United States. In early studies using simulation methods, Johnson and Browning (1983) and Burkhauser and Finegan (1989) show that a moderate reduction of the minimum wage could reduce income inequality. Since the 1990s, studies have commonly used regression methods. Neumark, Schweitzer, and Wascher (2005), who apply a nonparametric method to estimate the minimum wage effect on income inequality, analyze several inequality measures (e.g., Gini coefficient, coefficient of variation, standard deviation, and Atkinson index) and find that a rise in the minimum wage can increase inequality. However, using data from 1979 to 1991 at the state level, Lee (1999) finds that the falling real minimum wage can explain from 70% to 100% of the growth in wage inequality in the lower tail of the female wage distribution and argues the declining minimum wage accounts for a substantial part of the growth in inequality in the United States from 1979 to 1991. Autor, Manning, and Smith (2016) find

---

[7]It is important to note that, like many studies do, our analysis assumes that minimum wage increases do not have an impact on employment or hours worked. Therefore, our results should be interpreted cautiously since the estimates could overstate the effect of minimum wage on reducing inequality.

that the minimum wage reduces wage inequality in the lower tail of the wage distribution (the 50/10 wage ratio), but the effects are typically less than half as large as those reported in Lee (1999) and are almost negligible for males. Taken together, most findings from the United States show that if the target group for the study of distributional effects is at the bottom end of the income/wage distribution, the minimum wage can help reduce inequality.

Evidence outside the United States is also limited, focusing primarily on Central and South American countries. The World Bank (2006) finds that the distributional effects of the minimum wage are ambiguous in Central and Southern America. Both positive and negative effects are found; however, the results show that the minimum wage has no effect on poverty and that the effect on inequality varies from country to country. Neumark, Cunningham, and Siga (2006) use a before-and-after method to study whether the minimum wage can help improve income inequality in Brazil and find that although the minimum wage has a positive effect on the income distribution at the 20th percentile, there is no effect at the 10th and 30th percentiles. Moreover, when a lagged minimum wage is added, the results show a significant negative effect. They also find that the results are not robust in different model specifications, and they ultimately conclude that the evidence from Brazil shows that the minimum wage does not reduce inequality. Gindling and Terrell (2007) use industry-level data from 2001 to 2004 in Honduras to study the effect of the minimum wage on the income distribution and find that the minimum wage has an effect on reducing inequality. Bosch and Manacorda (2010) study the effect of the minimum wage on earnings inequality in Mexico from the late 1980s to the early 2000s. They find that the Mexican minimum wage can explain a large part of earnings inequality in Mexico, and they show that at the bottom end of the earnings distribution, most of the growing inequality can be attributed to the rapid decline in the real value of the minimum wage.

Research on the effect of the minimum wage on inequality in China is limited. In the first empirical study, Wen (2007) uses pooled cross-sectional data from 2004 to 2006 at the provincial level to estimate the effect of the minimum wage on the employment and income distribution of rural migrant workers. He finds that the minimum wage has a positive effect on the employment and income distribution of rural migrants over the period of analysis. Wang (2011) discusses the effect of the minimum wage on patterns in income distribution and economic development, and he argues that the minimum wage could have possibly reduced the income gap in China. Using the time-series data from Chongqing City for the period between

1997 and 2010, Chen (2012) finds that increasing the minimum wage could help mitigate the growing income gap between urban and rural areas.

Wang (2013) uses a simulation method and shows that increases in the minimum wage can reduce earnings inequality and that the effect of minimum wage policy increases with the strength of its enforcement. Jia (2013) uses microdata sets from three different surveys conducted between 1995 and 2008 to study the effect of the minimum wage on wage inequality, and he finds that increasing the effective minimum wage can help reduce wage differentials in the lower tail of the wage distribution. In the only study to offer a different view of the minimum wage effect, Quan and Li (2011) test the growing income gap between urban and rural regions in Shanghai and show that the distributional effect of the minimum wage is limited.

In sum, almost all the limited studies on the minimum wage effect from China use aggregated data (published statistics), such as cross-sectional or time-series data. In contrast, information on the minimum wage (all at the provincial level) for calculating the mean minimum wage is insufficient. More important, the representativeness of the sample in previous studies is questionable. This study aims to address these concerns and to fill this research gap by providing a better data set, richer models and more complex estimation methods.

THE MINIMUM WAGE POLICY IN CHINA

Prior to 1994, China had no minimum wage law. In 1984, the country simply acknowledged the 1928 "Minimum Wage-Fixing Machinery Convention" of the International Labour Organization (Su, 1993). Because of sluggish wage growth and high inflation in the late 1980s, Zhuhai of Guangdong Province implemented the first local minimum wage regulations in 1989, and similar regulations followed in Shenzhen, Guangzhou, and Jiangmen in the same year. It was not until the eruption of private enterprises in 1992, when labor disputes became frequent, that the Chinese Central Government began to consider minimum wage legislation (Yang, 2006). In 1993, China issued the first national minimum wage regulations, and in July 1994, these regulations were written into China's new version of the Labor Law.

The 1994 legislation required that all employers pay wages no less than the local minimum wage to employees. Further, all provincial, autonomous-region, and municipal governments were required to set the minimum wage according to five principles and report them to the State Council of the Central Government. Specifically, the five principles indicated that the setting and adjustment of the local minimum wage should synthetically consider the lowest living expenses of workers, the average number of dependents that workers support, local average wages, the level of labor productivity, the level of local employment, and the level of economic development among regions. These conditions provided considerable flexibility for provinces in setting minimum wage standards, with the economic development principle giving them the flexibility to limit the minimum wage to attract foreign investment (Frost, 2002; Wang & Gunderson, 2011). By December 1994, 7 of 31 provinces had set their own minimum wage, and by the end of 1995, that number had increased to 24.

In the early 2000s, the slowly increasing minimum wage, along with growing concerns for uncovered/disadvantaged workers, began to increase the government's focus on new minimum wage regulations. In December 2003, the Ministry of Labor and Social Security passed "The Minimum Wage Regulations" and promulgated the new law in January 2004. Regarding its main features, this law extends coverage to employees in state-owned and private enterprises, self-employed businesses, and private nonenterprise units. In particular, the new law establishes two types of minimum wages: a monthly minimum wage applied to full-time workers and an hourly minimum wage applied to non-full-time employees. Moreover, the minimum wage standards are set and adjusted jointly by the local government, trade union, and enterprise confederation of each province. A draft for the minimum wage standards are submitted to the Ministry of Labor and Social Security for review, and the Ministry then asks for opinions from the All-China Federation of Trade Unions and the China Enterprise Confederation. The Ministry of Labor and Social Security can request a revision within 14 days of receiving the proposed draft. If no revision is brought up after the 14-day period, the proposed new minimum wage scheme is considered to be passed.

In addition, the new regulation requires that local governments renew their minimum wage standards at least once every two years, and penalties for violations increased from 20−100% of the owed wage to 100−500% of the owed wage.[8] Moreover, employers cannot include subsidies such as

---

[8]The increase in penalties for violations has significantly affected compliance. According to our calculation using 2002−2009 data, throughout the country, the share of workers who earn less than the minimum wage continuously declined, decreasing from 7.28% to 5.62% in the pre- and post-2004 periods (2002−2003, 2004−2009), respectively. In particular, the number decreased from 8.08% to 5.33% in the Eastern region between the same periods, whereas the number decreased from 6.19% to 5.46% in the Central region.

overtime pay or canteen and traveling supplements as part of employees' wages when calculating the minimum wage. The new regulations were entered into force on March 1, 2004, and they have led to substantial increases in the minimum wage across China.

DATA AND RESEARCH DESIGN

Although there is considerable interest in studying the effect of the minimum wage on inequality in China, research on this topic has been hampered by difficulties in collecting data. First, because provinces, municipalities, and autonomous regions in China have considerable flexibility in setting their minimum wage according to local conditions, at least 3 or 4 levels of minimum wage standards are often applicable to various cities in most provinces.[9] Each city is responsible for documenting its own minimum wage standards; hence, city-level minimum wage data containing relevant information on the dates and extent of minimum wage increases are not readily available.[10] Second, in China, it is difficult to obtain microdata that can reasonably be considered representative of the population and that may be influenced by minimum wage increases. Furthermore, some provinces, such as Beijing and Shanghai, do not include social security payments and housing provident funds as part of wages when calculating the minimum wage, rendering their "official" minimum wage higher than the real minimum

---

[9]For expositional convenience, we refer to "provinces, municipalities, and autonomous regions" as provinces.

[10]The implementation date of a new minimum wage standard of a city can also differ across geographically contiguous neighbors within the same province. For example, Liaoning Province has the most complicated minimum wage scheme, in which 14 jurisdictions may enact their own standards on different dates. For instance, in 2007, the cities of Shenyang, Benxi, Dandong, and Panjin did not increase their minimum wage. In contrast, on December 20, the cities of Dalian and Anshan increased their minimum wage from 600 to 700 RMB, the cities of Jinzhou and Liaoyang increased their minimum wage from 480 to 580 RMB, and the city of Chaoyang increased its minimum wage from 350 to 530 RMB. Furthermore, the cities of Fushun and Huludao increased their minimum wage from 400 to 480 RMB on January 1, whereas the city of Yingkou increased its minimum wage from 380 to 480 RMB, the city of Fuxin increased its minimum wage from 350 to 420 RMB, and the city of Tieling increased its minimum wage from 380 to 420 RMB the following year.

wage.[11] The data and research design were chosen to estimate the effect of the minimum wage on earnings inequality and to attempt to address some of the aforementioned challenges in research on the effect of the minimum wage on inequality. Hence, our study uses two data sources: (1) the annual Urban Household Survey (UHS) collected by NBS of China from 2002 to 2009 (more details in the "Data" section) and (2) minimum wage data collected by authors at the city level (four-digit area code) between 1994 and 2012.[12]

Data

The UHS is a continuous, large-scale, socio-economic survey conducted by the NBS to study the conditions and standard of living of urban households, which include agricultural residents, nonagricultural residents, nonresidents who have lived in a city for at least six months and some migrant households with local residency. By using sampling techniques and daily accounting methods, the survey collects data from households in different cities and counties in all 31 provinces in Mainland China for each quarter. In late December, survey teams from all provinces are required to verify and then upload the aggregated annual data to the Division of City Socioeconomic Survey of the NBS through Intranet by January 10 of the following year. The UHS data contain information on households, such as

---

[11]The housing provident fund is a long-term, compulsory, indemnificatory and mutual aid housing fund program that is open to employees of government agencies, state enterprises, universities, hospitals, and some semi-state companies. It was founded as a form of involuntary savings to assist home financing. Workers who join the program agree to have their salary (between 4% and 10%) deposited into a special account in a state-owned bank and the participants' employer provides a one-for-one match for the amount that the employee deposits into the account. Designated banks would further supplement the fund with individual housing loans through a mortgage system. In other words, the difference between accounting for and not accounting for this issue can be substantial. For instance, the mean monthly minimum wage was 651 and 767 RMB in Beijing and Shanghai between 2004 and 2009; however, the average expenses of both social security payments and housing provident funds in Beijing and Shanghai were as high as 376 and 452 RMB over the same period, amounting to 58% and 59% of the nominal minimum wage, respectively. We discuss how we address this issue in the Data section.

[12]Because such detailed minimum wage data by city are not readily available to the public, we collected the data together with a team at Beijing Normal University.

income, earnings, and consumption expenditures; demographic characteristics; work and employment; housing; and other family-related matters.

Fig. 3 shows the 16-province sample for the analysis (represented by darker areas), which includes two major municipalities, Beijing and Shanghai; four economically important provinces in the Eastern region (more prosperous), Guangdong, Jiangsu, Shandong, and Liaoning; five provinces in the Central region (developing), Henan, Anhui, Hubei, Jiangxi, and Shanxi; and four provinces in the Western region (less developed), Chongqing, Gansu, Sichuan, and Yunnan. Overall, our 16-province sample

Fig. 3. Coverage of Sample Provinces in the Analysis. *Notes*: The data used in the analysis include 16 provinces (darker areas in the map) covering three regions in Mainland China. The East includes Liaoning, Beijing, Shandong, Jiangsu, and Guangdong; the Central region includes Heilongjiang, Shanxi, Henan, Anhui, Hubei, and Jiangxi; and the West includes Gansu, Chongqing, Sichuan, and Yunnan.

contains 65% of the total population in China and covers 60% of the cities in the country (National Bureau of Statistics of China, 2010).[13]

Our primary objective is to thoroughly and accurately acquire relevant information on the minimum wage for each city. In China, provinces have considerable flexibility in setting their minimum wage standards according to local economic conditions; thus, there are several levels of standards across cities within the same province. Moreover, the adjustment date of a city's new minimum wage standards can also differ from its geographically contiguous neighbors within the same province, rendering the estimation of minimum wage effects more challenging. To effectively address this issue, we collected our minimum wage data from every local government website and carefully recorded the minimum wage information for every year from 1994 to 2012. As such, our data contain the monthly minimum wage for full-time employees, the hourly minimum wage for part-time employees, the effective dates of the minimum wage standards and the extent to which social security payments and/or housing provident funds were included as part of the minimum wage calculations. We then merge the minimum wage data with the UHS data, a 16-province data set containing individual/household socio-economic information for the period 2002–2009.

In Table 1, we present a brief summary of the minimum wage data used in our main analysis for the period following the implementation of new minimum wage regulations (2004). Columns (1), (2), and (3) correspond to the mean of the monthly minimum wage, the standard deviation, and the number of counties for the three regions and the 16 provinces in 2004, respectively.[14] When calculating the mean minimum wage, we use a time-weighted method, as suggested in Rama (2001), to address the issue of different adjustment dates among cities in a province within a year. The mean minimum wage is adjusted for inflation and converted into 2,005 RMB by using the urban resident CPI for comparison over time. In addition, to account for the differing living costs among provinces, we apply the PPP-adjusted deflator developed by Brandt and Holz (2006).[15] The last row reports the mean of the minimum wage for all provinces, its standard deviation, and the total number of counties for each year.

---

[13]Note that the UHS data are not publicly available. The NBS allows limited access to the microdata for up to 16 provinces under certain conditions for academic research. Nonetheless, the 16-province sample includes almost all economically important provinces in China.

[14]Note that there was no minimum wage increase in 2009 because of the global financial crisis.

[15]The updated version, which is extended to 2010, is available at http://ihome.ust.hk/~socholz/SpatialDeflators.html

Table 1. Minimum Wages across Various Jurisdictions in China, 2004–2009.

Province	2004			2005			2006			2007			2008			2009		
	MW	S.D.	Obs.	MW	S.D.	Obs.	MW	S.D.	Obs.	MW	S.D.	Obs.	MW	S.D.	Obs.	MW	S.D.	Obs.
East																		
Beijing	509.5	0	2	562.5	0	2	611.8	0	2	665.4	0	2	735.4	0	2	820.1	0	2
Shanghai	590.3	0	2	662.5	0	2	712.1	0	2	757.7	0	2	894.0	0	2	984.2	0	2
Liaoning	282.3	46.0	96	361.9	36.6	96	405.5	41.2	96	465.8	48.7	96	550.1	59.9	97	587.8	63.2	97
Shandong	348.4	35.2	129	440.9	50.0	129	454.6	53.5	129	476.2	66.3	129	571.9	75.6	129	609.9	80.6	129
Jiangsu	416.2	59.9	66	457.6	66.8	66	517.9	70.4	66	591.0	78.0	75	647.8	88.1	75	694.4	94.7	75
Guangdong	361.2	59.9	104	442.1	80.6	104	475.0	84.9	104	516.6	88.5	104	574.3	88.2	104	636.1	98.2	104
All East	349.1	68.5	339	426.7	72.1	339	460.6	76.0	399	507.4	86.5	399	583.6	87.6	408	629.7	95.7	409
Central																		
Heilongjiang	282.0	28.1	30	287.8	28.7	30	384.0	45.7	30	418.0	53.6	30	456.0	58.6	30	486.3	62.5	30
Anhui	304.6	11.7	86	330.7	17.1	86	350.1	19.1	86	400.7	27.1	86	420.4	29.2	86	448.3	31.2	86
Jiangxi	246.7	6.6	99	317.7	8.9	100	328.9	9.4	100	427.5	15.2	100	460.3	21.8	100	490.9	23.3	100
Shanxi	348.2	21.8	119	445.4	22.3	119	454.2	22.4	119	476.3	21.6	119	536.6	22.8	119	642.5	28.6	119
Hubei	271.9	34.9	89	320.6	36.8	89	330.2	37.2	89	402.4	39.1	89	453.4	45.6	89	541.5	58.5	89
Henan	251.5	15.5	127	278.5	17.0	127	345.0	27.9	127	371.1	25.7	127	477.2	42.5	127	509.0	45.3	127
All Central	284.8	43.6	550	337.1	63.8	550	366.2	54.7	551	416.3	46.3	551	473.1	51.7	551	529.1	77.0	551
West																		
Gansu	298.2	8.5	87	304.4	8.7	87	322.1	16.3	87	344.6	35.1	87	471.6	36.3	87	549.4	39.2	87
Chongqing	334.7	21.7	42	365.7	24.6	42	409.0	30.1	42	477.8	39.8	42	554.8	44.5	42	591.7	47.4	42
Sichuan	295.4	32.1	50	352.2	41.9	50	392.2	43.8	50	425.0	42.3	181	477.9	53.0	181	509.7	56.5	181
Yunnan	297.5	18.0	138	365.2	23.4	138	403.6	23.4	138	427.0	22.8	138	527.2	31.5	138	562.3	33.6	138
All West	302.3	23.3	317	346.5	36.1	317	380.1	45.0	317	414.9	51.8	317	499.1	52.3	448	541.3	54.1	448
All provinces	309.5	56.7	1266	367.7	73.1	1266	399.4	73.3	1267	442.3	74.8	1407	513.5	79.2	1408	562.2	88.3	1408

Note: MW represents the mean of time-weighted monthly minimum wages calculated using all counties in a jurisdiction, and it has been adjusted for inflation and converted into 2,005 RMB.

Table 1 reveals several important patterns. First, the mean nominal minimum wage increased by 80% (from 310 to 562 RMB) between 2004 and 2009 throughout China.[16] Second, the Eastern region has the highest minimum wage during this period, with an average of 522 RMB per month, and the Western (436 RMB) and Central regions (424 RMB) follow. Surprisingly, the minimum wage shows a similar annual growth rate of 13% for the three regions.[17] Third, the minimum wage was sometimes raised more than once in a year. For example, Beijing increased its minimum wage in January and July of 2004, and Jiangsu raised its minimum wage in April and July of 2008.

We restrict the analysis to salaried workers between the ages of 16 and 59 who are employed in the civilian labor force, report positive annual earnings, are not self-employed, and are not enrolled in school. To reduce the effect from outliers, we winsorize the top two percentiles of the earnings distribution in each city-year group by assigning the value of the 97th percentile to the 98th and 99th percentiles.[18] Sampling weights are used in all calculations.

In Table 2, we provide summary statistics for the workers in our sample for the period 2004−2009. The total number of observations is 289,009.

Table 2.   Summary Statistics of Salaried Worker Age 16−59, 2004−2009.

Variable	Mean	Standard Deviation
Age	40.71	9.09
Men	0.55	0.50
Earnings (annual, RMB)	23,716	18,811
Years of schooling	12.87	2.74
Han ethnicity	0.97	0.17
Married with spouse present	0.88	0.32
Local hukou (household registration)	0.97	0.16
Work experience (year)	21.81	10.07
Years of residence	31.19	14.60

Notes: The number of observations is 289,002. Earnings has been adjusted for inflation and accounted for the differing living costs among provinces by applying the PPP-adjusted deflator developed by Brandt and Holz (2006).

---

[16]In fact, the average real minimum wage has also grown at a similar rate.
[17]The average annual growth rate of the minimum wage is 12.7% in the Eastern region, 13.2% in the Central region, and 12.5% in the Western region over the period 2004−2009.
[18]Alternatively, we also drop the top 99th percentile and the bottom 1st percentile, and the results are not affected.

The mean age is approximately 41 years, and men comprise 55% of the sample. Furthermore, the workers earn 237,716 RMB on average annually, the average number of years of schooling is 12.87, and approximately 97% of the workers are of Han ethnicity. Regarding marital status, 88% of the workers are married with a spouse present. Because of the nature of the UHS, not surprisingly, 97% of the workers have local hukou (legal household registration in a city), and the average length of residence in a city is 31 years. Finally, the average work experience is approximately 22 years.

In Table 3, we summarize the characteristics of the minimum wage standards in China. The first row of Table 3 shows that approximately 6.81% of all workers earn less than the minimum wage and that 1.88% earn the minimum wage, indicating that 8.69% of Chinese employees are minimum wage workers during the period 2004−2009.[19] Among those who earned the minimum wage or less than the minimum wage, 63.81% and 62.38% are females, respectively. Furthermore, the minimum-to-average-wage ratio of workers receiving less than the minimum wage is 2.35, indicating that these disadvantaged workers earn a wage that is only approximately one-quarter of the official standard. Regarding regional differences, in the Eastern and Central regions, approximately 92% of the workers earn a wage above the minimum wage, whereas the corresponding figure for the Western region is 89%.

Regarding the different age cohorts, Table 3 shows that teenagers (age 16−19) are very likely to be minimum wage workers, as approximately 47% of teenagers in our sample are minimum wage workers. The percentage of minimum wage workers decreases substantially as workers' age

---

[19]Our number of the average 93.2% compliance rate (16 representative provinces) over 2004−2009 is close to Ye, Gindling, and Li's (2015) who use a matched Chinese firm-employee data from 6 provinces in 2009 and find that compliance rates are as high as 96.5% for full-time workers. Although the 2004 regulation raised the penalties for violations substantially (see the section "The Minimum Wage Policy in China"), penalties for violating the minimum wage are still small. In practice, almost all firms that are found to be violating the regulations correct the violation after receiving warnings from the government labor authorities (no fines). Very few firms are required to pay fines and almost none are referred to the judicial authorities (Ye et al., 2015), resulting in some workers still being paid below the minimum wage despite the high overall compliance rate. Nevertheless, bindingness of the minimum wage can affect our analysis. Due to data limitation, we are not able to investigate this issue so our results should be interpreted with caution. Several studies have attempted to deal with the issues of enforcement and compliance such as Gindling, Mossaad, and Trejos (2015) for Costa Rica, Bhorat, Kanbur, and Mayet (2012) for South Africa, Ronconi (2010) for Argentina, and Ye et al. (2015) for China.

Table 3. Characteristics of Minimum Wage Standards in China, 2004–2009.

Variable	Less than the Minimum	The Minimum	Above the Minimum
Percent of total	6.81	1.88	91.31
Percent of female	62.38	63.81	43.36
Minimum-to-average wage ratio	2.35	1.00	0.36
	(4.34)	(0.03)	(0.21)
Region (%)			
East	6.43	1.84	91.73
Central	6.64	1.79	91.57
West	8.61	2.23	89.17
Age cohort (%)			
Age 16–19	41.48	5.34	53.18
Age 20–29	10.77	2.30	86.93
Age 30–39	5.77	1.62	92.61
Age 40–49	6.14	1.95	91.91
Age 50–59	6.74	1.86	91.41
Educational attainment (%)			
Elementary school or below	19.71	4.71	75.58
Junior high school	11.61	3.34	85.04
High school	8.12	2.35	89.53
Vocational school	5.84	1.58	92.57
Junior college	3.52	0.96	95.52
Occupation (%)			
Administrative persons of enterprises, state organs and party organizations	2.54	0.55	96.91
Professional and technical staff	2.49	0.61	96.90
Clerical and related staff	4.19	1.21	94.60
Commercial service worker	14.57	4.24	81.19
Agricultural worker	14.85	3.89	81.26
Production, transport equipment operator or related worker	7.34	2.30	90.37
Other	17.78	4.76	77.46
Industry (%)			
Mining	3.71	1.05	95.24
Manufacturing	6.73	1.84	91.44
Power production and supply	2.99	0.82	96.19
Construction	6.88	1.77	91.34
Transportation and postal service	4.74	1.23	94.03
Information technology	6.14	1.38	92.48
Wholesale and retail sales	12.81	3.55	83.64
Hotel and restaurant	12.43	3.55	84.03
Banking and finance	3.12	0.73	96.15
Real estate	6.80	1.65	91.55
Leasing and commercial service	8.01	1.84	90.15

Table 3.   (*Continued*)

Variable	Less than the Minimum	The Minimum	Above the Minimum
Scientific research	2.49	0.47	97.04
Environment and public facility	4.72	1.40	93.88
Housekeeping	15.37	4.45	80.17
Education	3.29	0.78	95.94
Health care	4.11	1.02	94.88
Sports and entertainment	4.83	0.99	94.17
Public service	2.87	1.06	96.07

Notes: Standard deviations are in parentheses. There are 289,002 salaried workers aged 16–59 in this period. "Less than the Minimum" are workers earning wages at or below 95% of the minimum wage. Minimum wage workers earn wages above 95% and up to 105% of the minimum wage. Above minimum wage workers earn wages above 105% of the minimum wage. The East includes Liaoning, Beijing, Shandong, Jiangsu, and Guangdong; the Central region includes Heilongjiang, Shanxi, Henan, Anhui, Hubei, and Jiangxi; and the West includes Gansu, Chongqing, Sichuan, and Yunnan.

increases. A similar decreasing pattern is observed with respect to skill, as measured by educational attainment. Regarding the characteristics of workers by occupation and industry, Table 3 shows that 19% of workers in clerical and related occupations and commercial service occupations combined earn less than the minimum wage. The housekeeping industry has the largest share of minimum wage workers, with approximately 20% of housekeepers earning the minimum wage or less. In both the wholesale and retail sector and the hotel and restaurant sector, approximately 16% of workers earn the minimum wage or less.

Research Design

Our objective is to assess the effect of the minimum wage on the earnings distribution in China. As noted in the section "Literature on the Distributional Effect of the Minimum Wage," nearly all existing studies on the minimum wage in China use pooled time-series/cross-section data at the provincial level and report mixed results, implying that a "consensus" regarding distributional effects of the minimum wage remains to be established. Our study attempts to reconcile existing findings by using detailed/complete minimum wage data, which allow us to employ a panel structure analysis of minimum wage effects, to exploit the greater variation in the relative minimum wage at the city level and to avoid the measurement error caused by using a uniform provincial minimum wage. Moreover, unlike previous studies that use aggregate published statistics, our study uses household survey microdata, which allow us to calculate the dependent variable — earnings differentials — at the city level. Thus, the dependent variable contains more variation and information on local conditions. Ideally, this feature should facilitate more reliable estimates of the distributional effects of the minimum wage in China.[20]

Following Lee (1999) and Autor et al. (2016), we parameterize the minimum wage effect as a quadratic function of the difference between the log minimum wage and the pth percentile of the actual log earnings distribution by expressing the q to p percentile differential $w_{ct}^q - w_{ct}^p$ as a function of the latent wage differential plus a minimum wage effect. That is, our estimation equation is

$$w_{ct}^q - w_{ct}^p = \beta_1^q \left(\mathrm{MW}_{ct} - w_{ct}^p \right) + \beta_2^q \left(\mathrm{MW}_{ct} - w_{ct}^p \right)^2 + X_{ct}' \gamma^q + \alpha_c^q + \alpha_t^q + u_{cqt} \quad (1)$$

where $\mathrm{MW}_{ct} - w_{ct}^p$ is the "effective" minimum wage variable of city c in year t, denoting the minimum wage relative to some level of local earnings that is unaffected by the minimum wage and that proxies for local living standards. We include a quadratic term "$\left(\mathrm{MW}_{ct} - w_{ct}^p \right)^2$" in the equation to capture the property that $w_{ct}^q - w_{ct}^p$ exhibits "flatten[ing] to the left," as proposed by Lee (1999) and shown in Fig. 4; for example, the quadratic term for 2008 is statistically significant at the 5% level. In estimating Eq. (1), w_{ct}^p is defined as the median wage. Further, X is a set of control variables used to capture aggregate business cycle effects; α_t^q is a set of year fixed effects; and α_c^q is a set of city fixed effects. The disturbance term u is assumed to be independent of city and year effects.[21]

Lee (1999) assumes the errors are orthogonal to the independent variables (the effective minimum wage and its square) in his estimation. However, Autor et al. (2016) point out the problem with the OLS

---

[20]As stated in the "Introduction" section, our analysis assumes minimum wages have no effects on employment or hours. We discuss how this assumption affects the interpretation of our results in the last paragraph of the section "Minimum Wage Effects on Earnings Differentials."

[21]We also include several control variables in the equation to try to reduce the concern of endogeneity. First, the city's GDP per capita and CPI (city level) capture aggregate business cycle effects and control for the global financial crisis. Second, the city's level of foreign direct investment (FDI) is used to control for provinces that may restrain the minimum wage to attract foreign investors (Frost, 2002).

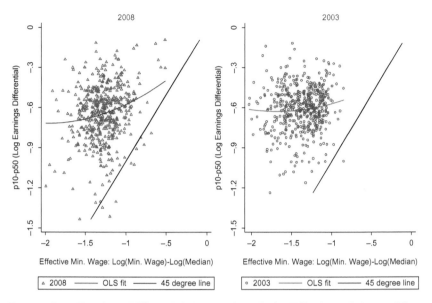

Fig. 4. Log Earnings Differential (p10-p50) and the Effective Minimum Wage across cities in 2003 and 2008. *Notes*: The estimated coefficient on the quadratic term for 2008 is statistically different from zero at the 0.05 level; while it is insignificant for 2003.

estimation of Eq. (1) is that potential measurement errors will lead to upward biased estimates of the effect of the minimum wage on inequality in both the lower and upper tail of the earnings/wage distribution. Hence, Autor et al. (2016) follow the approach in Durbin (1954) by applying IVs to address the bias caused by such a measurement error problem. Likewise, Bosch and Manacorda (2010) apply the IV approach to address this issue in their study on Mexico. Since we use Lee's methodology, we need instruments to deal with the problem of measurement error. In the 2SLS regressions, we instrument the observed effective minimum wage and its square by using three instruments as in Autor et al. (2016): (1) the log of the real minimum wage, (2) the square of the log of the real minimum wage, and (3) the interaction between the log minimum wage and the average log median real wage for the city over the sample period. In such specification, identification for the effective minimum wage $\left(\mathrm{MW}_{ct} - w_{ct}^p\right)$ in Eq. (1) fully comes from the variation of (1) the log of the real minimum wage and identification for the quadratic term $\left(\mathrm{MW}_{ct} - w_{ct}^p\right)^2$ comes from (2) the square of the log of the real minimum wage and (3) the interaction term.

Counterfactual Estimates of Changes in Earnings Inequality

To measure the contribution of the increase in the effective minimum wage to the observed rise in China's earnings inequality over the period 2004–2009, we compare actual and counterfactual estimates of changes in earnings differentials. Conceptually, we calculate counterfactual estimates of changes in latent earnings differentials without the rise in the minimum wage – that is, the change in the earnings gap that would have been observed had the minimum wage been held at a constant, real benchmark.

Lee (1999) and Autor et al. (2016) propose the following simple procedure to estimate changes in latent earnings differentials. For each observation in the data set, we calculate its rank in its respective city-year earnings distribution. Then, to simulate the earnings of the qth percentile worker in city c in t_1 (such as 2009) with the minimum wage at its t_0 (such as 2004) relative level, we adjust each worker's actual log earnings by the quantity:

$$\Delta w_{ct}^q = \hat{\bar{\beta}}_1^q \left(\tilde{\text{MW}}_{c,t_0} - \tilde{\text{MW}}_{c,t_1} \right) + \hat{\bar{\beta}}_2^q \left(\tilde{\text{MW}}_{c,t_0}^2 - \tilde{\text{MW}}_{c,t_1}^2 \right) \tag{2}$$

where $\tilde{\text{MW}}_{c,t_1}$ is the observed end-of-period effective minimum wage in city c in t_1, $\tilde{\text{MW}}_{c,t_0}$ is the corresponding beginning-of-period effective minimum in t_0, $\hat{\bar{\beta}}_1^q$ and $\hat{\bar{\beta}}_2^q$ are estimated coefficients from Tables A1 and A2. Take $t_0 = 2004$ and $t_1 = 2009$ example, adding Δw_{ct}^q to each observed earnings in 2009 would adjust the 2009 earnings distribution to its counterfactual under the realized effective minimum wage in 2004. Next, we pool these adjusted earnings distribution to get a counterfactual national earnings distribution, and then compare changes in earnings inequality between the observed earnings distribution and the simulated distribution obtained from the above method.[22] Finally, standard errors are calculated by bootstrapping the estimates within the city-year panel.[23]

---

[22]$\tilde{\text{MW}}$ is calculated by correcting the estimation for changes in the minimum wage and changes in the city's median earnings, while Lee (1999) and Autor et al. (2016) use national and state median wages when calculating $\tilde{\text{MW}}$.

[23]As in Autor et al. (2016), we start by drawing cities with replacement in our sample and then estimate Eq. (1) and apply the coefficients to compute the counterfactual in Eq. (2). We report the standard deviation using 200 replications in Table 5.

EMPIRICAL RESULTS AND DISCUSSION

Minimum Wage Effects on Earnings Differentials

We first present the estimation results of minimum wage effects on earnings differentials in Table 4. In each column, we estimate Eq. (1) by using a fixed-effects model with four different specifications. All regressions are weighted by the size of the city's population, and standard errors (in parentheses) are clustered at the city level. Entries in the tables refer to the estimated first derivative (marginal effect) of each dependent variable with respect to the effective minimum wage evaluated at the population-weighted average across cities and years.[24] In addition to OLS, we use 2SLS regression to address potential endogeneity issues as suggested in Autor et al. (2016). To check the validity of our instruments, we report results for the weak identification test and overidentification test (Hansen J statistics) in Tables A1–A4. Except specification (1) for the p75-p90 and p90-p50 earnings differentials in Tables A3 and A4, which reject the exogeneity of the instruments, all other test results show that our instruments are valid.[25]

We report the OLS and 2SLS results in terms of the marginal effects of four specifications for each percentile gap. Each entry refers to a separate regression, where each row refers to the differential between the 10th, 25th, 75th, and 90th percentiles of the earnings distribution and the median. The first column of Table 4 reports the estimates with cluster-robust standard errors at the city level presented in parentheses for the specification using fixed year and city effects. In the second column, we report the estimates of the specification with fixed year and city effects and the interaction of the province and year dummies. This specification allows us to abstract from the differential changes in the minimum wage and latent wages across cities. The estimation of the third column further contains city trends, whereas in the fourth column, we additionally include city covariates to control for the local economic conditions and business cycle effects.

---

[24]That is, each entry mean is $\beta_1^q + 2\beta_2^q(\mathrm{MW} - w^p)$, where variables without the ct subscript refer to the sample mean values over all cities and all periods.

[25]For all 2SLS models, the weak identification test shows that the instruments are highly significant and able to pass standard diagnostic tests for weak instruments, as suggested in Stock, Wright, and Yogo (2002).

Table 4. Marginal Effects of the Minimum Wage on Earnings Differentials, 2004–2009.

Earnings Differential	(1)		(2)		(3)		(4)	
	OLS	2SLS	OLS	2SLS	OLS	2SLS	OLS	2SLS
p50-p10	-.118**	-.277*	-.113**	-.237*	-.137***	-.206**	-.094**	-.117*
	(.047)	(.154)	(.048)	(.143)	(.051)	(.091)	(.049)	(.064)
p50-p25	-.094***	-.163**	-.101***	-.146**	-.107***	-.146***	-.116***	-.131***
	(.028)	(.070)	(.028)	(.063)	(.034)	(.056)	(.036)	(.047)
p75-p50	.025	.027	.025	.024	.026	.024	.025	.024
	(.028)	(.068)	(.030)	(.081)	(.026)	(.064)	(.028)	(.050)
p90-p50	.037	.040	.036	.034	.037	.036	.038	.036
	(.040)	(.101)	(.043)	(.124)	(.037)	(.089)	(.039)	(.073)
Observation	989		989		989		989	
City fixed effects	Yes		Yes		Yes		Yes	
Province × Year (interactions)			Yes		Yes		Yes	
City trends					Yes		Yes	
City controls							Yes	
Weak identification test	Reject		Reject		Reject		Reject	
Overidentification test	Not reject[a]		Not reject		Not reject		Not reject	

Notes: Cluster-robust standard errors at the city level are in parentheses. Entries in the table refer to the estimated first derivative of each dependent variable with respect to the effective minimum wage evaluated at the sample mean which is $\beta_1^q + 2\beta_2^q(MW - w^p)$, where variables without the *ct* subscript refer to sample means over all cities and all periods. The statistics of weak identification and overidentification tests for each earnings differential are in the Appendix Tables A1–A4.

[a]Note that except specification (1) for the p75-p50 and p90-p50 earnings differentials which reject the exogeneity of the instruments, all other test results do not reject the null hypothesis that the instruments are exogenous.

*** Statistically significant at the 1% level; ** at the 5% level; * at the 10% level.

The significance of our results is compelling: Overall, we find that the minimum wage can reduce the earnings differentials at the bottom end of the earnings distribution (i.e., p50-p10 and p50-p25); in contrast, as a placebo test, we do not find a statistically significant effect at the upper end of the earnings distribution (e.g., p75-p50 and p90-p50). For example, the OLS estimates of −.118 and −.094 in column (1) show that a 10% increase in the effective minimum wage leads to statistically significant 1.18% and .94% reductions in the p50-p10 and p50-p25 earnings differentials, and the corresponding reductions according to the marginal effects of the 2SLS results are 2.77% and 1.63%, which are also statistically significant. As expected, the point estimates tend to be smaller for the p50-p25 earnings differential than for the p50-p10 earnings differential, implying some spillover, but the effect is attenuated as we move up the earnings distribution ladder.[26] Note that the OLS and 2SLS results at the upper end (p75-p50 and p90-p50) are not statistically significant, suggesting the minimum wage does not have an effect on earnings above the median.

In column (2) of Table 4, we additionally control for the interaction of the year dummies with the province dummies. By including province-year interaction fixed effects, we control for province-specific factors that have been shown to be important predictors of changes in the earnings structure. These regressions effectively identify the effect of the minimum wage based on its differential variation across cities. Compared with the results in column (1), the 2SLS results in column (2) show weaker effects of the minimum wage on the earnings distribution by reducing the earnings gaps at the bottom end of the distribution.

Column (3) of Table 4 additionally controls for city-specific linear time trends. As shown, the marginal effects decrease in absolute value for the p50-p10 and p50-p25 earnings differentials in the 2SLS estimates. The

---

[26]The spillover effects of the minimum wage are quite evident from our results. However, Autor et al. (2016) provide a mundane but plausible explanation for their findings of spillover effects using US data, which is that it is measurement error. Since we are using household survey data, and survey data on sensitive questions such as earnings often have considerable measurement error, it is possible that the spillover effects we find may be due to measurement error. On the other hand, Jia and Zhang (2013) find spillover effects of minimum wages in China using longitudinal data at the individual level from the China Health and Nutrition Survey. Their results indicate that spillover effects of the minimum wage increase can reach to 1.50 and 1.25 times of minimum wages on male and female wage distribution, respectively. Although we cannot rule out the possibility of measurement error, our use of IV regression can substantially reduce this concern as shown in Autor et al. (2016).

marginal effects are statistically significant up to the median and are not significant afterward, implying pronounced spillover effects of the minimum wage that propagate to higher percentiles of the earnings distribution at the bottom but not the upper end of the earnings distribution. For example, the 2SLS result in column (3) for the period 2004−2009 suggests that a 10% increase in the effective minimum wage reduces the p50-p10 earnings differential by almost .206 log points and the p50-p25 earnings differential by .146 log points.

Potential concerns regarding the results in the previous columns are that the correlation between earnings inequality and the minimum wage might be contaminated by the opening of the Chinese economy after China became an official member of the WTO in December of 2001 and that soaring FDI might have contributed to shaping the trends in earnings inequality, as others have claimed. To address these possible issues, we additionally control for factors that might be correlated with the trend in the effective minimum wage. The marginal effects that include these additional controls are presented in column (4) of Table 4, and they are smaller than those in columns (1), (2), and (3). In short, we find that minimum wage changes have reduced earnings inequality in China by essentially decreasing earnings gaps at the bottom end of the earnings distribution.[27]

Note that our results are based on the assumption that minimum wages have effects on employment or hours. However, recent studies that use firm level or household surveys to examine the employment effect of minimum wages in China have found either negative or no effects (Fang & Lin, 2015; Huang, Loungani, & Wang, 2014; Mayneris, Poncet, & Zhang, 2014). In particular, Ye et al. (2015) use 2009 matched firm-employee data which contains detailed wage information (basic monthly wages, bonus, supplements, and hours) and find evidence that Chinese firms adjust to the higher

---

[27]Note that if the endogeneity problem we try to instrument for mainly comes from measurement error, we would expect the 2SLS estimates in Table 4 to be smaller (in absolute value) than the OLS estimates. As expected, the upper end of the earnings distribution (p75-p50 and p90-p50) shows that the 2SLS estimates are smaller than the OLS estimates (except specification 1). However, for the lower end (p50-p10 and p50-p25) shows the opposite. There can be two possible reasons. First, it could be possible that the measurement error problem is not the major endogeneity issue (not as severe as we expect in the lower end of the earnings distribution in the data). Second, our instruments marginally pass the Stock & Yogo's weak instrument test, signaling we might have weak instrument issues. Due to lack of data, we are not able to pursue further. Although we cannot rule out these concerns, our conclusions do not change and should be interpreted with caution.

minimum wage by increasing hours worked of those low-skilled workers in the most labor-intensive firms. If we were to consider these findings that employment and hours go down in response to a minimum wage change, our estimates could overstate the effect of minimum wages on reducing earnings inequality in China and should be interpreted with caution.

Results of Counterfactual Estimates of Changes in Earnings Inequality

Table 5 presents the results of the counterfactual estimates of changes in the p50-p10 and p50-p25 earnings differentials. The calculations are done at the city level by using the estimated coefficients from Tables A1 and A2 and the method illustrated in the section "Counterfactual Estimates of Changes in Earnings Inequality." The third column reports the earnings differentials in log points for 2004 and 2009. The fourth column presents the observed actual change, which equals the difference in the log gaps of 2004 and 2009 times 100, whereas the fifth and the sixth columns provide the counterfactual estimates of the latent change (100 times the log change) based on the OLS and 2SLS results from the four model specifications.

Because the minimum wage policy particularly aims to help low-earning workers, we are interested in how the minimum wage affects inequality at the bottom half of the earnings distribution. Take the p50-p10 earnings differential as an example: The actual log earnings gap is .892 in 2004 and .922 in 2009. Hence, the actual change is −.0296 log points between the two years, indicating that the earnings inequality deteriorates. Had there been no minimum wage increase between 2004 and 2009, what would the p50-p10 earnings gap be in 2009? We answer this counterfactual question by reporting the latent changes:

Table 5. Actual and Latent Changes in Earnings Differentials, 2004−2009.

Earnings Differential	Year	Log Gap	Actual Change	Latent Change (OLS)				Latent Change (2SLS)			
				(1)	(2)	(3)	(4)	(1)	(2)	(3)	(4)
p50-p10	2004	.892	−.0296	−.0415	−.0396	−.0375	−.0335	−.0495	−.0436	−.0395	−.0360
	2009	.922		(.010)	(.011)	(.015)	(.015)	(.009)	(.012)	(.015)	(.015)
p50-p25	2004	.463	−.0047	−.0059	−.0053	−.0052	−.0051	−.0055	−.0051	−.0050	−.0049
	2009	.468		(.001)	(.001)	(.002)	(.002)	(.001)	(.001)	(.002)	(.002)

Notes: Actual and latent changes are in log points calculated at city level. Actual change = [log gap (2004)− log gap (2009)]. Marginal effects are bootstrapped and standard deviations associated with the estimates are in parentheses.

The numbers are larger for both the OLS and the 2SLS models and for all specifications. For example, the latent change in 2SLS specifications (1) and (4) is −.0495 and −.0360 log points, respectively, which indicates that the p50-p10 earnings gap in 2009 would have been 67−22% higher if the minimum wage had not increased. Note that the numbers are lower than those in Lee (1999) but close to those in Autor et al. (2016). The results for the p50-p25 earnings differential tell a similar story, that is, that the inequality would have been higher if there were no minimum wage increase in China between 2004 and 2009.

CONCLUSIONS

We use a large set of panel data at the city level that contains relevant information on the minimum wage, combined with a longitudinal household survey of 16 representative provinces, to estimate the distributional effect of minimum wage changes in China over the period 2004−2009. Compared with previous studies using provincial-level data and reporting mixed results, our study shows that minimum wage changes significantly help reduce the earnings gap at the bottom end of the earnings distribution. In a placebo test, we do not find that minimum wage changes have an effect on the earnings gap at the upper end of the distribution.

To gauge the contribution of minimum wage increases to reducing earnings inequality, we calculate the counterfactual changes in earnings differentials and decompose the total change in China's earnings distribution. Indeed, we find that minimum wage changes substantially contribute to reducing the earnings gap at the bottom end of the distribution. Likewise, the results for the Gini coefficients and variance in our analysis suggest that the minimum wage helps reduce earnings inequality.

In sum, our findings are consistent with recent studies reporting that the minimum wage plays an essential role in earnings/wage inequality. Both the United States and Mexico have exhibited a declining minimum wage (both real and effective) and rising inequality, and empirical evidence shows that the declining minimum wage accounts for a substantial part of the growth in inequality in both countries over the past three decades (Autor et al., 2016; Bosch & Manacorda, 2010; Lee, 1999). In contrast, China has experienced a rapid increase in the minimum wage and rapidly increasing inequality in the past 10 years, which provides an opportunity to study the effect of the minimum wage on inequality in an environment that differs from that in prior research (e.g., United States and Mexico). Our finding that minimum wage increases have reduced inequality – by reducing earnings gaps particularly at the bottom end of the earnings distribution – has both regional relevance and general implications in the context of the minimum wage literature.

ACKNOWLEDGMENTS

This paper is supported by Grant #106753 from IDRC (International Development Research Centre) Canada. Myeong-Su Yun's work is supported by Inha University Research Grant (INHA-53347). We are grateful to the editors, and two anonymous referees for their helpful suggestions and insightful comments. We thank Thomas Lemieux, Stephen Machin, and participants at IZA Workshop on Inequality: Causes and Consequences in Bonn, Germany (March 20–21, 2015); Kaushik Basu, Jan Svejnar, Ravi Kanbur, Haroon Bhorat, Rajeev Dehejia, Henry Wan, and participants at the World Bank Conference on Markets, Labor and Regulation in New Delhi, India (December 17–18, 2014); Yaohui Zhao, Xiaoyan Lei, Lixing Li, Dandan Zhang, Maoliang Ye, and seminar participants at National School of Development of Peking University; Li Yu, Simon Chang, Sophie Wang, and seminar participants at China Center for Human Capital and Labor Market Research of Central University of Finance and Economics in Beijing; Ming Lu and Ninghua Zhong, and seminar participants at Tonji University in Shanghai; Sylvie Démurger and seminar participants at the Groupe d'Analyse et de Théorie Economique (GATE Lyon Saint-Etienne, CNRS) in Lyon, France; Sang-bong Oh at the Korea Labor Institute (KLI) seminar; Chunbing Xing at ORF University of Western Ontario-BNU Joint Workshop on Labor Market in China; Eric S. Lin and seminar participants at Tsing Hua Conference on the Economics of Public Policy of National Tsing Hua University, Taiwan (2014); Shihe Fu and all conference participants in the 2014 Chinese Economists Society (CES) Annual Conference in Guangzhou of China, 2014 Chinese Economic Association (Europe/UK) at University of Gothenburg in Sweden, 2014 Asia Economic Community Forum (ACEF) in Incheon, South Korea, Conference on Reforming Minimum Wage and Labor Regulation Policy in Developing and Transition Economies (Beijing Normal University, October 18, 2014), 2015 Eastern Economic Association Conference in New York, seminars at National Taipei University, IDRC India, Industrial Canada, Carleton University, and Bucknell University. Finally, we are grateful for Shi Li (Beijing Normal University) for his tremendous support and the three editors Lorenzo Cappellari, Solomon Polachek, and Konstantinos Tatsiramos for their encouragement and patience with the final draft. All errors are our own. Send an email to the corresponding author, Myeong-Su Yun (msyun@inha.ac.kr), for any further inquiry.

REFERENCES

Autor, D. H., Manning, A., & Smith, C. L. (2016). The contribution of the minimum wage to US wage inequality over three decades: A reassessment. *American Economic Journal: Applied Economics, 8*(1), 58–99.

Bhorat, H., Kanbur, R., & Mayet, N. (2012). Estimating the causal effect of enforcement on minimum wage compliance: The case of South Africa. *Review of Development Economics, 16*, 608–623.

Bosch, M., & Manacorda, M. (2010). Minimum wages and earnings inequality in urban Mexico. *American Economic Journal: Applied Economics, 2*(4), 128–149.

Brandt, L., & Holz, C. A. (2006). Spatial price differences in China: Estimates and implications. *Economic Development and Cultural Change, 55*(1), 43–86.

Burkhauser, R. V., & Finegan, T. A. (1989). The minimum wage and the poor: The end of a relationship. *Journal of Policy Analysis and Management, 8*(1), 53–71.

Chan, A. (2001). *China's workers under assault: The exploitation of labor in a globalizing economy*. New York: ME Sharpe.

Chen, J. (2012). *The employment effect and income distribution effect from the minimum wage standard: Evidence of chongqing*. Chongqing Normal University (in Chinese).

Cheung, S. N. S. (2004). Another eye on minimum wages. *Southern Weekly*.

Cheung, S. N. S. (2010). The lethality of minimum wages. *Economic Information Daily*.

Cooke, F. L. (2005). *HRM, work and employment in China*. New York: Routledge.

Durbin, J. (1954). Errors in variables. *Revue de l'Institut International de Statistique [Review of the International Statistical Institute], 22*(1–3), 23–32.

Fang, T., & Lin, C. (2015). Minimum wages and employment in China. *IZA Journal of Labor Policy, 4*, 1–30.

Frost, S. (2002). Labour standards in China: The business and investment challenge. Association for Sustainable and Responsible Investment in Asia.

Gindling, T. H., Mossaad, N., & Trejos, J. D. (2015). The consequences of increased enforcement of legal minimum wages in a developing country: An evaluation of the impact of the campaña nacional de salarios mínimos in Costa Rica. *ILR Review, 68*(3), 666–707.

Gindling, T. H., & Terrell, K. (2007). The effects of multiple minimum wages throughout the labor market: The case of Costa Rica. *Labour Economics, 14*(3), 485–511.

Huang, Y., Loungani, P., & Wang, G. (2014). *Minimum wages and firm employment: Evidence from China*. IMF Working Paper No. WP/14/184.

Jia, P. (2013). *Minimum wage effects on employment and income distribution*. Jilin: Jilin University. (in Chinese)

Jia, P., & Zhang, S. (2013). Spillover effects of minimum wages increase. *Statistical Research, 30*(4), 37–41. (in Chinese)

Johnson, W. R., & Browning, E. K. (1983). The distributional and efficiency effects of increasing the minimum wage: A simulation. *American Economic Review, 73*, 204–211.

Lee, D. S. (1999). Wage inequality in the United States during the 1980s: Rising dispersion or falling minimum wage? *The Quarterly Journal of Economics*, *114*(3), 977–1023.

Li, S., & Luo, C. (2011). How unequal is China? *Economic Research Journal*, *4*, 68–78. (in Chinese)

Li, S., & Zhao, R. (1999). Re-examining the income distribution in China. *Economic Research Journal*, *4*, 3–17. (in Chinese)

Mayneris, F., Poncet, S., & Zhang, T. (2014). *The cleansing effect of minimum wage: Minimum wage rules, firm dynamics and aggregate productivity in China.* CEPII Working Paper No. 2014-16.

National Bureau of Statistics of China. (2010). The 6th China population census.

National Bureau of Statistics of China. (2013). China labour statistical year book.

Neumark, D., Cunningham, W., & Siga, L. (2006). The effects of the minimum wage in Brazil on the distribution of family incomes: 1996–2001. *Journal of Development Economics*, *80*(1), 136–159.

Neumark, D., Schweitzer, M., & Wascher, W. (2005). The effects of minimum wages on the distribution of family incomes: A nonparametric analysis. *Journal of Human Resources*, *40*(4), 867–894.

Neumark, D., & Wascher, W. L. (2008). *Minimum wages.* Cambridge, MA: MIT Press.

Quan, H., & Li, L. (2011). The income distribution effect of minimum wage in Shanghai: Evidence and simulation. *Shanghai Economic Research*, *4*, 96–109.

Rama, M. (2001). The consequences of doubling the minimum wage: The case of Indonesia. *Industrial and Labor Relations Review*, *54*(4), 864–881.

Ronconi, L. (2010). Enforcement and compliance with labor regulations in Argentina. *Industrial & Labor Relations Review*, *63*(4), 719–736.

Stock, J. H., Wright, J. H., & Yogo, M. (2002). A survey of weak instruments and weak identification in generalized method of moments. *Journal of Business & Economic Statistics*, *20*(4), 518–529.

Su, H. (1993). Research on the legislation of minimum wage law of China. *Review of Economic Research*, *Z1*, 26–36 (in Chinese).

Wang, D. (2011). On the minimum wage system of China: Probable effects on income distribution and economic development. *Zhejiang Social Sciences*, *2*, 11–17 (in Chinese).

Wang, D. (2013). *Minimum wage effects on income distribution.* Jilin: Jilin University (in Chinese).

Wang, H. (2007). *Income distribution and income liquidity of residents in China.* Guangzhou: Sun Yat-Sen University (in Chinese).

Wang, J., & Gunderson, M. (2011). Minimum wage impacts in China: Estimates from a pre-specified research design, 2000–2007. *Contemporary Economic Policy*, *29*(3), 392–406.

Wen, Q. (2007). *Research on the effect of minimum wages on rural migrants' employment and income distribution.* Chengdu: University of Electronic Science and Technology of China (in Chinese).

World Bank. (2006). *Minimum wages in Latin America and the Caribbean: The impact on employment, inequality, and poverty.* Washington, DC: Office of the Chief Economist.

Yang, T. (2006). What is the social background when China implemented its minimum wage law? *People's Daily*.

Ye, L., Gindling, T. H., & Li, S. (2015). Compliance with legal minimum wages and overtime pay regulations in China. *IZA Journal of Labor & Development*, *4*(16), 1–35.

APPENDIX

Table A1. OLS and 2SLS Estimates of Minimum Wages on p50-p10 Earnings Differential: 2004–2009.

Dependent Variable: p50-p10	Model							
	(1)		(2)		(3)		(4)	
Independent Variable	OLS	2SLS	OLS	2SLS	OLS	2SLS	OLS	2SLS
Effective MW	-.173	-.386	-.124	-.351	-.108	-.215	-.053	-.142
	(.306)	(.225)	(.299)	(.232)	(.290)	(.121)	(.297)	(.091)
(Effective MW)^2	-.024	-.154	-.005	-.140	.012	-.083	.018	-.056
	(.125)	(.091)	(.120)	(.094)	(.121)	(.049)	(.125)	(.038)
Observations	989		989		989		989	
City fixed effects	YES		YES		YES		YES	
Province × Year (interactions)			YES		YES		YES	
City controls					YES		YES	
City trends							YES	
Weak identification test	12.861		10.410		13.657		21.208	
Overidentification test	0.120		0.746		0.797		0.833	
(*p*-value)	(0.73)		(0.39)		(0.31)		(0.27)	

Note: The instruments are (1) the log of the real minimum wage, (2) the square of the log of the real minimum wage, and (3) the interaction between the log minimum wage and the average log median real wage for the city over the sample period.

Table A2. OLS and 2SLS Estimates of Minimum Wages on p50-p25 Earnings Differential: 2004–2009.

Dependent Variable: p50-p25	Model							
	(1)		(2)		(3)		(4)	
Independent Variable	OLS	2SLS	OLS	2SLS	OLS	2SLS	OLS	2SLS
Effective MW	-.327	-.194	-.305	-.156	-.226	-.137	-.309	-.120
	(.182)	(.103)	(.180)	(.101)	(.193)	(.077)	(.218)	(.062)
(Effective MW)^2	-.100	-.076	-.088	-.061	-.051	-.053	-.083	-.046
	(.077)	(.042)	(.075)	(.041)	(.080)	(.031)	(.091)	(.025)
Observations	989		989		989		989	
City fixed effects	YES		YES		YES		YES	
Province ×Year (interactions)			YES		YES		YES	
City controls					YES		YES	
City trends							YES	
Weak identification test	12.861		10.410		13.657		21.208	
Overidentification test	0.387		0.908		0.997		1.189	
(p-value)	(0.53)		(0.34)		(0.30)		(0.24)	

Note: The instruments are (1) the log of the real minimum wage, (2) the square of the log of the real minimum wage, and (3) the interaction between the log minimum wage and the average log median real wage for the city over the sample period.

Table A3. OLS and 2SLS Estimates of Minimum Wages on p75-p50 Earnings Differential: 2004–2009.

Dependent Variable: p75-p50	Model							
	(1)		(2)		(3)		(4)	
Independent Variable	OLS	2SLS	OLS	2SLS	OLS	2SLS	OLS	2SLS
Effective MW	.338	.425	.332	.520	.410	.353	.581	.296
	(.180)	(.142)	(.180)	(.186)	(.176)	(.104)	(.173)	(.068)
(Effective MW)²	.034	.164	.033	.205	.068	.136	.139	.114
	(.069)	(.578)	(.068)	(.076)	(.071)	(.042)	(.068)	(.029)
Observations	989		989		989		989	
City fixed effects	YES		YES		YES		YES	
Province ×Year (interactions)			YES		YES		YES	
City controls					YES		YES	
City trends							YES	
Weak identification test	12.861		10.410		13.657		21.208	
Overidentification test	3.651		0.644		0.528		0.501	
(p-value)	(0.06)		(0.42)		(0.38)		(0.36)	

Note: The instruments are (1) the log of the real minimum wage, (2) the square of the log of the real minimum wage, and (3) the interaction between the log minimum wage and the average log median real wage for the city over the sample period.

Table A4. OLS and 2SLS Estimates of Minimum Wages on p90-p50 Earnings Differential: 2004–2009.

Dependent Variable: p90-p50	Model							
	(1)		(2)		(3)		(4)	
Independent Variable	OLS	2SLS	OLS	2SLS	OLS	2SLS	OLS	2SLS
Effective MW	.569	.650	.577	.811	.540	.489	.722	.439
	(.258)	(.208)	(.262)	(.273)	(.226)	(.137)	(.230)	(.097)
(Effective MW)^2	.083	.252	.090	.321	.069	.187	.145	.169
	(.098)	(.085)	(.098)	(.012)	(.088)	(.563)	(.088)	(.041)
Observations	989		989		989		989	
City fixed effects	YES		YES		YES		YES	
Province × Year (interactions)			YES		YES		YES	
City controls					YES		YES	
City trends							YES	
Weak identification test	12.861		10.410		13.657		21.208	
Overidentification test	4.721		0.521		0.901		1.310	
(*p*-value)	(0.03)		(0.47)		(0.34)		(0.21)	

Note: The instruments are (1) the log of the real minimum wage, (2) the square of the log of the real minimum wage, and (3) the interaction between the log minimum wage and the average log median real wage for the city over the sample period.

TRADING PLACES: A DECADE OF EARNINGS MOBILITY IN CHILE AND NICARAGUA

Rafael Novella, Laura Ripani, Agustina Suaya, Luis Tejerina and Claudia Vazquez

Inter-American Development Bank

ABSTRACT

Using longitudinal datasets from Chile and Nicaragua, we compare intragenerational earnings mobility over a decade for two economies with similar inequality levels but divergent positions in equality of opportunities within the Latin American region. Our results suggest that earnings mobility, in terms of origin independence of individual ranking in the earnings distribution, is greater in Chile than in Nicaragua.

Keywords: Earnings mobility; Rankings; Chile; Nicaragua

JEL classification: D31; J3; J6; O54

Income Inequality Around the World
Research in Labor Economics, Volume 44, 213–237
Copyright © 2016 by Emerald Group Publishing Limited
All rights of reproduction in any form reserved
ISSN: 0147-9121/doi:10.1108/S0147-912120160000044013

INTRODUCTION

Economists have studied the evolution of the welfare status of populations mainly through comparisons of per capita income, inequality, and poverty indexes over time.[1] These metrics are generally calculated from a given income distribution based on anonymous cross sections, considering individuals, households, or population groups as the main unit of analysis. Although important, those snapshots are static and do not permit assessing dynamic phenomena of income distributions, such as mobility (changes in socioeconomic status over time). Along with static characteristics such as inequality and per capita income, the *dynamics* of income distribution can be a significant factor of social welfare. As Friedman (1962) and many others claim, two societies with the same level of inequality may have different welfare levels if one society is more rigid such that the people with low incomes are consistently the same, while the other society has more socioeconomic mobility.

Socioeconomic standing can be captured by different measures: while sociologists have generally concentrated on occupational status and social classes' mobility, economists tend to focus on individual earnings and household income. Mobility levels found in empirical research differ depending on the measure used and the defined unit of analysis.[2] In this paper, we consider the individual worker as the unit of analysis and use earnings (labor income) to measure socioeconomic position, excluding any other sources of income.[3]

The timeframe of our study is also set by our focus on the individual worker. Intragenerational studies focus on changes in the economic status within the lifetime of the same individual on the basis of longitudinal or retrospective data. Intergenerational studies, on the other hand, analyze

---

[1]For example, using abbreviated social welfare functions (Lambert, 2001).

[2]Each of these measures presents advantages and disadvantages. For example, social classes and occupations present fewer issues in terms of recall and reliability than measures of earnings and incomes (which are particularly important in the case of intergenerational studies based on questions about economic status of parents). Also, earnings and income more commonly suffer from measurement errors. In particular, some authors claim that occupation may be a more reliable indicator of permanent economic standing than single-year income measures, which may be affected by shocks (Goldberger, 1989). On the other hand, occupations and classes are highly aggregated groups that miss important variation in economic status.

[3]In particular, we use real gross earnings, so the impact of taxation or of state transfers is not accounted for.

changes in socioeconomic status between generations (e.g., children and their parents), so the analysis spans a longer time period and the unit is not an individual, but a family or dynasty. In this paper, accordingly, we are interested in mobility in individual earnings over the medium term (over a decade). In particular, we aim to compare the level of intragenerational earnings mobility in two Latin America and the Caribbean (LAC) countries: Chile and Nicaragua.

Yet as a multivariate phenomenon, measuring earnings mobility is not straightforward, and earnings mobility may mean different things. Fields and Ok (1999a) identify two facets of mobility that do not always coincide: earnings *movements* in the aggregate and *origin independence* (the degree to which future income does not depend on current income).[4] To illustrate these aspects, the authors present the following example: Assume a society has two persons and an initial distribution of earnings given by the vector $x = (1, 3)$. Then consider two separate transformations: For $I : x = (1, 3) \rightarrow (3, 1) = y$, and for $II : x = (1, 3) \rightarrow (2, 2) = z$. Which transformation involves more mobility? It depends on the definition of mobility: Process I shows larger earnings changes (movement aspect), and process II shows no dependence of one's final earnings on the initial earnings, compared with the perfect (negative) correlation in process I (origin independence).

There are also different definitions of mobility depending on whether it is considered an absolute or relative phenomenon. Most measures are based on a relative definition of mobility. This means that if x is the initial vector of earnings distribution and y is the final earnings distribution, a relative measure will report some level of mobility if $y \neq \lambda x$, with $\lambda \geq 0$. In other words, there is a change in earnings' shares and not just a proportional change in earnings. Another approach, also based on the idea of relative mobility, focuses on rank orders (positional mobility). In this paper, we measure mobility in Chile and Nicaragua in two ways. First, we focus on *positional movement*, since we are especially interested in (relative) low-income persistence. Second, we measure mobility as (conditional) *origin independence*, since this concept is closely related to equality of opportunities which largely motivates our study.

Indeed, the main reason for choosing Chile and Nicaragua to study earnings mobility is that while both countries show a similar and relatively high level of anonymous inequality, they are located in opposite extremes

---

[4]The authors clarify that these definitions are not the only aspects of the income mobility concept.

in the distribution of the *Human Opportunity Index* (HOI). As discussed in the section "Economic Settings," the HOI is an indicator proposed by Molinas et al. (2010) that measures the equality of opportunities in the access to key goods and services for human capital formation. Therefore, we expect that comparing mobility levels in Chile and Nicaragua could shed light on the importance of equal access to opportunities for social mobility.

Longitudinal data to track the evolution of agents' income over time is required for mobility studies, but information availability regularly limits the study of mobility, especially in LAC countries where panels are relatively scarce.[5] The data used in this study comes from Chile's National Socioeconomic Characterization Survey (CASEN) panel dataset for the years 1996, 2001, and 2006 and the Nicaraguan Living Standards Measurement Survey (LSMS) surveys for the years 1998, 2001, and 2005. Chile and Nicaragua are the only two countries in the region for which it is possible to find data for such a long period of time. Hence, unlike most studies in LAC, we can measure intragenerational mobility levels in the medium term.

This paper seeks to contribute to the literature on comparative earnings mobility in LAC. We compare intragenerational earnings mobility in two LAC countries that have received relatively less attention in the literature. We measure positional movements and analyze origin independence through transition matrices and the estimation of an autoregressive model, where the ranking of each individual depends on their past ranking, conditional on a set of characteristics. Following the literature, we use an instrumental variables approach based on Arellano and Bond (1991) to overcome the potential endogeneity problem that arises with dynamic panels.

Our results suggest that earnings mobility is lower in Nicaragua than in Chile, particularly in regard to origin independence. In Nicaragua, after controlling for relevant individual characteristics such as age, education, and working hours, previous rankings still play a significant role in explaining the individual's current position in the income distribution. In Chile, on the other hand, previous rankings are not significant in explaining the position of individuals in the distribution, suggesting no time dependence after controlling for other factors.

The paper is structured as follows: the following section reviews the literature on mobility for LAC countries, focusing on comparative studies and

---

[5]As Fields et al. (2006) suggest, the recent availability of longitudinal data has been accompanied by an increase in the number of studies on economic mobility in LAC countries. For a detailed review of these studies, see Sections 3 and 4 of Fields et al. (2006).

evidence for Chile and Nicaragua. The next section describes the economic performance of both countries during our period of study and also presents the situation of both countries regarding inequality and human opportunities. The section "Methodology and Data" describes the methodology and the data. The next section presents the results, and final section concludes.

EVIDENCE ON INCOME MOBILITY IN LAC

Empirical studies have analyzed economic mobility in LAC mostly from a country-specific perspective, but there are some comparative studies measuring different aspects of mobility using different methodologies and types of data. This section briefly discusses the main findings of some comparative studies and the previous literature on Chile and Nicaragua.

Fields et al. (2015) examine changes in individual earnings using sequences of short panels in Argentina, Mexico, and Venezuela. They test two main hypotheses. First, they ask whether income changes favor the income recipients who started at the top of the income distribution (*divergent* mobility) or those who started at the bottom (*convergent* mobility). The second hypothesis they test is whether the groups that gain the most when the economy is growing lose the most when the economy is contracting (*symmetry* of mobility). The authors do not find empirical support for the divergent mobility hypothesis, and they find that poorer individuals gained more than others regardless of whether the economy was contracting or growing, so they reject the symmetry hypothesis. In the same direction, Fields and Sánchez-Puerta (2010) do not find any evidence of divergent mobility in Argentina for 1996–2003. In both studies, the weak evidence of divergent mobility contrasts with the rising inequality in the region during the years studied, which the authors contend is explained by the different outcomes of panels and cross-sectional analysis.

Using pseudo-panel data,[6] Cuesta et al. (2011) analyze mobility patterns in 14 LAC countries for 1992–2003. They concentrate on the time

---

[6]A pseudo-panel is formed creating synthetic observations obtained from averaging observations with similar characteristics (for instance, year of birth and educational level) in a sequence of repeated cross-sectional datasets. The main disadvantage of using cohorts is that aggregation probably distorts the individual dynamic, which is the dimension we are interested in when analyzing mobility. However, using information of three countries where panel data also exists (Chile, Nicaragua, and Peru), Cruces et al. (2013) analyze whether pseudo-panels can be used as a substitute of panel data in the estimation of intragenerational mobility

dependence aspect of mobility and use the log of per capita household incomes as the dependent variable, finding that very high levels of income immobility exist in the region as a whole (the estimate of the unconditional mobility is 0.966 when no control is considered). The study highlights the importance of controlling for personal and socioeconomic characteristics. Once controlling for these characteristics, immobility decreases more than 30 percent (the estimates of time dependence income mobility was reduced to 0.601). Country-specific analysis indicates that the estimated conditional mobility is low in Brazil, Colombia, and Costa Rica (βexceeding 0.75), while it is moderate in Chile (0.605). Nicaragua was not included in the analysis because it failed to report non-labor incomes in its household surveys. Also using pseudo-panels, Calónico (2006) analyzes the time-dependence facet of mobility in eight Latin American countries. He focuses on labor income as the variable of interest and finds that Chile show one of the highest levels of mobility within the region.

In the case of Chile, Scott and Litchfield (1994) study income mobility and the evolution of inequality from 1968 to 1986 for rural households. They use a transition matrix between absolute income classes and different models (ordinary least squares and order logit models) for the determination of directional income movements. According to the transition matrix, half of the population moved to a higher income class, around a quarter moved down, and, in what is very interesting, 1 in 10 initially poor households moved upward.[7] Their analysis shows that of all the households that moved, most were not very far from their initial positions, though those that moved upward moved further. The multivariate analysis performed shows the importance of age, education of the household head, amount of land owned, and initial per capita income as determinants of upward income mobility.

The CASEN longitudinal dataset from Chile has been used in studies of income mobility. Contreras et al. (2005) use the first two waves of this survey, 1996 and 2001, to study poverty dynamics, following a methodology similar to Scott and Litchfield (1994), using transition matrix and logistic

---

measures. They found that synthetic panels perform well, in the sense that mobility calculated with panels most often lies within the two bounds estimated using cross-sectional surveys, supporting the application of this methodology in contexts where panel data are absent.

[7]This fact is analyzed in detail by Scott (2000), who shows that the upward mobility for around 60 percent of the initial poor households who moved was not enough to overcome the poverty line.

regressions. Contreras et al. (2005) find significant positional mobility across the lowest seven deciles of the income distribution, which indicates, according to the authors, a high vulnerability of non-poor households to become poor. In another study of Chile for the same period, Contreras et al. (2007) analyze the distributional effects of growth using parametric and non-parametric techniques to determine percentages of income changes. They find some evidence of convergent mobility mainly in the lower tails of the income distribution (i.e., growth in Chile has contributed to the reduction of the poverty rates). Paredes and Zubizarreta (2005) use the CASEN 1996 and 2001 datasets to compare mobility among poor, extreme-poor, and non-poor households. The study reports high transition rates out of extreme poverty conditions. Additionally, the factors determining the mobility of extreme−poor households are different from those determining mobility of poor households. According to the authors, these findings provide critical information to policymakers and can be used to design better poverty alleviation policies.

Economic literature on intragenerational mobility in Nicaragua is very scarce. Andersen (2003) uses panel data from the 1998 and 2001 LSMS surveys to calculate Markov transition matrices and finds significant differences in the mobility rates by type of household. Households located in urban areas that comprise fewer children and have a higher level of education have less vulnerability and the highest degrees of upward mobility. An interesting finding is that more education is robustly related to less vulnerability, higher probability of upward mobility, and lower probability of downward mobility. Living in urban areas and having fewer young members in the household shows similar relations with vulnerability and upward/downward mobility.

The revision of the existing literature on economic mobility in LAC shows that many studies use total income as their variable of interest, while there is a lack of literature on studies focusing on labor income/earnings mobility. Moreover, it is evident that there is a lack of empirical evidence in Nicaragua, which this paper seeks to address.

ECONOMIC SETTINGS

This section presents a brief description on the economic performance of Chile and Nicaragua during the period of our study. It also offers a review of where the two countries are compared with the rest of LAC in terms of inequality in results and opportunities.

Chile has had high growth rates and a stable macroeconomic situation
for the last 20 years. During this period, the country reduced the poverty
rates significantly, achieving the highest improvement on this indicator in
the whole region. While in 1987 almost 19 percent of the population was
living on less than two dollars a day, in 2006 only 3 percent were (World
Bank Databank). In only three decades, Chile was able to move from one
of the poorest LAC countries (early 1980s) to the wealthiest (2009). From
1983 to 1998, Chile increased its per capita GDP to over 110 percent, sur-
passing LAC and global growth rates (12.6 and 27.2 percent, respectively).
Between 1998 and 2002, while most of the region was not growing,
Chile was an exception, with a modest yet positive per capita growth rate
(1 percent). Finally, the last decade presented unique opportunities, with an
important increase in commodity prices and low interest rates that fueled
the economy to annual growth of almost 5 percent for six consecutive years
(IDB, 2006).

While Chile had a high growth rate during the 1980s, Nicaragua and the
rest of Central America was facing a substantial economic crisis (see Fig. 1
for the GDP growth in Chile, Nicaragua, and LAC). The 1990s were a decade of economic stabilization, allowing Nicaragua to achieve a positive per
capita GDP growth in the second half of the decade, thought it was still
lower than those observed in the 1960s and the 1970s. Among the factors
that could explain the economic expansion, Ros (2004) identifies four key
elements: access to international markets, macroeconomic stabilization,
political stability, and establishment of a new development strategy based
on exports of manufactured goods. Even though Nicaragua had a positive
growth rate from the second half of the 1990s to the early 2000s, the

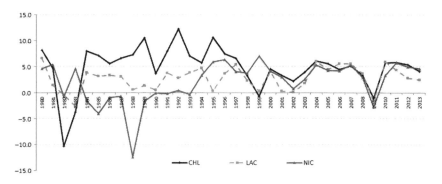

Fig. 1.   GDP Growth 1980−2013 (percent). *Source*: The World Bank.

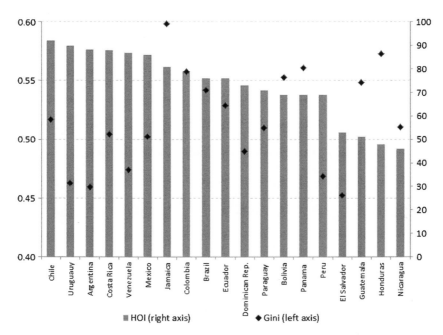

Fig. 2. Human Opportunity and Gini Indices (circa 2008). *Source*: Authors' elaboration based on Molinas et al. (2010) and SEDLAC (CEDLAS and The World Bank).

improvement was not enough to produce a significant decrease in poverty rates.

Fig. 2 shows the two countries' distribution of results and opportunities in the region and summarizes the distribution of households' per capita income in each country using the Gini coefficient.[8] The figure also shows that Chile and Nicaragua perform very similarly on inequality of income distribution, with Gini coefficients of 0.52 and 0.51, respectively. Therefore, in terms of static anonymous distribution, both countries remain close to the average level of the region.

On the other hand, the two countries contrast on inequality of opportunities. Literature on the topic emphasizes the importance of distinguishing between factors that an individual chooses and those beyond their control.

---

[8]See Table A.2 for more detail on income distribution indexes, HOI components, and survey years.

The latter is usually called *circumstances*, referring to gender, ethnicity, and parental background, among others. While results of the economic process (income, consumption) depend, at least in part, on decisions made by individuals – hence, some degree of inequality may be perceived as fair – inequality that arises as a result of differences in circumstances is called inequality of opportunities and is perceived as unfair.

Thus, equality of opportunities means that the distribution of a certain variable is not correlated with circumstances beyond the control of the individual. Equality of opportunities is particularly relevant in the labor market and children's access to goods and services that affect the possibilities of pursuing a life of their choosing, such as education, health services, minimum nutrition, and citizenship rights. The HOI is a synthetic scalar measure for monitoring both the average coverage rate of key goods and services and how equitably they have been allocated among circumstance groups. Thus, the HOI assesses the whole empirical distribution of the provision of opportunities to access a specific good or service (see Molinas et al., 2010, for details on HOI construction).

Fig. 2 presents the HOI for 18 countries in LAC. Chile and Nicaragua hold extreme positions in the distribution of this index for 2008; while static inequality is equally high in both countries, the HOI suggests a very different situation regarding the opportunities distribution, which shapes different contexts for socioeconomic mobility. If equal opportunities and mobility are positively associated, similar static inequality in both countries (i.e., cross-section anonymous indicators) may be compatible with very different intertemporal inequality situations and social welfare.

METHODOLOGY AND DATA

Our objective is to compare intragenerational mobility levels in Nicaragua and Chile based on earnings. We will measure two aspects of mobility: earnings movements and origin independence. We focus on positional mobility, namely changes in individuals' position (quintiles, ranks) in the earnings distribution. In order to compare earnings *movements*, we measure average changes in ranks within the distribution of earnings in each country using the following indicator:

$$M_R = \frac{1}{N}\sum_i |r_{it+1} - r_{it}| \tag{1}$$

where r_{it} is the ranking of individual i in period t divided by the total number of earnings n.[9] This indicator aims at measuring changes in rankings regardless of direction (Fields and Ok, 1999b).

After summarizing the magnitude of movements in the rankings, we concentrate on the origin independence aspect of mobility, which refers to the degree to which the economic situation of one individual is determined by their past economic situation. To start we aggregate data, presenting transition mobility matrices among quintiles of earnings. The rows of these matrices indicate the quintile of the earning distribution to which the worker belongs in the initial period, and columns indicate the worker's location in the final period. An identity matrix represents the case of complete time dependence, while a matrix with all equal cells represents the case of complete time independence. Then we measure the origin independence based on the difference between the observed matrix and the perfect independence matrix, as proposed in Gasparini et al. (2012),

$$I_m = \sum_f \sum_c \frac{(m_{fc} - m^i_{fc})^2}{m^i_{fc}} \tag{2}$$

where m_{fc} is the number of observations in the cell fc in the observed matrix and m^i_{fc} is the number of observations in the cell fc in the independence matrix.[10]

Finally, to measure conditional time dependence, we assume that the ranking of individuals follows the autoregressive dynamic in the following equation:

$$r_{it} = \alpha + \beta r_{it-1} + \gamma z_{it} + v_{it}, \quad v_{it} = \mu_i + \epsilon_{it} \tag{3}$$

where r_{it} is the rank order of individual i at moment t,[11] z_i is a vector of time-variant characteristics, ϵ_{it} reflects shocks, and $1 - \beta$ is a measure of conditional mobility. Although the value of β is not bounded in principle, it empirically lies between zero and one — an estimate of β closer to one

---

[9]The rank was created in ascending order so that the highest value of earnings would indicate a higher rank. Equal observations were assigned the average rank. Then we divided for the total number of earnings for a scale invariance property.

[10]I_m follows a chi-squared distribution.

[11]In this model, r_{it} is the absolute ranking — that is, number of individuals with less or equal earnings than i — and is not divided by the number of earnings as in Eq. (1).

indicates low mobility while $\beta = 0$ means a lack of dependence on the past (i.e., full mobility).

The model in Eq. (3) is a dynamic panel. By construction, the unobserved time-invariant heterogeneity μ_i is correlated with the lagged dependent variable r_{it-1} and ordinary least square estimators are inconsistent. A fixed-effect estimator would be inconsistent too. For instance, when we eliminate the individual fixed effect by taking first-differences in Eq. (3), Δr_{it-1} in Eq. (4) is correlated with $\Delta \epsilon_{it}$ [12]

$$\Delta r_{it} = \beta \Delta r_{it-1} + \gamma \Delta z_{it} + \Delta \epsilon_{it}. \tag{4}$$

We address this issue using an instrumental variables approach. In particular, we use a consistent estimator from Arellano and Bond (1991) that consists of using further lags of the dependent variable (i.e., r_{t-2}) as an instrument for $\Delta r_{it-1} = (r_{t-1} - r_{t-2})$. The instrument r_{it-2} is correlated with Δr_{it-1} but will not be correlated with $\Delta \epsilon_{it} = \epsilon_{it} - \epsilon_{it-1}$ as long as the error does not present serial correlation.

Data

The data used in this study comes from the CASEN panel datasets for the years 1996, 2001, and 2006 and from the Nicaraguan LSMS surveys for the years 1998, 2001, and 2005. To define our sample, we combine different criteria. First, we use a balanced panel with complete information on the three waves for each country. Second, we restrict the sample to those workers with positive labor income in all the periods. We do this to be able to calculate a ranking position for each individual in the sample. Third, we restrict the sample to those workers whose age was between 25 and 65 years over the whole period of analysis. The resulting data contains 1,383 workers in Chile and 1,087 in Nicaragua.

Table 1 shows some descriptive statistics from the Chilean CASEN, corresponding to 1996, 2001, and 2006; hours worked per week; and monthly real earnings increase on average during the period. Table 2 shows some descriptive statistics of the main variables of interest of the sample of Nicaragua. For example, over the years, workers increased their level of

---

[12] By construction, $\Delta \epsilon_{it}$ contains ϵ_{it-1} which is correlated with r_{it-1}.

Table 1. Summary Statistics for the Chilean CASEN 1996, 2001, and 2006.

	1996		2001		2006	
	Mean	SD	Mean	SD	Mean	SD
Male	0.78	0.41	0.78	0.41	0.78	0.41
Age	37.91	7.90	43.07	7.96	48.06	7.95
Years of education	8.81	3.82	8.73	3.88	9.03	3.95
Weekly working hours	44.90	13.88	44.17	14.59	46.55	12.63
Monthly earnings	333.35	224.72	395.66	252.57	604.92	398.93
Manufacture = 1	0.16	0.37	0.15	0.36	0.14	0.35
Commerce = 1	0.16	0.37	0.16	0.37	0.18	0.39
Services = 1	0.23	0.42	0.24	0.43	0.23	0.42
Agriculture = 1	0.23	0.42	0.21	0.41	0.20	0.40
Others = 1	0.22	0.42	0.24	0.43	0.25	0.43
Employer = 1	0.01	0.11	0.03	0.16	0.03	0.18
Self-employed = 1	0.22	0.41	0.21	0.41	0.23	0.42
Employee	0.77	0.42	0.76	0.43	0.73	0.44

Source: Authors' elaboration based on CASEN. *Notes*: Earnings are expressed in US$ PPP and correspond to monthly earnings. The difference between employers and self-employed is that employers hire paid staff, whereas self-employed work by themselves.

education. Unlike in Chile, in Nicaragua the number of working hours per week is constant over the period, though real wages increase but remain below those in Chile. On average, workers in Nicaragua work five more hours per week than workers in Chile, but their real monthly wage represents around three-quarters of one average worker in Chile. Some additional differences appear when comparing the two countries: On average, Chilean workers have almost three more years of schooling and have completed secondary education in higher proportion compared to Nicaraguan workers. It is also interesting to highlight that the proportion of individuals who are employers and self-employed are higher in Nicaragua than in Chile.[13] In contrast, the proportion of employees is much higher in Chile

---

[13]The difference between employers and the self-employed is that employers hire and pay staff, whereas the self-employed work by themselves.

Table 2. Summary Statistics for the Nicaraguan LSMS 1998, 2001, and 2005.

	1998		2001		2005	
	Mean	SD	Mean	SD	Mean	SD
Male = 1	0.63	0.48	0.63	0.48	0.63	0.48
Age	38.30	8.70	41.27	8.71	45.48	8.70
Years of education	5.74	4.35	5.86	4.82	6.48	5.25
Weekly working hours	50.21	20.7	49.85	17.71	50.73	16.12
Monthly earnings	252.28	227.21	349.80	337.14	430.48	337.23
Manufacture = 1	0.07	0.26	0.08	0.27	0.08	0.27
Commerce = 1	0.22	0.41	0.21	0.41	0.20	0.40
Services = 1	0.11	0.31	0.12	0.32	0.12	0.32
Agriculture = 1	0.31	0.46	0.32	0.47	0.33	0.47
Others = 1	0.29	0.45	0.27	0.45	0.27	0.44
Employer = 1	0.06	0.24	0.09	0.29	0.07	0.26
Self-employed = 1	0.35	0.48	0.36	0.48	0.44	0.50
Employee	0.58	0.49	0.55	0.50	0.48	0.50

Source: Authors' elaboration based on LSMS. *Notes*: Earnings are expressed in US$ PPP and correspond to monthly earnings. The difference between employers and self-employed is that employers hire paid staff, whereas self-employed work by themselves.

than in Nicaragua. These differences likely reflect institutional and human capital differences between the two countries.

RESULTS

Since our main interest is on the changes in rankings over time, we begin this section presenting descriptive statistics for the two countries in the study on earnings movements. Fig. 3 shows the indicator in Eq. (1) reflecting the average of relative movements in rankings (proportion of individuals with earnings less than or equal to the earnings of individual i in period t). M_R is calculated for the different periods in each sample. On average, and without controlling for additional characteristics, workers in Nicaragua appear to have moved more in relative terms than those in Chile.

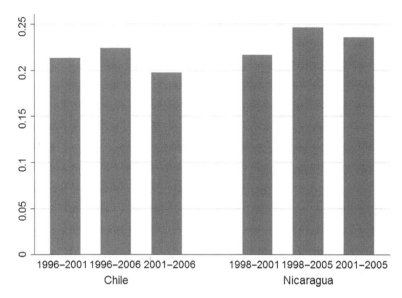

Fig. 3. Average Changes in Relative Rankings for Chile and Nicaragua. *Source*: Authors' own elaboration.

We now turn to the origin independence aspect of mobility. Tables 3 and 4 present transition matrices, a typical instrument for analyzing income mobility. In this case, rows indicate the quintile in the earnings distribution to which the individual belongs in the initial year, and columns indicate the individual's quintile in the final year. Table 3 presents two transition matrices for Chile, one for each wave pairwise combination, and Table 4 presents the same for Nicaragua.[14] For the four matrices presented, we reject the null hypothesis of independence — see Eq. (2) — in the Pearson's chi-squared test with a p-value < 0.000, suggesting that some degree of unconditional immobility is present in both countries. Moreover, the percentage of individuals who remain in the same quintile in 1996 and 2006 for Chile and in 1998 and 2005 for Nicaragua is similar: 34 percent and 33 percent, respectively.

Unconditional immobility seems to be higher in the extremes of income distribution. For example, 53.4 percent of Chilean individuals in the richest quintile in 1996 remained in that quintile five years later, and

---

[14]Table A.1 shows the transition matrix for the entire period.

Table 3. Transition Matrices Based on Chilean Labor Income (1996, 2001, and 2006).

Quintile in 1996	Quintile in 2001				
	1	2	3	4	5
1	44.6	28.6	13.0	10.5	3.3
2	19.9	27.8	27.8	18.1	6.5
3	16.3	23.9	26.5	21.0	12.3
4	12.6	13.0	21.3	28.5	24.6
5	6.5	6.9	11.2	22.0	53.4

Quintile in 2001	Quintile in 2006				
	1	2	3	4	5
1	49.6	21.4	15.2	8.0	5.8
2	23.5	32.5	21.3	18.8	4.0
3	13.8	28.3	28.3	20.3	9.4
4	10.8	13.0	23.8	30.3	22.0
5	2.2	5.1	11.2	22.7	58.8

Source: Authors' own elaboration.

Table 4. Transition Matrices Based on Nicaraguan Labor Income (1998, 2001, and 2005).

Quintile in 1998	Quintile in 2001				
	1	2	3	4	5
1	45.6	26.3	13.8	9.2	5.1
2	24.4	29.5	21.7	16.6	7.8
3	16.1	20.2	29.8	18.4	15.6
4	3.7	14.3	24.9	31.3	25.8
5	10.1	9.6	10.1	24.3	45.9

Quintile in 2001	Quintile in 2005				
	1	2	3	4	5
1	37.8	28.1	15.7	11.1	7.4
2	24.9	26.3	22.1	16.1	10.6
3	15.6	19.3	29.4	23.4	12.4
4	13.4	14.8	24.0	26.3	21.7
5	8.3	11.5	9.2	22.9	48.2

Source: Authors' own elaboration.

the proportion grew to 58.8 percent between 2001 and 2006. Moreover, the percentage of individuals who remained in the poorest quintile increased from 44.6 percent in 1996–2001 to 49.6 percent in 2001–2006. Transition matrices for Nicaragua also show higher values on the diagonal, especially at the extreme quintiles. However, while immobility among the richest also increased (the percentage remaining in the fifth quintile increased from 45.9 percent in 1998–2001 to 48.2 percent in 2001–2005), the percentage remaining in the first quintile decreased from 45.6 percent to 37.8 percent in 2001–2006.

In conclusion, we are not able to clearly identify different patterns in social mobility between the two countries with unconditional and aggregated mobility matrices. We now turn to analyzing mobility in a regression framework, controlling for others factor affecting rankings. We estimate the model in equation (3) using Arellano and Bond (1991) instrumental variables estimators and the two-step estimator with Windmeijer bias-corrected robust errors. Table 5 presents results for Chile and Nicaragua on four specifications.

Our estimates for the main variable of interest, the coefficient of past ranking, are not statistically significant in any specification for Chile, but they are for Nicaragua. Depending on the controls included, β estimates for Nicaragua range from 0.20 to 0.24. Therefore, our results suggest that the two countries differ in the degree of conditional mobility, with Chile being a more dynamic economy in terms of individual labor income. These findings are related to those of Calónico (2006), who analyzes labor income mobility in eight countries in the region using pseudo-panel data and finds that Chile shows one of the highest levels of mobility.

Regarding other variables in the model, education is positive and significantly associated with rank orders in Chile but not in Nicaragua. Age and its square are significantly associated with rank order in both countries, indicating that holding everything else constant, individuals tend to progress in positions, but at a decreasing rate the older they get. Results for Chile are similar to those of Scott and Litchfield (1994), despite studying a different period of time and unit of analysis (Scott and Litchfield looked at households instead of workers). In the conditional analysis, their results also indicate that variables such as age and education are important determinants of upward mobility.

As we expected, the specifications in column III of Table 5, which add other controls to the regression, show that rank positions are positively correlated with weekly hours worked in both Chile and Nicaragua. In

Table 5. Estimated Results of Conditional Mobility in Chile and Nicaragua.

Variables	Chile			
	I	II	III	IV
$rank_{t-1}$	0.054	0.058	0.066	0.080
	(0.066)	(0.065)	(0.066)	(0.066)
Age	34.076***	33.262***	30.421**	27.740**
	(12.217)	(12.219)	(12.283)	(12.261)
Age^2	−0.371***	−0.369***	−0.367***	−0.330**
	(0.134)	(0.134)	(0.135)	(0.134)
Education	-	12.783**	12.001**	12.106**
	-	(5.418)	(5.434)	(5.468)
Formal	-	-	111.189***	97.824***
	-	-	(28.541)	(28.811)
Hours worked	-	-	2.266***	2.377***
	-	-	(0.684)	(0.695)
Self-employment	-	-	-	−129.913***
	-	-	-	(34.373)
Manufacture	-	-	-	89.272**
	-	-	-	(42.175)
Commerce	-	-	-	42.918
	-	-	-	(40.970)
Services	-	-	-	79.209
	-	-	-	(49.013)
Others	-	-	-	72.848*
	-	-	-	(41.249)
Constant	−112.506	−197.218	−265.496	−254.246
	(284.864)	(286.637)	(289.922)	(290.514)
Observations	1,383	1,383	1,383	1,383

Variables	Nicaragua			
	I	II	III	IV
$rank_{t-1}$	0.230***	0.236***	0.206***	0.213***
	(0.070)	(0.070)	(0.069)	(0.069)
Age	27.051**	25.517*	23.844*	25.317*
	(13.142)	(13.440)	(13.452)	(13.590)

Table 5. *(Continued)*

Variables	Nicaragua			
	I	II	III	IV
Age^2	−0.309**	−0.300*	−0.284*	−0.281*
	(0.153)	(0.154)	(0.154)	(0.155)
Education	-	5.108	4.570	2.778
	-	(6.366)	(6.386)	(6.400)
Formal	-	-	61.116*	58.170
	-	-	(34.443)	(35.558)
Hours worked	-	-	3.938***	3.816***
	-	-	(0.557)	(0.555)
Self-employment	-	-	-	−52.620*
	-	-	-	(27.758)
Manufacture	-	-	-	138.197**
	-	-	-	(66.588)
Commerce	-	-	-	128.480***
	-	-	-	(44.167)
Services	-	-	-	86.757*
	-	-	-	(50.147)
Others	-	-	-	138.346***
	-	-	-	(43.114)
Constant	−149.906	−135.585	−288.148	−408.974
	(289.115)	(291.331)	(293.129)	(297.732)
Observations	1,087	1,087	1,087	1,087

Source: Authors' own elaboration.
*$p < 0.1$, **$p < 0.05$, ***$p < 0.01$.

Chile, ranks are also correlated with employment formality.[15] Formality is more important in Chile, where, holding everything else constant, workers contributing to the pension system improve their ranking position in 111 places (8 percent in terms of proportion) relative to their informal counterparts. On the other hand, self-employment is negatively associated

---

[15]We defined *formal* as a dummy variable that takes the value of 1 when the individual is listed in any pension system.

with ranking, especially in Chile, where, holding everything else constant, being self-employed is associated with an average decreased in almost 130 positions in the ranking (9 percent).

Finally, the specification in column IV of Table 5 includes a set of dummies for economic sector. Economic sectors seem to play a more significant role explaining the rankings in Nicaragua than in Chile. Relative to agriculture, the base category, being employed in manufacturing is significantly associated with higher ranking positions in both countries, but being employed in commerce and services is only correlated with a better position within income distribution in Nicaragua.

We estimated the same specifications of Table 5 for separate male and female samples in each country. We found that in Chile, estimates for the parameter of interest ($rank_{it-1}$) coefficient − are not significant and are very similar in magnitude in the male and female samples, ranging from 0.04 to 0.08, depending on the specification. On the contrary, in Nicaragua estimates are significant and relatively large for males (ranging from 0.27 to 0.32) but close to zero and not statistically significant for females.[16]

CONCLUSIONS

In this study, we analyze income mobility using longitudinal datasets for Chile and Nicaragua. These Latin American countries are useful for a comparative study on mobility because they have a similar level of static inequality in income distribution but contrast considerably both in the distribution of opportunities and in recent macroeconomic performance. Certainly, both countries have a relatively high inequality, with Gini coefficients slightly above the regional average. However, inequality measures such as the Gini coefficient are static, as they are calculated using different cross-section datasets. In this paper, we discuss the dynamic concept of mobility.

Mobility is related with inequality in numerous ways, because it affects the way income inequality is experienced intertemporally. Moreover, the concept of mobility is closely related with inequality of opportunities, in particular, with opportunities in the access to key goods and services for human capital formation. Molinas et al. (2010) calculate the HOI for Latin American countries to describe the situation of the region regarding

---

[16]Tables are not presented here, but are available upon request.

equality of opportunities. Chile and Nicaragua hold opposing positions in this indicator: Chile has the highest value in the HOI for 2008 and Nicaragua the lowest. This fact motivates the comparative analysis in these countries, since we would expect to see different degrees of mobility regardless inequality levels in income distribution. Additionally, the availability of data for both countries makes it possible to compare measures of mobility for over a decade.

The data used in this study came from Chile's CASEN panel dataset for the years 1996, 2001, and 2006, and from the Nicaraguan LSMS surveys for the years 1998, 2001, and 2005. We present transition matrices for the two subperiods and estimate models for individuals' ranking time-dependence controlling for a set of individual and labor market characteristics. The estimation uses an instrumental variable approach based on Arellano and Bond (1991) to address the methodological problems that arise in dynamic panels.

Our results suggest that workers in Chile experience a higher degree of earnings mobility, in the sense of origin independence, than those in Nicaragua. As mentioned above, these results are plausible given the differences in both countries regarding equality of opportunities and other important institutional (e.g. informality in the labor market) and socioeconomic dimensions (e.g. access to basic education; gender disparities in the access to education and labor markets; the share of people living in rural areas).

This paper highlights the fact that income mobility can be affected by the pairing of governments' economic policies with social policies for improving access to education, health, nutrition, and other services that are key to human capital formation. Such policies in Chile and Nicaragua led to improvements in the degree of individuals' mobility in income distributions.

In the last decade, LAC countries have (in general) been improving in terms of equality. However, the region is still one of the most unequal in the world. In order to improve the welfare of people in the region, especially the poor, it is necessary to continue efforts toward equalizing opportunities. All citizens should have a more equal starting point, which will help to unlock their potential in terms of the capacity to have decent earnings that could move them up the socioeconomic ladder.

Policy recommendations to expand opportunities and improving earnings include, but are not limited to: (i) policies that can improve market outcomes for low-income families (better labor market regulations that protect workers); (ii) skills development programs, such as on-the-job training and apprenticeship programs, also serve as a good way to open up learning opportunities for those who are disconnected from the formal labor market; (iii) intermediation services to connect the unconnected with good quality jobs; and (iv) nutrition assistance and health programs to have healthy and productive workers.

To better understand which specific measures should be taken by governments such as Nicaragua in terms of accelerating income mobility, we would also need to comprehend which policies affect the temporary poor versus the permanently poor and evaluate those impacts in specific environments. This is an interesting topic for future research.

ACKNOWLEDGMENTS

We would like to thank Maria Cecilia Soto for her excellent contribution in preliminary versions of this paper and participants at the 5th IZA/World Bank conference "Employment and Development" 2010 and the 17th Network on Inequality and Poverty (NIP) workshop 2011 for their helpful suggestions. We also want to thank comments from Javier Olivera and two anonymous referees. The authors are responsible for all results and views, not representing the Inter-American Development Bank.

REFERENCES

Andersen, L. (2003). *Population and poverty projections for Nicaragua 1995–2015. Working Paper Series No. 03/2003*, Institute for Advance Development Studies.

Arellano, M., & Bond, S. (1991). Some tests of specification for panel data: Monte Carlo evidence and an application to employment equations. *The Review of Economic Studies, 58*(2), 277–297.

Calonico, S. (2006). Pseudo-panel analysis of earnings dynamics and mobility in Latin America. *Paper prepared for the 2006 LACEA-LAMES Conference. Latin American and Caribbean Economic Association*, Mexico City.

Contreras, D., Cooper, R., Hermann, J., & Neilson, C. (2005). *Poverty dynamics and relative income mobility: Chile 1996 and 2001*. Technical Report, University of Chile.

Contreras, D., Cooper, R., & Neilson, C. (2007). Crecimiento pro pobre en Chile. *El Trimestre Economico, 75*(300), 931–944.

Cruces, G., Fields, G., & Viollaz, M. (2013). Can the limitations of panel datasets be overcome by using pseudo-panels to estimate income mobility? *8th IZA/World Bank Conference on Employment and Development.*

Cuesta, J., Nopo, H., & Pizzolitto, G. (2011). Using pseudo-panels to measure income mobility in Latin America. *Review of Income and Wealth, 57*, 224–246.

Fields, G., Duval-Hernandez, S., Freije, R., & Sanchez Puerta, S. (2015). Earnings mobility, inequality, and economic growth in Argentina, Mexico, and Venezuela. *The Journal of Economic Inequality*, *1*, 13.

Fields, G. S., Duval-Hernandez, R., Freije-Rodriguez, S., & Sanchez-Puerta, M. L. (2006). *Income mobility in Latin America*. Working paper No. 12, Cornell University.

Fields, G., Morgan, S., & Grusky, D. (2006). *Mohility and inequality: Frontiers of research from sociology and economics*. Stanford, CA: Stanford University Press.

Fields, G. S., & Ok, E. A. (1999a). The measurement of income mobility: An introduction to the literature. In J. Silber (Ed.), *Handbook on income inequality measurement*. Boston, MA: Kluwer Academic Publishers.

Fields, G. S., & Ok, E. A. (1999b). Measuring movement of incomes. *Economica*, *66*(264), 455–471.

Fields, G., & Sainchez-Puerta, M. (2010). Earnings mobility in times of growth and decline: Argentina from 1996 to 2003. *World Development*, *38*(6), 870–880.

Friedman, M. (1962). *Capitalism and freedom*. Chicago, IL: University of Chicago Press.

Gasparini, L., Cicowiez, M., & Escudero, W. S. (2012). *Pohreza y desigualdad en Amoerica Latina*, Temas Grupo Editorial.

Goldberger, A. S. (1989). Economic and mechanical models of intergenerational transmission. *The American Economic Review*, *79*(3), 504–513.

Lambert, P. (2001). *The distribution and redistribution of income*. Manchester: Manchester University Press.

Molinas, J. R., de Barros, R. P., Saavedra, J., & Giugale, M. (2010). Do our children have a chance, *The 2010 Human Opportunity Report for Latin America and the Caribbean. Conference Edition*.

Paredes, R., & Zubizarreta, J. (2005). *Focusing on the extremely poor: Income dynamics and policies in Chile. Working Paper No. 183*, Pontificia Universidad Católica de Chile.

Ros, J. (2004). El crecimiento económico en México y Centroamérica: Desempeño reciente y perspectivas (Vol. 18). United Nations Publications.

Scott, C. (2000). Mixed fortunes: A study of poverty mobility among small farm households in Chile, 1968–86. *Journal of Development Studies*, *36*, 155–180.

Scott, C., & Litchfield, J. (1994). *Inequality, mobility and the determinants of income among the rural poor in Chile, 1968–1986*. Development Economics Research Programme, Suntory-Toyota International Centre for Economics and Related Disciplines, London School of Economics.

APPENDIX

Table A1. Transition Matrices Based on Labor Income in Chile
and Nicaragua.

	Chile				
Quintile in 1996	Quintile in 2006				
	1	2	3	4	5
1	40.9	24.3	22.5	7.6	4.7
2	24.6	31.4	22.4	13.4	8.3
3	16.3	21.4	20.3	26.5	15.6
4	9.4	17.0	22.0	28.9	22.7
5	8.7	6.1	12.6	23.8	48.7
	Nicaragua				
Quintile in 1998	Quintile in 2005				
	1	2	3	4	5
1	39.2	24.4	15.7	10.6	10.1
2	23.5	26.3	21.7	17.5	11.1
3	13.3	23.9	26.6	21.6	14.7
4	12.4	15.2	22.1	30.4	19.8
5	11.5	10.1	14.2	19.7	44.5

Source: Authors' own elaboration.

Table A2.   HOI and Inequality Indices (circa 2008).

	Human Opportunity			Per capita income		Year of survey
	Index	Coverage	Penalty	Gini	Theil	
Chile	92	94	2	0.52	0.56	2006
Uruguauy	90	93	2	0.46	0.40	2008
Argentina	88	91	2	0.46	0.39	2008
Costa Rica	88	91	2	0.50	0.49	2009
Venezuela	87	90	3	0.47	0.45	2005
Mexico	86	90	4	0.50	0.54	2008
Jamaica	81	84	2	0.60	0.73	2002
Colombia	79	85	6	0.56	0.65	2008
Brazil	76	80	5	0.54	0.60	2008
Ecuador	76	82	6	0.53	0.75	2006
Dominican Rep.	73	78	6	0.49	0.49	2008
Paraguay	71	76	5	0.51	0.57	2008
Bolivia	69	77	-	0.55	0.59	2007
Panama	69	76	8	0.56	0.61	2003
Peru	69	76	8	0.47	0.42	2008
El Salvador	53	61	8	0.45	0.41	2007
Guatemala	51	59	8	0.55	0.64	2006
Honduras	48	57	9	0.57	0.68	2006
Nicaragua	46	56	9	0.51	0.57	2005

Source: Molinas et al. (2010); SEDLAC (CEDLAS and The World Bank).